STRATEGIC THINKING IN CRIMINAL INTELLIGENCE

STRATEGIC THINKING IN CRIMINAL INTELLIGENCE

Second edition

Editor
Jerry Ratcliffe, PhD

THE FEDERATION PRESS
2009

Published in Sydney by:
>   The Federation Press
>   PO Box 45, Annandale, NSW, 2038
>   71 John St, Leichhardt, NSW, 2040
>   Ph (02) 9552 2200 Fax (02) 9552 1681
>   E-mail: info@federationpress.com.au
>   Website: http://www.federationpress.com.au

First edition 2004
Reprinted 2004, 2007
Second edition 2009

National Library of Australia
Cataloguing-in-Publication entry

>   Strategic thinking in criminal intelligence. 2nd ed.
>   Editor: Jerry Ratcliffe

>   Includes index.
>   ISBN 978 186287 734 4

>   Criminal investigation. Intelligence service. Strategic planning.

363.25

Typeset by The Federation Press, Leichhardt, NSW.
>   Printed by Ligare Pty Ltd, Riverwood, NSW.

Preface

This structured text brings together some of the foremost practitioners and academics in the area of strategic criminal intelligence. With invited chapters from leaders in the field from around the world, the book explores the origins of strategic thinking, provides a road map to strategic criminal intelligence analysis, and concludes with chapters that probe the future of strategic thinking in law enforcement.

This book is designed to complement the drive for more effective strategic planning in law enforcement crime prevention and detection. It is part perspective, part instructional and part polemic. The first chapters lay the foundation for the place of strategic intelligence in current law enforcement thinking, by examining the development of the field in Australia and in the United Kingdom, leading up to the development of the National Intelligence Model. The central chapters provide a roadmap for the production of strategic intelligence and guide the reader through the components of the intelligence cycle as they apply to strategic thinking. Finally, the last three chapters dissect the issues surrounding collaborative multi-agency partnerships, the implementation of intelligence systems and explore the opportunities to develop more strategic thinking in the business of law enforcement. Every chapter is written by a practitioner or researcher closely involved with the law enforcement strategic intelligence field. Drawn from agencies such as the Australian Crime Commission, the Royal Canadian Mounted Police, the United Kingdom's Serious Organised Crime Agency, the Australian Federal Police, Criminal Intelligence Service Canada, and the New Zealand Police, they represent some of the leading specialists in the expanding field of strategic criminal intelligence. This book is designed and structured to be a resource for intelligence practitioners, crime analysts, law enforcement managers and advanced students of policing. Primarily it aims to give readers an insight into the philosophy and practice of leading strategic intelligence analysts.

Every chapter in this edition is either revised or new. Kevin Rogers adds a polemical call for organisational change at the level of the Australian federal government so that the Australian Crime Commission can attain greater policy significance within the strategic sector. John Grieve has added a table chronicling police intelligence in the United Kingdom dating back to 1725. Roger Gaspar joins Brian Flood and together they explain the origins of the National Intelligence Model and how it earned its name. Jonathan Nicholl updates the key tasking form, and adds a new section discussing explicit and implicit engagement with clients. Oliver Higgins has embarked on a major revision of his chapter, and in doing so develops varying collection models and includes a new section on debriefing investigators and covert collectors of intelligence. I have updated a number of case studies and added a new section on accessing security networks. Corey Heldon has added a section on the importance of structured thinking in the strategic domain. Natasha Tusikov and Robert Fahlman provide a new chapter that details the innovative work being conducted by strategic agencies in Canada in the development of new risk assessment tools. Neil Quarmby adds new examples to his chapter, and this is followed by a new chapter from Mark Evans on the integration of products with operational policing. Patrick Walsh has updated a case study with recent work conducted by the Victoria Police in Australia. Ray Guidetti provides numerous approaches to more collaborative partnerships among law enforcement agencies, a chapter that should be required reading for fusion centre managers everywhere. Steve Christopher and Nina Cope expand on many of the themes in this book by discussing how to embed intelligence into police practice. Finally, James Sheptycki and I look at a range of intelligence issues for the future of strategic thinking, and expand on the potential benefits of a social harm approach to crime problems.

What is unusual about this book is that the invited authors were assigned topics by the editor, and this gives the book a structure that deliberately aims to encompass both the process of strategic intelligence production as well as the current issues in strategic direction and policy determination within law enforcement. I would like to thank all of the authors for their contributions to this book, especially given the constraining nature of the brief that I provided. I am also appreciative that the authors appear to have tolerated my relentless badgering even though the workload of intelligence agencies in the new century appears to be forever increasing with no respite in sight. The book is also richer for the contributions of numerous people who provided comment and guidance on various chapters, including Deborah Osborne, Philippa Ratcliffe, and Ann Cunningham of Federation Press.

The book is undoubtedly richer for the contributions of many authors who are currently active in the area of strategic intelligence on behalf of their respective governments. That they could find the time to contribute to the broader field through the pages of this book is a tribute to their dedication to the craft of strategic thinking.

Jerry Ratcliffe
Philadelphia, April 2009

Contents

Preface   *v*

Contributors   *ix*

CHAPTER 1
The structure of strategic thinking   1
Jerry Ratcliffe

CHAPTER 2
Developments in Australian strategic criminal intelligence   13
Kevin Rogers

CHAPTER 3
Developments in UK criminal intelligence   28
John Grieve

CHAPTER 4
Strategic aspects of the UK National Intelligence Model   47
Brian Flood and Roger Gaspar

CHAPTER 5
Task definition   66
Jonathan Nicholl

CHAPTER 6
The theory and practice of intelligence collection   85
Oliver Higgins

CHAPTER 7
Intelligence research   108
Jerry Ratcliffe

CHAPTER 8
Exploratory intelligence tools   124
Corey E Heldon

CHAPTER 9
Threat and risk assessments   147
Natasha Tusikov and Robert Fahlman

CHAPTER 10
Futures work in strategic criminal intelligence   165
Neil Quarmby

CHAPTER 11
Influencing decision-makers with intelligence
and analytical products   187
R Mark Evans

CHAPTER 12
Project management   204
Patrick F Walsh

CHAPTER 13
Collaborative intelligence production   222
Ray Guidetti

CHAPTER 14
A practitioner's perspective of UK strategic intelligence   235
Steve Christopher and Nina Cope

CHAPTER 15
Setting the strategic agenda   248
Jerry Ratcliffe and James Sheptycki

Index   269

Contributors

Jerry Ratcliffe was a police officer for a decade with the Metropolitan Police (London, UK) until a winter mountaineering accident precipitated a move to academia. Academic and research positions include a number of years as lecturer in policing (intelligence) with Charles Sturt University (Australia), a stint as senior research analyst with the Australian Institute of Criminology, and he is a former academic coordinator of Australia's National Strategic Intelligence Course. He has a BSc and PhD from the University of Nottingham, and is the author of four books and numerous articles on the subjects of crime mapping and intelligence-led policing. He is a Professor of Criminal Justice at Temple University, Philadelphia.

Steve Christopher joined South Wales Police in 1979 and prior to his recent retirement was a crime manager on a Basic Command Unit with responsibility for the investigation of volume, serious and public protection crime. Prior to this, he was head of force intelligence where he co-ordinated the management of the force intelligence bureau and intelligence provision for organised crime and homicide investigations. He has been a member of various Association of Chief Police Officers (ACPO) working groups into covert policing and initiated the concept of a source registry that has been advocated as good practice by Her Majesty's Inspectorate of Constabulary (HMIC). Steve obtained a honours degree in Psychology and Criminology from Cardiff University and, as a serving officer, conducted research for the Home Office. Since retiring from the police service, Steve has been conducting research into dangerous and severe personality disorder (DSPD) for his doctorate at Aberystwyth University. Steve is senior lecturer and Deputy Director of the Centre Investigative, Security and Police Sciences (CISPIS) at The City University, London.

Nina Cope is employed as a consultant to the public sector. As the time of writing the chapter she was employed by the Metropolitan Police Service (London), where she has worked as an adviser to Senior Management and led the development and implementation of a major change program that aimed to develop the organisation's intelligence and crime analysis capability. She previously worked as a lecturer and researcher at the Universities of Warwick, Cambridge and Surrey. She has a range of research interests in policing and crime, including analysis, youth offending and the use of drugs. Her PhD from the University of Warwick researched the experience of young offenders' drug use in prison.

Mark Evans began a long career in intelligence as an analyst with the Defence Intelligence Staff (Ministry of Defence, London), work that took him to the Middle East, South-East Asia, Afghanistan, and subsequently to Canberra working on a joint project with the Australian Department of Defence. In 1993 he joined the Northern Ireland Office (Belfast) as Head of Research and Intelligence working on national security and organised crime priorities, until his appointment as the first Director, Analytical Services of the Royal Ulster Constabulary (later Police Service of Northern Ireland) Analysis Centre in 1999. Mark was made OBE in the 2005/06 New Year's Honours list for public service in Northern Ireland and joined the New Zealand Police as National Manager: Intelligence in September 2007.

Robert Fahlman, former Interpol General Secretariat Assistant Director responsible for Interpol's global Criminal Intelligence Program, is a career professional intelligence officer with the Royal Canadian Mounted Police (RCMP). From 2002 to 2008, he was attached to Criminal Intelligence Service Canada completing his service there as acting Director General. Robert was promoted to Director General, Criminal Intelligence, RCMP in May 2008. He is responsible for criminal intelligence policy, governance and doctrine, professional standards and training, domestic and international partnerships, and research, development and innovation.

Brian Flood joined the British police service in 1967. He served for 31 years in the national security, drugs and general criminal intelligence fields both at home and in Europe before transferring in 1998 to the National Criminal Intelligence Service where he was Assistant Director (Corporate Development). Following the creation of the UK's Serious Organised Crime Agency (SOCA) in 2006, he was appointed director of the agency's principal information business change program. Brian Flood was responsible for much early work in UK law enforcement on the setting of standards for human rights compliance in covert operations. He was one of the principal architects of intelligence-led policing and a leading designer of the UK's National Intelligence Model. He was awarded the Queen's Police Medal in 1998 and an MBE on his retirement in early 2008.

Roger Gaspar joined the Metropolitan Police in 1966 and worked principally in operational detective, crime policy and training roles, rising to the rank of Commander. He was appointed Deputy Director General and Director of Intelligence of the National Criminal Intelligence Service from 1998 to 2002 and was awarded the Queen's Police Medal in 1998. He led major reviews on the quality of evidence and national work on Investigative Interviewing, Hi-Tech Crime, Communication Data access and the UK National Intelligence Model.

John Grieve served with the Metropolitan Police (London) from 1966 to 2002. As the first Director of Intelligence for the Metropolitan Police, he led the MPS Intelligence Project and the Anti-Terrorist Squad as National Co-ordinator during the 1996-1998 bombing campaigns by the IRA. In August 1998, he became the first Director of the Racial and Violent Crime Task Force. He has an Honours Degree in Philosophy and Psychology from Newcastle University and a Masters Degree from Cranfield University. He is now Senior Research Fellow at Portsmouth University; Professor Emeritus at London Metropolitan University; Honorary Fellow at Roehampton Institute, Surrey University; and an Honorary Doctor at London Metropolitan University. He has served as a Commissioner of the International Independent Monitoring Commission for the Peace Process in Northern Ireland since 2004, and was in 2008 appointed Independent Chair of the Home Office/Ministry of Justice Independent Advisory Group on Hate Crime. He was awarded the Queen's Police Medal in 1997 and appointed CBE in the Millennium Honours list.

Ray Guidetti has served with the New Jersey State Police across a range of staff, intelligence and investigative assignments, which include organised crime and counter terrorism. At the rank of lieutenant, he is currently an intelligence manager with the interagency New Jersey Regional Operations Intelligence Center. He has a Masters Degree with Seton Hall University and the Naval Postgraduate School. His applied research efforts are aimed at strengthening organisational intelligence capacities and interagency collaboration.

Corey Heldon is a Superintendent with the Australian Federal Police and has been with the AFP for the past 19 years. During this time she has had opportunities to work in diverse areas such as community policing, close personal protection, intelligence and as a trainer in the School of Law Enforcement Intelligence at the Australian Federal Police College in Canberra. She has recently served in East Timor, and is currently at Headquarters in an intelligence capacity. She has a Graduate Certificate of Criminal Intelligence and Graduate Diploma in Criminal Intelligence with Charles Sturt University. Corey is a member of the Australian Institute of Professional Intelligence Officers.

Oliver Higgins is a Senior Manager working for the UK's Serious Organised Crime Agency (SOCA). He has worked in a number of strategic and operational roles within law enforcement over the past 13 years. In the past he has led the delivery of the UK Threat Assessment, contributed to the Joint Intelligence Committee process and led one of the intelligence teams working in SOCA's enforcement arm.

Jonathan Nicholl has substantial experience in the national security and criminal intelligence fields, occupying positions including Manager Intelligence Analysis at the National Crime Authority, Principal Policy Advisor to the Commissioner of the Australian Federal Police and as a

Specialist Advisor to a military headquarters. Jonathan is currently Head of the Australian Crime Commission's National Indigenous Intelligence Task Force and Special Intelligence Operation examining the nature and extent of child sexual abuse and violence in indigenous communities.

Neil Quarmby has a long career across a range of intelligence fields. He served for over 20 years in the Australian Defence Force, with appointments in signals intelligence, on a command appointment with the British forces conducting counter-intelligence and counter-terrorist duties, and in staff roles providing intelligence support to Defence's Strategic Command. He also completed a range of intelligence training and capability development appointments in Defence including multi-national interoperability roles. On retirement from the Army as a lieutenant colonel in 2001, Neil served as a senior analyst in, and then manager of, a national strategic crime assessments agency in the Attorney General's Department and then developed and managed a strategic intelligence capability in the Australian Crime Commission on its formation in 2003. He subsequently moved on to build and manage an integrated compliance risk and intelligence system in a key regulator in Australia's health system, targeting fraud and non-compliance.

Kevin Rogers developed a firsthand understanding of strategic intelligence as a strategic analyst with the Australian Department of Defence – as Head, Protective Security Coordination Centre in the Attorney-General's Department, and as Director Intelligence and Strategic Policy with the National Crime Authority. He lectured in policing (intelligence) at Charles Sturt University before taking up consulting and *pro bono* work. He is a graduate of the Joint Services Staff College and holds a degree in law from the Australian National University.

James Sheptycki is Professor of Criminology at York University, Toronto, Canada. He completed his PhD at the London School of Economics in 1991 after which he later moved to a Fellowship in the School of Law at Edinburgh University, where he stayed until 2000. He is best known for his work on transnational crime and policing and has written on a variety of topics including intelligence systems, organised crime, witness protection programs and cross-border policing. His current work concerns guns, crime and social order.

Natasha Tusikov has worked as a strategic analyst at Criminal Intelligence Service Canada (CISC) in Ottawa since 2000. She was a lead analyst responsible for developing the CISC National Threat Assessment on Organized Crime and the CISC governmental threat assessment, the National Criminal Intelligence Estimate. She is currently the acting manager of the National Research and Methodology Development Unit at CISC where she is developing risk analysis methodology to assess the threats and harms from organized crime. Since 2000, she has analysed Asian organised crime, outlaw motorcycle gangs, mortgage fraud, counterfeit pharmaceuticals and money laundering. Natasha holds a Master's degree in English Literature from Queen's University.

Patrick Walsh is a Senior Lecturer in Criminal Intelligence at the Australian Graduate School of Policing, Charles Sturt University, where he is Course Coordinator for the Graduate Criminal Intelligence Program. Prior to his appointment at Charles Sturt University, Patrick was a Senior Strategic Intelligence Analyst at the Australian Crime Commission and the National Crime Authority in Sydney. In these positions, his main area of responsibility was the development and management of various new criminal intelligence projects. Prior to working in federal law enforcement intelligence, Patrick was a Transnational Security Analyst at the Office of National Assessments in Canberra. He has written on a range of intelligence related topics, including; project management in intelligence, intelligence-led policing, intelligence education and management. His research areas include intelligence theory and doctrine, international policing and transnational security issues.

CHAPTER 1

The structure of strategic thinking

Jerry Ratcliffe

At the beginning of the first edition of this book, I wrote, at no time in history is law enforcement more in need of strategic direction. The rapid changes in the criminal environment over recent years have taken many in law enforcement by surprise. Transnational crime has become more transnational, organised criminals have become more organised, and the ever expanding role of law enforcement to combat a broader array of ills has not been matched with a corresponding expansion in resources. If anything, the situation since 2004 appears to have exacerbated. To be effective, law enforcement is now required to predict into the short and long term, anticipate the behaviour of organised crime groups, think strategically and be judicious with resource allocation. This 'intelligent' level of business planning has long been neglected by a police establishment fixated (as it has been until now) with tactical investigations and short-term operational outcomes. 'Worry about tomorrow: next year is somebody else's problem', has until recently been the mantra.

However, the increase in crises that could be considered 'Black Swans' – improbable and unpredictable events[1] – such as the 7 July 2005 London bombings and the 2001 attacks on the World Trade Center and Pentagon, have made decision-makers sorely aware of the uncertainties inherent in our understanding of everything from local crime to national security.[2] Inquisitions such as the Hutton and Butler inquiries in the UK (into the death of Dr David Kelly and intelligence on Iraq respectively) highlighted the uncertainty surrounding the decision-making process, and brought into public focus the lack of objectivity in processes designed to manage risk based on incomplete information.

Changes compelled by legislation and government inquiries have, in many countries, forced a more critical examination of law enforcement

---

1   A 'Black Swan' is an event of extreme impact that is an outlier (at least in terms of being outside of regular expectation), yet might appear retrospectively predictable (Taleb, 2007: xvii). The term originates with the widespread belief in most of the world that all swans were white, a notion finally dispelled by the discovery of black swans in Australia in the 17th century.
2   A fundamental part of the definition of a Black Swan event is the largely unpredictable nature of the event before it takes place, yet this is precisely the type of crisis that intelligence is expected to predict.

planning and the management of risk. The pressure is on senior executives to justify decisions and manage a wide variety of threats to public life. In turn, some decision-makers are now looking for a level of knowledge that can make sense of an increasingly complex and dynamic criminal environment, so that resource priority decisions can be made in the present, and developing criminal endeavours anticipated and managed in the future.

Priorities are usually determined on the basis of an understanding of the impending risks that an organisation or community will face. Greater emphasis on the pre-emptive mitigation of risk rather than reactive management of the aftermath of crime suggests *proactive* crime prevention, and proactivity requires an ability to anticipate crime. This is only possible when law enforcement agencies have the capacity to identify the *predictability* in criminal behaviour, a predictability that is usually only observable from the identification of *patterns* (see Figure 1.1).

Figure 1.1 The relationship between prevention and patterns of crime and criminality

Prevention

requires

Proactivity

requires

Predictability

requires

Patterns

Pattern recognition is therefore the aim of the intelligence process, while reduction in observable patterns is the aim of operational units and crime prevention agencies. Patterns can be used as a foundation for dictating priorities for enforcement, further intelligence gathering, and prevention (NCPE, 2005; Ratcliffe, 2008) and are synonymous with action. Patterns provide knowledge of the criminal environment, and as John Grieve argues in this volume, intelligence is knowledge designed for action. The overarching aim is therefore reduction of patterns with the corollary that the end result of a successful crime prevention strategy will be random or chaotic criminal activity with no discernible pattern or model. Complete eradication of criminal activity is perhaps overly ambitious; reduction to effectively random patterns of crime may be a more realistic goal.

By providing a model to explain criminal behaviour, intelligence offers an avenue for intervention. This, Phillips (2009: 29) suggests, becomes a theory of crime control; a notion of patterns leading to responses that policing scholars will recognise from the problem-oriented policing literature and concept (Goldstein, 1990; Scott, 2000; Goldstein, 2003). Without intervention, without the ability for the intelligence process to influence the thinking of decision-makers who then implement strategies that impact on the criminal environment, there is no intelligence-led policing (Ratcliffe, 2008).

Normalising strategic intelligence

With this seemingly incessant process of change in the modern criminal environment, the opportunities presented by an objective strategic intelligence system that can absorb, filter, analyse and disseminate relevant intelligence on an issue of strategic importance would appear to be a godsend for senior law enforcement management. And yet the discipline of strategic criminal intelligence remains at a crossroads, still struggling in some areas to generate interest and prove its relevance. As one of the more recent innovations within law enforcement, it is still finding its feet. Many analysts are convinced of the craft's relevance: the issue is one of convincing policy makers. This situation is aggravated by decision-makers in policing who are unable to see beyond the evidential focus of policing and cannot see the value of intelligence for prioritisation and resource allocation. Crime prevention is still the ugly stepchild to the more glamorous prosecution.

A further reality is that a strategic assessment must compete for the attention of decision-makers in the law enforcement field. While a military tactician may work in a remote theatre of conflict and find that intelligence is the only decision-making information available, senior managers in law enforcement often have to juggle a bewildering number of competing pressures before coming to a decision regarding law enforcement policy. No police service has the resources to fully combat the combined perils of offences such as illicit drugs, illegal immigration, electronic fraud, violent crime, property offences and Internet crime to everyone's satisfaction. It is an actuality of modern law enforcement that a triage process is inevitable, resulting in priorities that should balance risks and threats against law enforcement capabilities and the opportunities afforded by vulnerabilities in criminal groups.

Crime analysts and intelligence practitioners should stand up and do battle to promote an objective criminal intelligence assessment over less objective demands such as pressure from the media, political forces and single-issue community groups, all of whom are less inclined to recognise the complex mosaic of the 'bigger picture'. This is not to dismiss the political realities of life as a law enforcement executive, but rather recognition that an intelligence product can provide a police commissioner with the necessary objective ammunition to justify resource allocation decisions, and to fend off criticism from external bodies who are not held accountable for the larger crime-fighting domain and whose subjective demands are not necessarily in the interests of the broader community.

Within this organisational context, the worldwide move towards intelligence-led policing is to be welcomed. It is defined thus; 'Intelligence-led policing is a business model and managerial philosophy where data analysis and crime intelligence are pivotal to an objective, decision-making framework that facilitates crime and problem reduction, disruption and prevention through both strategic management and effective enforcement strategies that target prolific and serious offenders' (Ratcliffe, 2008: 89). A key requirement that challenges policing to engage with strategic products and management is the defined need for an objective, decision-making framework. Identifying, working within, and supporting such a framework may be the greatest challenge facing strategic criminal intelligence analysts.

While competition with external pressures is one complication with the acceptance of a strategic product, there are other reasons why strategic crime analysis and intelligence outputs are not as yet fully endorsed by policy makers. These include the inexperience of senior managers in handling intelligence material, the apparent irrelevance of the strategic domain to street-level officers, and that training in strategic intelligence practice is rare, resulting in uncertainty about the tasking of practitioners or the interpretation of intelligence products.

Intelligence is still a new discipline within law enforcement, as opposed to the more established process of investigation. Many senior officers are former detectives, as a detective background is often seen as a prerequisite for the highest levels of police management. Detectives often see the intelligence role as an investigative aid, suborning the process to the tactical assistance necessary to crack an individual case. Intelligence and crime analysis at this level merely becomes a tool to increase the arrest rate. Though this can help determine an individual case, it makes no contribution at a broader, strategic level. How this problem manifests is in the gulf between expectations of certainty from inexperienced managers, and the realities of the intelligence world where an incomplete picture will not explicitly provide the definitive 'answer' that many decision-makers seek. While a degree of uncertainty is inevitable, many executives fail to recognise that it is mitigated by a strong intelligence product.

A second problem is that the apparent lack of connectivity between strategic decision-making and tactical issues means that few street level officers appreciate the value of strategic intelligence; to them, a broader, longer-term view of the criminal environment can often seem irrelevant. A common complaint heard around police stations is that the intelligence section is a 'black hole', where information goes in but nothing comes out. This can even be heard from some crime analysts in regard to the strategic process. Yet this apparent gulf between the tactical and strategic levels is rarely real. It is more a reflection of a lack of communication to explain policy positions in the law enforcement world. It is also possible that some in strategic intelligence fail to accept that they must continue to 'sell' the strategic product at all levels of an organisation. As chapter authors in this book point out, intelligence is intelligence: it can be equally valuable on different levels. Christopher and Cope make this point in their chapter, writing; 'Intelligence is a highly reusable resource, which is better labelled when it is applied to the area where the intention is to add value or inform a particular decision, rather than when it is gathered'.

A third problem is that strategic intelligence is a new discipline, still developing methodologies and mechanisms. This can result in different standards and techniques, and even different definitions of intelligence. At this relatively young stage of a craft, many would regard a developmental and experimental approach to the business as a positive development, allowing innovation and new ideas to flourish. It can, however, confuse decision-makers, especially in multi-agency task forces. Different agencies usually have different definitions of strategic intelligence, and some in the field can get awfully hung up on this issue. However, the broad intention is usually the same. As Brian Flood and Roger Gaspar note in this book, the UK National Intelligence Model views the term 'strategic' not as one that is reserved for 'exclusively national or whole law enforcement perspectives but as one that is applied to the process of business planning and resource allocation at each of the structural levels within UK policing'. This may differ from the view of an analyst with, say, the Australian Crime Commission who is tasked with advising the higher levels of government on law enforcement policy; however, there is sufficient overlap in intent to achieve a high degree of agreement on the important issues.

To better understand how these different systems have evolved, the first chapters of this book aim to provide the reader with a contextual basis for the current state of strategic intelligence in the UK and Australia. Kevin Rogers provides an eloquent account of the development of strategic thinking in Australia up to the creation of the Australian Crime Commission. From a long and distinguished career in Australian criminal intelligence, Rogers draws attention to the cycle of government inquiries and legislation that have shaped the criminal intelligence environment. John Grieve, former Director of Intelligence at New Scotland Yard, relates the development of criminal intelligence in the UK, and specifically the Metropolitan Police, as a process of individual initiatives finding their way into policy through a process of trial and error. Flood and Gaspar pick up from Grieve by identifying the limitations of traditional business planning within law enforcement that resulted in the need to develop the National Intelligence Model. This chapter provides the reader with a rare insight into the philosophy and thinking of the architects of the UK's National Intelligence Model and is their only publicly available co-authored work.

This contextual perspective lays the foundation for the chapters that follow; chapters that seek to provide a mixture of instruction and discussion of issues relevant to the intelligence process at the strategic level.

The intelligence process

Many agencies have different definitions of intelligence and the various perceived levels of intelligence. Some definitions are short and succinct, while others run to paragraphs (Palmer and McGillicuddy, 1991). Many analysts reading this will have been first exposed to criminal intelligence at the tactical level. Tactical intelligence can be seen as the creation of an intelligence product which supports front-line areas, investigations and other operational areas in taking case-specific action to achieve enforcement objectives.[3] The tactical level is often the entry level to law enforcement criminal intelligence, especially in the US where the overwhelming number of small agencies limits the tactical process to an investigative aid much of the time. The tactical level is also the one that appears to most police officers to have the maximum utility. The problem with this view is the myopia that a case-by-case focus can have on the establishment and pursuit of agency direction and priorities.

There is a growing need to establish more long-term crime reduction planning at the operational level, from the use of crime reduction partnerships and the processes of intelligence-led policing that are evident in Australia, the UK and beyond (NCIS, 2000; Ratcliffe, 2003, 2008). This level of operational thinking and problem-solving demands a degree of operational support beyond the provision of case-specific tactical intelligence. We can define operational intelligence as the creation of an intelligence product which supports area commanders and regional operational managers in planning crime reduction activity and deploying resources to achieve operational objectives. For many smaller agencies, the operational level, as defined here, works as their strategic plane. In other words, decisions regarding the deployment of resources are considered 'strategic' thinking for a smaller police service agency. In this regard, although a large agency would consider local district resource allocation an operational command process, this represents the pinnacle of business planning for a small outfit.

The level of intelligence product that is the primary concern of this book is the strategic product, which aims to provide insight or understanding, and make a contribution to broad strategies, policies and resources. It is primarily directed to the achievement of long-term organisational objectives. This definition stresses the product aspect of law enforcement intelligence, but intelligence is more than a product, it is also a process. Providing decision-makers with advice that attempts to anticipate future criminal trends is no mean feat, and the undertaking is usually conducted by following, or at least making a passing reference to, the intelligence cycle.

The intelligence cycle is a repetitive set of actions that has been used within defence and military circles prior to its adoption by law

---

3   For discussions of this definition and the subsequent definitions of operational and strategic intelligence, see ACS (2000) and Ratcliffe (2008).

enforcement. While variations exist, the basic intelligence cycle (Figure 1.2) consists of five stages: direction; collation; analysis; dissemination; feedback and review (SCOCCI, 1997).[4] The direction (task definition) phase, as Jonathan Nicholl points out in Chapter 5, is the first crucial stage in the process. Errors made at this point may be significant as early mistakes compound in the later stages of the cycle. As Nicholl observes, a fundamental role of the analyst (often overlooked in recruitment criteria) is the need to maintain an honest and trustworthy relationship with the client in order to ensure the best conditions for the success of the project.

Figure 1.2. The intelligence cycle

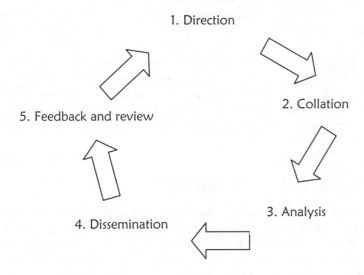

1. Direction

5. Feedback and review

2. Collation

3. Analysis

4. Dissemination

Oliver Higgins picks up on the next stage (collation) from his perspective at the Serious Organised Crime Agency in the UK. Establishing a formal and reliable process for thorough and effective data collection is essential to the development of an objective intelligence product that maintains operational credibility and integrity. Higgins reviews the pros and cons of a number of different collation strategies.

A chapter on intelligence research seeks to set the basic intelligence research processes in their context as an extension of social science research methodology, before four experienced practitioners describe specific analysis techniques that are of value to all strategic intelligence workers. Corey Heldon tackles a range of techniques that can help an analyst visualise the scope of a strategic issue, methods that are useful to the analyst both as analytical tools and as briefing mechanisms for senior

---

4   For a variation, Lisa Palmieri refers to the intelligence cycle as; planning, collection, collation, analysis, dissemination, feedback (cited in Ratcliffe, 2008: 153).

managers and clients. Natasha Tusikov and Robert Fahlman bring their experience from the Royal Canadian Mounted Police and Criminal Intelligence Service Canada respectively to bear on the issue of organised crime by outlining new approaches to risk and threat assessment. Neil Quarmby then delves into rarely charted territory by outlining techniques that can enable an analyst to visualise a range of possible future scenarios. Techniques to estimate the possible criminal environment in the future are rarely employed within law enforcement, yet they arguably wrestle with the searching questions that are foremost in the minds of policy makers.

After these chapters address the analytical stage of the intelligence cycle, Mark Evans draws on his time with the Police Service of Northern Ireland and as National Manager (Intelligence) for the New Zealand Police to frame various intelligence products and dissemination strategies within an operational context. Patrick Walsh completes the cycle by examining the management of the whole strategic intelligence process, incorporating feedback and review into the project. In this way, the central chapters of this book aim to provide new analysts with a roadmap for strategic intelligence product creation, and experienced analysts with a wider appreciation of the issues inherent in each stage of the intelligence cycle.

Influencing decision-makers

A reader having moved through the central parts of the book might be left with the impression that strategic intelligence products are the mainstay of law enforcement decision-making. This is unfortunately, and often inexplicably, not always the case. The issues identified earlier in this chapter are still problems: senior decision-makers do not understand or appreciate strategic documents, the law enforcement front-line are often sceptical, and the developing range of strategic tools are still to be set in stone, evaluated and applied with confidence.

Of all of the issues (these and others) one of the most difficult to counter is the lack of strategic thinking within law enforcement. Senior managers can be given a strategic intelligence report, but the bottom line is that they often don't have a clue what to do with it. Having rarely been trained how to convert an intelligence document into a crime reduction policy, many simply don't understand how to incorporate a strategic product into their organisational thinking. An unfortunate limitation on the quality of intelligence products is the sophistication of the decision-making process. As Phillips (2009: 28) cynically but accurately laments; 'commanders have a strong and sometimes sorry record of relying on their preconceptions rather than a current and measured appraisal of the problem in hand. Strong leaders can be personally effective and strategically weak'.

While defence purists may argue that intelligence should not have an opinion, but should allow the client to interpret the result of sifted, analysed and interpreted information, this assumes that the defence and law enforcement intelligence and policy environments operate in an identical manner. But of course they do not: defence managers are educated to interpret and appreciate intelligence early in their careers, while the use of crime analysis and intelligence is still relatively new to law enforcement. A police operational commander is far less likely to have been trained to appreciate and act on a complex intelligence or crime analysis report than his or her military counterpart. It is not a truism that what is good for defence intelligence is good for law enforcement intelligence. Few police managers are trained in the art of interpreting criminal intelligence and crime analysis, and even fewer have the necessary training to convert that intelligence into practical and effective long-term crime reduction policies.

There is no shortage of evidence on the effectiveness of many crime prevention strategies. Unfortunately, said evidence is often academic, rarely concise, and often encumbered with caveats. As a result, it is rarely absorbed by police practitioners seeking a (frequently elusive) simple and unambiguous response to a crime problem. Analysts working outside of policing are often able to gain greater traction with crime prevention from agencies that have no enforcement or prosecution function, but rather rely on compliance and prevention.

While the intelligence cycle is useful for training purposes and conceptualising the analytical phases of strategic intelligence, it fails to emphasise the vital role of the decision-making context in determining the outcome of intelligence work.

The model shown at Figure 1.3 explicitly incorporates decision-making into the process. In this model, the arrow from the intelligence

Figure 1.3 A simplified (three-i) intelligence-led policing model

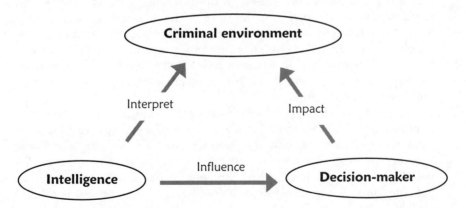

Source: Ratcliffe, 2003, p 3.

cell to the criminal environment stresses a requirement on the analyst to actively interpret the criminal environment rather than wait to receive intelligence (rather in the fashion of the old collators, as would be suggested by an arrow from criminal environment to intelligence). 'Pull' models to gather information from willing volunteers are rarely effective in practice. Rather, an analyst must actively seek out the necessary intelligence and strive to understand the criminal environment, rather than wait for the information to come to them. Even when they do that, the resulting interpretation is of no value unless used to influence the thinking of decision-makers so that intelligence becomes a key component of the strategic thinking of the organisation. These are major concerns that are addressed throughout this book. The final stage of intelligence-led policing requires that the intelligence is used by the decision-maker to have a positive impact on the criminal environment (Ratcliffe, 2003). As Kevin Rogers points out in Chapter 2, the 'practice of strategic crime intelligence is at its best when it is in counterpoise with strategic thinking. In other words, strategic analysts do their best work when they are closely engaged with a client who is thinking about strategic issues and wants to shape strategic policy'.

This *three-i* (interpret, influence, impact) model of intelligence-led policing is, of course, a simple description of what can be a much more complex process. Often, the decision-makers will direct the intelligence analyst, and sometimes it is media pressure and political necessity that has a greater influence over decision-makers: however, this basic structure is the aim of the intelligence process within law enforcement.

How successful intelligence analysts and decision-makers are at completing the three-i model varies. Greater employment of enforcement partnerships and non-police partners into the decision-maker/client mix certainly provides challenges for the intelligence community, especially if an excessive degree of secrecy pervades relationships between partners. However, when that is not the case, the more long-term and crime reduction goals of a strategic product can find a receptive audience with regulatory and community-based groups not looking for an enforcement solution. These non-police partners often have a strong preventative interest in a solution to crime problems that does not rely on maintaining a police focus. Ray Guidetti's chapter outlines a number of ways that intelligence managers can foster a collaborative environment between partners and is grounded in his experiences within New Jersey's intelligence fusion centre.

The last two chapters of this book deal specifically with the incorporation of the UK National Intelligence Model's strategic capacity into local law enforcement, and the broader issue of defining a national agenda. As Steve Christopher and Nina Cope point out in the book's penultimate chapter, intelligence remained in the 'murky backwater' of policing for over a hundred years before being 'thrust into the spotlight' of law enforcement practice in the last decade. This is a relatively short time to establish doctrine and processes which all levels of the organisation understand and subscribe to, and as they say, 'numerous and imposing challenges indicate the inhospitable context strategic intelligence has found itself'. In the last chapter, James Sheptycki and I argue that further work is necessary to establish strategic thinking in local policing. In doing so, we consider the mechanisms that are used to define national law enforcement agendas, and the limitations and opportunities for intelligence analysts to influence decision-makers.

Strategic intelligence is a business, and as such it revolves around clients.[5] It may be that this book, as one of the few books in this area (Grieve, 2009) and if only read by intelligence officers and crime analysts, is preaching to the choir. The real target audience should perhaps be law enforcement decision-makers and policy makers, the police chiefs who control resources and priorities. In this, Australia and the UK (like Canada, New Zealand and a host of other nations) have an advantage over colleagues in the United States, where the degree of jurisdictional overlap can create an added level of complexity. The eight police services in Australia, the 43 in England and Wales, eight in Scotland, and the Police Service of Northern Ireland, all maintain a geographical hegemony over their respective jurisdictions. By changing the thinking of a few key individuals, it is possible to positively influence the way that policing is conducted in large areas that cover millions of people.

It is the analyst who bears this considerable responsibility. The analyst's role is to construct an image of the criminal environment and convey that picture to decision-makers. This view of the criminal world is often perceived by decision-makers as the most objective intelligence available, and as such can form the basis of significant policy decisions that can affect the lives of many people. The opportunity to steer the crime reduction strategies of communities, or nations, is a great opportunity for analysts to play a role in the improvement of the quality of life across society, but it is also a burden that should not be taken lightly. The burden places a substantial duty on analysts to research thoroughly, read widely, analyse effectively and report findings and recommendations diligently and honestly. Recommendations that explore avenues for crime prevention and reduction operations will require the analyst to have a broad knowledge of crime prevention strategies, long-term crime reduction policies, and to know 'what works' in policing and crime reduction. All of this information must be conveyed to the decision-maker in a timely and accurate fashion, in such a way that the decision-maker embraces and employs the product to its maximum effect. This is a big task, and I hope that practitioners and researchers, new and experienced, find in this book ideas and tools that advance their strategic work and knowledge, so that we can all benefit from enhanced strategic thinking in criminal intelligence.

---

5   Some agencies and authors refer to the client as a customer. For continuity purposes, this book refers to the 'client' throughout.

References

ACS, 2000, *Intelligence Doctrine*, Australian Customs Service.

Goldstein, H, 1990, *Problem-Oriented Policing*, McGraw-Hill.

Goldstein, H, 2003, 'On further developing problem-oriented policing: The most critical need, the major impediments, and a proposal', in Knutsson, J (ed), *Problem-Oriented Policing: From Innovation to Mainstream*, Criminal Justice Press.

Grieve, JGD, 2008, 'Introduction to Part 1: Ideas in police intelligence', in Harfield, C, MacVean, A, Grieve, JGD, and Phillips, D (eds), *The Handbook of Intelligent Policing: Consilience, Crime Control, and Community Safety*, Oxford University Press.

NCIS, 2000, *The National Intelligence Model*, National Criminal Intelligence Service.

NCPE, 2005, *Guidance on the National Intelligence Model*, National Centre for Policing Excellence.

Palmer, B, and McGillicuddy, L, 1991, *Intelligence and Analysis (Definitions)*, Australian Bureau of Criminal Intelligence.

Phillips, D, 2008, 'Police intelligence systems as a strategic response', in Harfield, C, MacVean, A, Grieve, JGD, and Phillips, D (eds), *The Handbook of Intelligent Policing: Consilience, Crime Control, and Community Safety*, Oxford University Press.

Ratcliffe, JH, 2003, 'Intelligence-led policing', *Trends and Issues in Crime and Criminal Justice*, No 248, Australian Institute of Criminology.

Ratcliffe, JH, 2008, *Intelligence-Led Policing*, Willan Publishing.

SCOCCI, 1997, *Guiding principles for law enforcement intelligence*, Standing Advisory Committee on Organised Crime and Criminal Intelligence (Australia).

Scott, MS, 2000, *Problem-Oriented Policing: Reflections on the First 20 Years*, Washington DC, COPS Office.

Taleb, NN, 2007, *The Black Swan: The Impact of the Highly Improbable*, Random House.

CHAPTER 2

Developments in Australian strategic criminal intelligence

Kevin Rogers

Introduction

Practitioners of strategic crime intelligence in Australia pursue a pluralistic discipline – one that is pluralistic in its origins, its institutions, its modalities of practice, its skills base, and in the uses made of its findings. We should not, then, be surprised to find differences of opinion about the conceptual foundations of intelligence and about the place of strategic crime intelligence within law enforcement. One view – perhaps the prevailing view – sees strategic intelligence as a force that directs strategy and policy. Implicit here is the belief that intelligence of high quality will not only attract the attention of policy makers but also will, and should, direct their decisions.[1] Such a view, however, does not fully explain the multi-layered and multi-directional relationship between strategic intelligence and strategic thinking in an institutional context. The view offered here will be that strategic intelligence, as an institutional practice, is dependent on a strong culture of strategic thinking for its sustenance and enlivenment. Unless policy makers seek out strategic intelligence and integrate it into their thinking, the practice of strategic intelligence is unlikely to enjoy more than an occasional flowering. Where the culture of strategic thinking is weak, the practice of strategic intelligence will wither.

What then is the situation in Australia? Do we find, in Australia, a culture of sustained thinking about anti-crime strategies that would support an established and flourishing strategic intelligence practice? Where do we see this level of thinking? When, historically, does it begin?

---

1 The Mission Statement of the Australian Bureau of Criminal Intelligence saw criminal intelligence *driving* crime reduction strategy. The National Crime Authority saw strategic intelligence as giving *direction* to strategies and policies. See Calcutt (1994). The Australian Crime Commission seeks to optimise the policy *impact* of its work by incorporating a component of the Strategic Intelligence Program into the Strategic Outlook and Policy Division. See ACC (2008: 12).

From *Nation Without A Mind* to the Hilton bombing

Strategic thinking about crime begins, at a national level, in the 1970s and 1980s. After the Second World War, Australia experienced 20 or 30 years of domestic security. The population generally felt isolated from the influences of the social conditions that might be a cause of crime, particularly organised crime, in other parts of the world. If Australians were conscious of organised crime at home, they saw it as less virulent than examples overseas. Donald Horne captured the national mood in his work, *The Lucky Country* (Horne, 1964). Sub-headings such as *Innocent happiness*, and, *Nation without a mind*, do not encourage a view that Australia was, at the time, engaged in creative thinking about anti-crime strategies.

Nevertheless, the police commissioners of Australia's federated jurisdictions developed a collegiate culture of practical cooperation that softened jurisdictional rivalries and gave at least a national flavour to some aspects of policing. Within the Commonwealth Public Service, a small group of policy officers worked to find administrative solutions to some of the practical difficulties of a federal constitution that vested most of the general law enforcement powers in the States and Territories and away from the central government. As a response to this, by 1973 the Federal Government had seen the need for, and established, the Australian Institute of Criminology (AIC) to give a national focus to the study of crime and criminal justice in Australia and to disseminate criminal justice information.

Australia's sanguine view of its criminal environment would not last. Developments in the late 1960s and early 1970s brought with them the realisation that a benign view of crime was no longer sustainable. Australia's military engagement in Vietnam and its political aftermath brought about a sea change in Australia's view of itself. The social and criminal problems associated with the arrival of illicit drugs also began to enter the national consciousness. New communities of migrants, most noticeable in the cities of the eastern States, contributed to the sense of social change. Incidents of terrorism contributed to a feeling of vulnerability. The attack by the Black September faction on the Israeli contingent at the Munich Olympics on 7 September 1972 had a psychological effect similar to the attack on the World Trade Centre in New York on 11 September 2001. Australia, as a consequence stiffened its strategic response to a possible terrorist incident on Australian soil by establishing comprehensive plans for operations conducted jointly by the jurisdictional police services and the Australian Defence Force.

In 1977, the then Prime Minister, J Malcolm Fraser, sensitive to the contemporary geopolitical developments affecting Australia, and wanting to develop closer relationships with the countries of East and South East Asia, saw a need to establish the Office of National Assessments (ONA). This was done through the *Office of National Assessments*

Act 1977 (Cth). Because the government was thinking intently about its diplomatic strategy and posture, its decision-makers wanted and called for strategic assessments to assist the process. The ONA would offer assessments about international matters of political, strategic or economic significance to Australia. From its inception, however, the ONA has influenced the shape of strategic intelligence beyond its charter. It showed a wide audience, including the law enforcement community, what strategic intelligence looked like and how it might be used to support policy-making.

The detonation of an explosive device outside the Hilton Hotel in Sydney on 13 February 1978, during a Commonwealth Heads of Government Meeting, put strategic thinking about managing terrorist incidents in Australia high on the agenda of urgent and important national issues.

Almost immediately, Prime Minister Fraser established two inquiries. He appointed Sir Robert Marks (former Commissioner of the Metropolitan Police in London, United Kingdom) to review the Commonwealth's law enforcement arrangements (Marks, 1978), and appointed Justice RM Hope, to review Australia's protective security arrangements (Hope, 1979). Justice Hope's terms of reference included the relationship between the police services, the intelligence community, the Australian Defence Force and the public service departments. His report, *Protective Security Review,* tabled in Parliament in May 1979, promoted the role of intelligence and proclaimed as a truism that, 'the first line of defence against terrorism is intelligence' (Hope, 1979: 69).

These influential reviews swept up and consolidated the strands of strategic thinking that had been developing in Australia in the preceding years and acted, as did the events that were their provenance, as catalysts for an invigoration of law enforcement institutions and practices in Australia.

Coming of age – in a hurry

By the end of February 1978, before Marks and Hope had tendered their recommendations, Prime Minister Fraser proposed, in cooperation with the State Premiers and the Chief Minister of the Northern Territory, a national counter-terrorism committee. The committee, called the Standing Advisory Committee on Commonwealth/State Cooperation For Protection Against Violence (SAC-PAV) was to coordinate counter terrorism preparedness on a national basis.

The SAC-PAV, by combining police, civilian, security and military representatives in a single institution, significantly advanced the practice of strategic intelligence within law enforcement – at least with respect to counter-terrorism planning. The Committee needed strategic intelligence and sought it from, and through, the Australian Security and Intelligence Organisation (ASIO) which acted as the Committee's intelligence adviser. Consequently, the police services, both State and Federal, had, for the first time, a formal and frequently used institutional conduit to some of the strategic intelligence of the national intelligence agencies.

The Hope and Marks reviews had resulted in ASIO being given a legislative footing, under the *Australian Security and Intelligence Organisation Act 1979* (Cth). The reviews were also the immediate impetus for the amalgamation, also by legislation, of the Commonwealth and Australian Capital Territory Police to form the Australian Federal Police Force. Moreover, law enforcement was soon to get its own intelligence institution through the impetus of another Royal Commission – the Australian Royal Commission of Inquiry into Drugs, also known as the Williams Commission (Williams, 1980). The report, handed down in 1980, enthusiastically promoted the importance of intelligence and of establishing a national system of criminal drug intelligence, stating; '[I]ntelligence is the most important single weapon in the armoury of law enforcement generally and of drug law enforcement in particular. Evidence received by this commission left no doubt that good intelligence is an essential prerequisite to effective law enforcement' (Williams, 1980: D35).

Thus, in 1981, the Australian Bureau of Criminal Intelligence (ABCI) was established by an administrative agreement between the Commonwealth, the States and the Northern Territory. Its mission was to establish a cooperative national criminal intelligence service. It was not, however, to be a collector of intelligence; it had the more limited role of managing and analysing the intelligence repository provided by its law enforcement clients.

More inquiries followed. In the early 1980s, the Royal Commission into the Federated Ships Painters and Dockers Union (the Costigan Commission) investigated corruption associated with union activities on the waterfront. Costigan surprised the government and the public with the scale and the scope of the activities he uncovered. The then Attorney-General of the Commonwealth of Australia, Gareth Evans, conveyed a sense of the surprise to the Parliament:

> Until very recently, few people in Australia were aware of the existence and spread of organised crime in this country. Today, however, warned by a succession of reports by royal commissions and other enquiries, the great majority of Australians are conscious of the threat that organised crime represents to the economy, the amount of revenue available for spending on necessary and desirable forms of community activity and, indeed, to our whole way of life (Evans, 1983, Senate, Debates, Vol S 100: 2491).

Donald Horne's 'Innocent Happiness' was over. Australia needed an anti-crime strategy and an anti-crime agency for dealing with organised crime. Thus was born the National Crime Authority (NCA) with coercive powers to investigate organised criminal activity. The NCA would work in cooperation and partnership with the police services and other law enforcement agencies. Decisions about using the NCA's coercive powers would largely be made by an inter-governmental committee (the IGC-NCA) comprising law enforcement Ministers from each Australian jurisdiction. The NCA and the IGC-NCA needed strategic intelligence on organised crime to inform their decisions, and the NCA established a Strategic Intelligence Unit to supply it. Other agencies, notably the Australian Federal Police (AFP), also began to develop strategic intelligence.

Australia now had three law enforcement institutions that were national in structure and purpose – the ABCI, the SAC-PAV and the NCA. Almost by definition they had a strategic focus, and they were all using and producing strategic intelligence.

As we have seen, royal commissions or other forms of government-sponsored inquiry were influential in setting up the three national institutions. Royal commissions with coercive powers of inquiry are often used in Australia as powerful instruments for discovering (and publicising) the truth about issues and activities with implications for law enforcement policy. Almost invariably they attract a high political profile and can lay the groundwork for a change of public policy. Between 1973 and 1981, Australian governments established five royal commissions of inquiry into law enforcement matters: Moffit, 1973 (organised crime in clubs); Woodward, 1977 (drug trafficking); Williams, 1977 (drugs); Costigan, 1980 (painters and dockers); and, Stewart, 1981 (drug trafficking). Their findings and recommendations, particularly when considered as a whole, had a significant influence on strategic thinking about law enforcement well into the 1990s. Other forms of inquiry, including inquiries by parliamentary committees, were also undertaken. Indeed, in the decade between the early 1970s and the early 1980s Australian jurisdictions established a significant inquiry on an issue related to law enforcement at a rate of more than one a year.

As a consequence, by the early 1990s, Australia had a federation of nationally focused law enforcement institutions that included:

- The Australian Bureau of Criminal Intelligence;
- SAC-PAV;
- The Australasian Police Ministers' Council (with New Zealand);
- The National Police Research Unit;
- The National Crime Authority;
- The Australian Transaction Reports and Analysis Centre;
- The National Crime Statistics Unit;
- National Exchange of Police Information;
- The Federal Justice Office;
- The Australian Police Staff College; and
- The Australian Securities Commission.

The Australian Federal Police might also sensibly be included in the foregoing list along with some of the Australian Customs Service's functions. The work of both these federal agencies have a clear national dimension. Furthermore, new anti-crime institutions were also being created at the State level, notably, the New South Wales Crime Commission and the Queensland Criminal Justice Commission, with special powers capable of strategic contributions to the national law enforcement effort. And while not strictly law enforcement, the contributions of influential national institutions closely related to law enforcement, in particular, the Ministerial Council on Drugs Strategy and the Australian Institute of Criminology, must be recognised in any consideration of the build-up of law enforcement's strategic capability.

Throughout these developments, the frequent, regular and formal consultations under the auspices of the Australasian Police Commissioners' Conference continued to offer strategic direction and leadership, particularly in the form of coordination and joint planning.

From the mid-1970s to the late 1980s, the Australian jurisdictions sustained a remarkable effort of public administration. To design, establish and conduct a dozen or more significant inquiries over the period of about 20 years was, in itself, an achievement. But also to establish a suite of new law enforcement institutions, to evolve a complex and workable set of protocols for practical inter-jurisdictional cooperation, to shape new law enforcement policies and to manage the passage of supporting legislation through Parliament – this was a high point in the history of Australia's public administration. It surely deserves closer study.

The powerful composite of law enforcement and regulatory agencies that had emerged lacked, however, one feature that might have made easier the shaping of a coherent and comprehensive anti-crime strategy at a national level: it lacked an effective mechanism for taking the thinking of the law enforcement ministers and their professional advisers to a whole-of-government level either within the Commonwealth's own machinery of government or nationally.

In the late 1980s, the Federal Government, led by RJ Hawke, took a small, tentative but significant step towards improving the coordination of law enforcement policy within the Commonwealth. Soon after the federal election of 1987, the new Prime Minister established a law enforcement Ministry – the Ministry of Justice – as a junior Ministry within the Attorney-General's portfolio. The measure implied, possibly for the first time at a federal level, that law enforcement policy could be differentiated from the legal policy responsibilities of the Attorney-General. The measure did not, however, challenge the culturally dominant view of law enforcement as a legal economy. Consequently, law enforcement administration and policy remained under the supervision of the First Law Officer.

Regrouping – a chance to press on

After the sustained administrative activity of the 1970s and 1980s there was a need to draw breath and regroup. It came in 1993 in the form of a comprehensive Commonwealth Law Enforcement Arrangements Review (CLER) (Coad, 1994).

The CLER did not try to hide the tensions that had formed between some of the agencies nor the feelings of dissatisfaction about some of the contributions to the law enforcement effort (Coad, 1995). Nor does one need to read very closely between the lines to detect suggestions for a realignment of budgets and functions.

The NCA, for example, having been introduced in 1984 as a law enforcement flagship was, by 1994, running on a budget of $37 million – less than 1 per cent of national law enforcement funding. The ABCI was working on a budget of $5 million (plus some seconded staff) – a figure based on running cost estimates formed at its establishment in 1981 but now outdated by the cost of a new generation of computerised databases with continuous on-line access. Meanwhile, newer arrivals were being resourced on the basis of contemporary cost estimates. For example, the Australian Transaction Reports and Analysis Centre (AUSTRAC), estab-lished in 1988, was given a budget of just over $8 million, and the Australian Securities and Investments Commission (ASIC), established in 1991, had in 1993 a budget of $135 million.

As for strategic intelligence, the CLER saw a wide gap between expectation and performance. On one hand, CLER reinforced the enthu-siastic support for the idea, indeed, the ideal of strategic intelligence articulated by Hope, Williams and others, stating; 'The best quality strategic thinking and planning in law enforcement is critically depen-dent on the provision of high quality information about current and emerging criminal trends and methodologies and accurate assessments of the vulnerabilities of institutions, systems, and processes to criminal attack' (Coad, 1994: 151).

On the other hand, the CLER asserted that this much-to-be desired outcome had not been attained. Australia's strategic crime intelligence did not have the quality the CLER expected of it. Indeed, an accepted discipline of practice had not evolved. And agencies had adopted various definitions of intelligence and had differences of view about the types of intelligence to be developed. The CLER saw these differences as more than merely semantic; 'In some cases the different definitions used are based on major conceptual differences which make comparisons across agencies difficult. Judgments about whether or not an agency is provi-ding the appropriate level and quality of analysis depend partially on the definitional criteria selected' (Coad, 1994: 152).

As for the quality and effectiveness of the intelligence, the CLER was, with few exceptions, unenthusiastic; 'Despite the expansion of law enforcement intelligence in Australia over the past 10 years, the Review believes that neither the Commonwealth nor national law enforcement is receiving the intelligence service that is needed to gain the greatest impact out of the law enforcement effort' (Coad, 1994: 152).

Even the CLER's view of the better intelligence was heavily quali-fied. It could, for example, acknowledge only the *progress* made by the

AFP and the NCA *towards* a quality strategic intelligence capacity. Clearly there was much to be done, given that 'there is room for considerable development in the area of strategic intelligence' and that 'government is currently poorly served in the area of over-the-horizon strategic intelligence' (Coad, 1994: 153).

The ABCI was unable to attract even faint praise from the CLER, which noted that the strategic intelligence capability of the ABCI was 'inherently flawed'. A major problem was considered to be the staffing arrangements. Consequently, the CLER recommended a fundamental reshaping of the ABCI's capability. Minor staffing adjustments would not, the CLER considered, 'produce the significant increase in quality that is necessary for the production of the national strategic crime intelligence which Australian law enforcement agencies and government need' (Coad, 1994).

The CLER's views might be harsh. They were not shared by the ABCI or the Commissioners of Police who considered the ABCI's strategic intelligence to be satisfactory. But, even so, two questions arise: why did conceptual differences emerge over intelligence; and, why did some of the strategic intelligence capacity fail to gain universal approval?

Perhaps views like Justice Williams', that there is 'no mystery in intelligence' (1980: D35) had encouraged some agencies to form an oversimplified view of the practice of strategic intelligence. One might agree that there is no mystery in, for example, accountancy. Nevertheless, accountants must not only acquire by study and tutored experience a body of complex knowledge and skills but must also learn to apply them with fine judgment. A lack of mystery neither means that a craft is without inherent difficulty nor that the untutored can perform it effectively.

Justice Hope had already pointed out the importance for the intelligence function of having people who are both skilled and experienced in their craft. In his view, 'good intelligence officers are not created overnight. They require years of training' (Hope, 1979: 69). In light of this advice, it is noteworthy that when the ABCI was attempting to introduce its strategic intelligence capacity, several other institutions were also expanding into strategic intelligence for the first time. So not only were there issues of methodology for the law enforcement collective to sort out but there were also problems of supply and demand. Where would the skilled and experienced intelligence specialists come from to satisfy the burgeoning demand for strategic intelligence? What methodologies would constitute the practice of strategic crime intelligence? What changes in institutional procedures would be needed to connect with and make use of the newly available strategic intelligence? Should a program be introduced to 'fast track' intelligence analysts?

If the law enforcement institutions appreciated the need to develop a recognised discipline of strategic intelligence and a need to incubate educated practitioners of the discipline, they did little, at an industry level, to satisfy the need.

Historically and culturally, crime intelligence has been a development of the investigatory arm of law enforcement. Investigators have historically collected intelligence and controlled informants; and, largely, they still do. Investigators analysed their own intelligence; and, often, still do. Not until the modern era have we begun to see an intelligence speciality develop as a fully fledged career option within law enforcement institutions.

Against this backdrop, we can, in hindsight, understand why there was no program of development for strategic intelligence specialists. Strategic crime intelligence was treated as an extension of the milieu of investigations and investigatory intelligence. Thus, police officers were appointed to the positions established for strategic intelligence analysts and, without further professional development or the benefit of a settled strategic intelligence method, were asked to shape strategic intelligence. It was a lot to expect.

At the ABCI, analyst positions were filled by the secondment of police officers to temporary appointments – specialist intelligence experience was not a prerequisite. The NCA filled its strategic intelligence analyst positions with former police officers with a variety of backgrounds, former members of the security intelligence agencies (ASIO and Defence), and by recruiting graduates in relevant disciplines such as statistics and criminology. All of these appointees brought with them knowledge and skills that enriched the practice of strategic intelligence. And, equally, they brought with them the particular culture of their professional backgrounds. A pluralistic practice accommodating major conceptual differences resulted.

Some of the more experienced analysts were concerned to shape a coherent discipline. For example, senior analysts at the NCA published a handbook for the strategic intelligence community – *Strategic Crime Intelligence Explained* (Calcutt, 1994). With other agencies such as the ABCI, they regularly conducted a National Strategic Intelligence Course designed to introduce tactical analysts to the strategic craft. However, even with these efforts from the ranks of the analysts, a more comprehensive, and indeed institutional solution, was needed to foster and to manage 'strategic conversations' within law enforcement.

Having established one end of the conversation – a strategic intelligence capacity – what was to be done about the other – an institution to foster and manage strategic thinking about law enforcement; to integrate strategic thinking and intelligence; and to take the outcomes to government (at a cabinet or whole-of-government level)? A resolution of these issues did not emerge. Neither structures nor processes capable of doing the job were introduced.

Within the Commonwealth structure, while the National Security Committee of Cabinet, chaired by the Prime Minister, considers military, security and diplomatic strategies and also reviews intelligence assessments from the security agencies, there is not a similar Cabinet institution for addressing law enforcement strategies and crime intelligence. At a national level, the Council of Australian Governments has historically maintained, despite occasional exceptions, a role too broad and an agenda of responsibilities too extensive to provide either a focus for national law enforcement policies or a forum for sustained and continuing conversation about law enforcement strategies.

A bold new front

The CLER's answer was to establish the intellectual foundation for a bold new front for Australian law enforcement. It took a bead on the central problem, namely, weak connectivity between law enforcement institutions and government. Not only was there no mechanism by which the Commonwealth Government might hear 'the collective voice' of all major Commonwealth law enforcement agencies but, so the CLER found, even the agencies of the Attorney-General's portfolio could not advise the two portfolio Ministers with 'a single voice' on matters of common interest. This was a serious deficiency. As Coad noted, 'without collective responsibility there will be poor cooperation, duplication and gaps, inconsistent law enforcement techniques, lack of ability for the government to set priorities and a general attitude in the agencies of "going it alone"' (1994: 228).

Earlier measures, according to the CLER, had not been adequate for the task. A Law Enforcement Policy and Resources Committee that functioned between 1989 and 1992 had failed to build a consensus for an integrated law enforcement policy. And, while the forum known as the Heads of Commonwealth Operational Law Enforcement Agencies (HOCOLEA) successfully exchanged ideas and encouraged cooperation, its constitution was not suitable for collective decision-making.

CLER proposed a radical reshaping of the milieu in which law enforcement institutions and governments transact the business of strategy. The solution centred on a new institution, the Commonwealth Law Enforcement Board (CLEB) with the primary objective of improving the quality of the conversation about strategy between government and the law enforcement collective. CLEB would also have the responsibility of ensuring that the law enforcement collective attended to the government's priorities and implemented the government's strategies. Each year it would provide the government with an assessment of current strategies, an order of priorities for the coming year and, where appropriate, proposals for new directions.

Reporting to the Board would be a new strategic intelligence institution – the Office of Strategic Crime Assessments (OSCA) – with the primary objective of delivering *over-the-horizon* strategic intelligence to government to assist strategic thinking. OSCA also had the responsibility for setting national intelligence priorities and intelligence collection requirements. OSCA would provide Cabinet, through the Board, with an annual assessment of the criminal environment.

What strikes one forcibly about the proposed solution is the attempt to guarantee that the government would engage the law enforcement collective in conversation about strategy and strategic intelligence at least once a year through the mechanism of the strategic assessment provided by CLEB and the intelligence assessment provided by the OSCA.

For the CLER proposal to succeed, it needed a government not only ready to think comprehensively and in a structured way about law enforcement strategies, but also one with sufficient confidence in the proposed institutions and processes to establish and implement them by legislation. The latter requirement was not satisfied. The Cabinet established CLEB (and OSCA) by administrative means. The CLEB, without the authority to direct the priorities of other law enforcement agencies and to command their cooperation, was short-lived, with their last annual report being lodged for the year 1996-97.

Had there been time for Ministers to become familiar with the new structure, the CLEB might, with cooperation from the collective, have survived. But, in 1996, within two years of its establishment, the CLEB's sponsoring Ministers lost office to a new incoming government. The CLEB fell into desuetude.

The new government was, perhaps, uncomfortable with an institutionalised process that presented it with law enforcement priorities in its first year of office. And there are indications that national law enforcement issues were not high on the new Prime Minister's agenda. In particular, Prime Minister John Howard shed the Office of Attorney-General from Cabinet and abolished the office of Minister for Justice. The promise of strategic conversations about law enforcement held out by the CLER proposals remained unsatisfied.

Prime Minister Howard, however, soon reversed his decisions about the Attorney-General's portfolio. Two of the early policies personally sponsored by Mr Howard – the tough on drugs policy and the guns buy-back and control program – were within the ambit of the Attorney-General's portfolio. As a consequence perhaps, by October 1997 he had not only promoted the Attorney-General to Cabinet and re-established the portfolio's junior ministry but had also given it the additional responsibility of overseeing the Australian Customs Service.

The over-the-horizon strategic intelligence function, protected within OSCA, survived the demise of CLEB; but only just. OSCA had been reduced to a branch of the Attorney-General's department – a difficult position from which to have a potent influence on strategic thinking within law enforcement. OSCA, however, would re-emerge later as part of the Australian Crime Commission (ACC).

The CLER solution had been a Commonwealth creation. It did not include the States. State representatives must have adjudged that to some extent they were disadvantaged by the new arrangements. When Commonwealth delegates attended national forums such as the Senior Officers' Group or the Police Ministers' Conference they would already have Cabinet endorsement for their priorities thus leaving little room for the accommodation of State issues.

To counter the perceived hegemony of the CLEB and to encourage a national perspective, the States persuaded the Commonwealth to join them in a new institutional arrangement – the Standing Advisory Committee on Organised Crime and Criminal Intelligence (SCOCCI). The broad membership of SCOCCI included the heads of most of Australia's law enforcement agencies. Its charter was to sweep-up the intelligence available through member agencies and to direct it at national anti-crime strategies.

Like the CLEB, the SCOCCI was essentially a considered attempt to strengthen the processes of strategic thinking about anti-crime strategies at a national level. But the CLEB had been not only the SCOCCI's point of departure but also its counterpoint. Without the strategic analysis that had been expected of CLEB, SCOCCI was deprived of its counterpoise. Its functions were folded into the Senior Officers' Group, the body supporting the Police Commissioners' Conference. However, some of the essential elements of SCOCCI – national coordination of intelligence and oversight of the national intelligence process by a board comprising agency heads – have survived in the structure and function of the Australian Crime Commission.

The vision created by CLER also survived CLEB. Ideas embedded in the intellectual framework laid out in CLER's 437 pages lay in institutional memories waiting for an opportunity to re-emerge. The opportunity came with the creation of the Australian Crime Commission.

A bold new front reborn

The Australian Crime Commission opened for business in January 2003. It absorbed the NCA, the ABCI and OSCA, but arguably it did so in a way that made the new composite more powerful than the sum of its antecedent parts.

Its advantages derive from four considerations. First, the ACC has the dimension of an intelligence collection agency as well as an intelligence assessment agency (it also sets national law enforcement priorities). This significant development for Australian law enforcement culture brings the law enforcement intelligence model closer to the security intelligence model. Second, the governing Board of the ACC comprises the police commissioners, heads of law enforcement agencies and the Director-General of ASIO – the most powerful forgathering of law enforcement and security leaders in Australia's institutional history. Next, the Parliament has given a legislative basis to the intelligence activities of the former ABCI and OSCA – a significant advance in both recognition and authority. Last, the legislation recognises a comprehensive role for coordinated law enforcement intelligence in not only underpinning operations but also in informing Commonwealth, State and Territory law enforcement policies, in shaping national law enforcement directions and in providing advice to legislators.

In the interstices of the ACC's charter, one can see the continuation of some of the important themes developed by the CLER, including; the shaping of national intelligence priorities; the provision of a legislative basis for a strategic intelligence function; and, an attempt to formalise and regularise a strategic conversation with government.

Prospects

Clearly, the ACC has been vested with much of the responsibility for developing Australia's capacity for producing strategic crime intelligence. And the ACC undoubtedly carries high expectations that its intelligence will ultimately contribute to tangible results.

The task facing the ACC is difficult and long term. We must not allow our hopes to get too far ahead of reality. However, the ACC's performance over the first five years of its life might give some indication of its prospects. We must recognise, however, that much of the organisation's effort over the first years of its life would have been devoted to recruitment, structure, budget, accommodation, methodology, policy and other aspects of establishing itself.

Even so, the reports and publications available to the public from the ACC are, arguably, similar in quality and even in content to the material previously available from the former NCA and ABCI. Neither is there evidence of more or better insights into the nature, scope and scale of organised crime, nor a clear implication of how crime might be targeted or prioritised.

At a more tangible level, the statistics published in the ACC's annual reports show, at least when viewed alone, unremarkable results. For example, in 2006/07, there were 176 people charged with 429 charges. This is significantly down from 2004/05 figures of 294 and 1665 respectively. It might be argued validly that the ACC should be awarded substantial credit for charges laid by the jurisdictional police forces on the basis of ACC intelligence. However, this is not borne out by the figures. For example, the number of cases referred by the AFP to the Director of Public Prosecutions (DPP) has been in decline. In 2006/07 the AFP referred 225 cases to the DPP in which the defendant was tried on indictment (down from 461 cases tried on indictment in 1999/2000).

Professor Mark Findlay has suggested that the AFP has evolved from a minor police force to a super-agency whose jurisdiction extends well beyond Australia's borders (Maley, 2008). The huge resources being devoted by the AFP to counter-terrorism investigations, off-shore policing, intelligence gathering and international liaison work are less likely to yield convictions within Australia.

It can be argued that an over-reaching emphasis on counter-terrorism within Australia's security economy has largely overshadowed the work of the ACC. The terrorist attacks of 11 September 2001 in New York and in Bali on 12 April 2002 were the impetus for policy and organisational changes that not only caught up the ACC when it began its life in 2003 but in some senses overshadowed it.

When we recall that the Commissioner of the AFP is the Chair of the ACC's Board, we would not be surprised if the demands on the Commissioner in overseeing the development of the AFP as a 'super-agency' have resulted in the ACC finding itself a little lower on the list of priorities than might otherwise have been so. Although there are some voices asking whether the emphasis on and the resources devoted to counter-terrorism are excessive (see Maley, 2008), we are not likely to see a sudden reversal in the policy landscape.

There is however, reason for optimism. Amidst legitimate criticism of current levels of performance we should not lose sight of the fact that Australia's crime intelligence agencies are keeping pace with comparable overseas counterparts and in some instances taking a lead. Moreover, we are seeing a convergence of the nation's strategic intelligence capabilities. ONA's interests are more closely associated with law enforcement issues than at any time in its history because contemporary developments falling within its charter are attracting law enforcement implications. ASIO participates with law enforcement agencies in the National Terrorism Committee. It is also on the board of the ACC. This association of interests and the forging of institutional connections are likely to see law enforcement issues finding a more frequent place on the agenda of the National Security Committee of Cabinet.

Such a development is crucial for the development of high quality strategic crime intelligence. The practice of strategic crime intelligence is at its best when it is in counterpoise with strategic thinking. In other words, strategic analysts do their best work when they are closely engaged with a client who is thinking about strategic issues and wants to shape strategic policy.

Over the longer term, the ACC, at the strategic level, would benefit from a law enforcement policy institution with which to form a symbiotic relationship. Unfortunately for the ACC, Australia lacks the advantages of an institution with the strategic policy functions of, for example, the United Kingdom Home Office. The most promising path towards establishing an institution in Australia with responsibility for strategic law enforcement policy lies in removing the Ministry of Criminal Justice and Customs from is subordinate position within the Attorney-General's portfolio and establishing it as a portfolio in its own right. The biggest obstacle to achieving this result is the entrenched view that law enforcement policy and security policy are a subset of legal policy. The inevitable consequence is that policy development is seen to be the province of lawyers rather than experts in law enforcement.

Today, the scale and scope of law enforcement activity is strengthening its claims to an independent portfolio. And the scale and importance of the functions performed by the Minister for Justice and

Customs is also pointing to the introduction of an independent portfolio. Should this occur, the ACC will have an historical opportunity for its strategic intelligence capability to flourish.

References

ACC (2008) *Australian Crime Commission Annual Report 2007-2008,* Canberra: Australian Crime Commission.

Calcutt, B (ed), 1994, *Strategic Crime Intelligence Explained,* National Crime Authority.

Coad, B (ed), 1994, *Report of the Review of Commonwealth Law Enforcement Arrangements,* Australian Government Publishing Service.

Coad, B, 1995, 'Needs and Strategies to Meet National Criminal Intelligence Requirements', *Journal of the Australian Institute of Professional Intelligence Officers' Association,* vol 5, no 1, 33-45.

Evans, G, 1983, Senate, Debates, Vol S 100, p 2491.

Hope, RM, 1979, *Protective Security Review,* Australian Government Publishing Service.

Horne, D, 1964, *The Lucky Country,* Penguin.

Maley, P, 2008, 'AFP referrals to prosecutor halved', *The Australian,* 29 July 2008, Nation section, p 7.

Marks, R, 1978, *Report to the Minister for Administrative Services on the Organization of Police Resources in the Commonwealth Area and Related Matters,* Australian Government Publishing Service.

Williams, ES, 1980, *Australian Royal Commission of Inquiry into Drugs,* Australian Government Publishing Service.

CHAPTER 3

Developments in UK criminal intelligence

John Grieve

Introduction

> The reason why the enlightened are able to win whenever they lead and can achieve unsurpassed success is because of foreknowledge ... Only those who are sagacious and wise ... Only those who are benevolent and just ... Only those who are detailed and subtle can obtain and decipher the truth in intelligence (Sun Tzu[1]).

The chapter is part personal reminiscence, a peripatetic retrospective, and part the building of a chronology with some analysis. To borrow from historian Roy Porter these are fragments with many gaps and references to be filled by me and others.

To adapt an idea of Robert Reiner, 'intelligence, or intelligent led policing' may be seen as the opposite of 'stupidity led policing' (Reiner, 2000; personal communication) using examples of intelligence development as strategic policing leadership. The word *intelligence* is being used in this chapter as 'information designed for action' (Sims, 1993; Metropolitan Police Service, 1994, 1998a; Taylor and Tidy, 2000) but also as the word is unpacked by Hofstadter (1980).

Hofstadter (1980) provides a useful framework for considering the issues when looking at the use of the word intelligence in different settings. His criteria for instantiation includes the ability to:

- respond very flexibly to situations;
- take advantage of fortuitous circumstances;
- make sense of the ambiguous or contradictory while recognising the relative importance of different elements;
- find similarities between situations despite different elements in those situations; and
- be able to draw distinctions despite those similarities.

---

1   For discussions of the various versions of Sun Tzu see Harfield and Harfield (2008) and Grieve (2008).

Hofstadter's framework also includes the ability to synthesise new concepts by taking old concepts and putting them together as new ways of approaching tasks, ultimately coming up with ideas that are novel.

The emphasis, in intelligence as 'information designed for action', is on the word action. The *designed* element unpacks as maps, analysis, linking, agent handling, security and secrecy from the early days of intelligence. The map is said to be one of the oldest intelligence analysis tools, as is the informer and agent, both of which are recorded in the Bible. Hans Gross (1934) lists 'orientation' – 'finding his bearings' – as one of the investigator's primary tasks. The intelligence process is also part of 'designed for action'. The tools of intelligence can be described as a cyclical process involving collection of information, its evaluation, the development of the initial findings, analysis of those findings, dissemination to those who need to know and action leading back to further collection plans.

This chapter will follow a number of general agendas about leadership, the relationship of police tactics and operations with strategy, and there will be a strong focus on the Metropolitan Police, where I have greatest experience. Broadly my position is:

1. Strategy is tactics talked through a brass hat – or in other words, strategic direction comes from within hearing the click of the handcuffs.

2. The word intelligence needs to be reclaimed from the secret world, made less threatening to communities and used in their service. This broader interpretation has been discovered by the business world (Bernhardt, 1994) and in local communities through recent community impact assessments of crimes and incidents (Metropolitan Police Service, 1998b; Smith, 1996; Hiley, 1997).

3. At certain crucial moments in criminal intelligence development street level officers working closely with communities provided the strategic direction.

4. Intelligence-led policing is not derived from a negative; the response to the ineffectiveness or failure of patrol (Lowe, 2001; Audit Commission, 1993, 1996, 1998), but from a positive evolution of street tactics.

5. Credit should be give to a number of academics who have been a positive part of that evolution despite often describing themselves as critical criminologists. The model of operational intelligence is the interaction of academic research, data analysis and practitioner tactical innovation that characterised the Battle of the Atlantic, most noticeably from May 1943 (Travis, 2001).

There are some obvious gaps. I will not deal with those tactical aspects of intelligence that are or were secrets except where they are firmly in the public domain (for example, Harfield and Harfield, 2006). I do not intend my chronology to include the history of corruption scandals that are also catalysts for change, nor the history of the National Criminal Intelligence Service (NCIS) once it was set up from the Central Drugs Intelligence Unit. I have included fleeting references to the Home Office Research Units in their various guises, despite their importance both in respect of their research and to the career paths of a number of individuals I will mention. Nor do I consider the role of the Police Foundation, despite its huge importance to the development of my own strategic thought in the late 1980s and early 1990s. The table in the appendix of this chapter sets the context for some themes developed later; formalising the systems, street level intervention, the role of drug-related violence and analytic discipline.

Early developments

As the appendix table shows, intelligence as a discipline had been known to UK public policing at least since Wellington who nominated Sir Charles Rowan as one of the two first Commissioners of the Metropolitan Police. The table also helps set a chronological context of policy, legislation and case law. Rowan had worked as a staff officer in the Army with the vanguard and rear guard, partly in an intelligence role of Wellington's Peninsular Army under Black Bob Craufurd, the author incidentally of one of the forgotten treatises of policing, Robert Crau-furd's 'Standing Orders' (Fletcher, 1991: appendix). From the start of policing, gathering covert information from informants to surveillance was considered important. Accounts of the Whitechapel Murders in 1888 describe detectives in disguise, and Edwardian photographs show detectives disguised, or wearing workingmen's clothing and ready for action.

Since the 1920s, a card index of local thieves had been maintained in each Criminal Investigation Department (CID) office. During the dark winter nights, aides to CID both used and maintained the index while achieving the requisite standard of arrests to gain a coveted place on a CID course. The index, if not the selection procedure, was to my know-ledge still in use in the mid-1960s.

In the immediate aftermath of the Second World War, Detective Inspector Jack Capstick and later his Detective Sergeant John Gosling, led a small team of four experienced detectives called The Special Duty Squad who infiltrated a number of gangs. The aim was 'to create a Squad of selected officers to be employed solely for acquiring information concerning the activities of criminals' (Public Record Office document Mepo 3/2033).

Although a small squad, they were quite effective. For example, in one year (1948) they were responsible for 186 arrests and the recovery of over £56,000 of stolen property. Charges laid included over 50 arrests for burglary and nearly 50 arrests for handling stolen goods. However, despite considerable success against selected crimes and criminals, they were disbanded after five years and recombined with the Flying Squad and the embryonic intelligence section into a new intelligence section called C5(2).

Under George Hatherill, from 1954 'detectives were trained specifically to investigate certain types of crime'. This was necessary because 'the modern criminal, in the methods and techniques he used, was a far more intelligent type of crook than any that the police had had to deal with in earlier days, and unless an equally intelligent approach were made to dealing with his activities, the crime rate would obviously continue to rise' (Hatherill, 1971: 32). When Hatherill took over command of the CID, there were no specialist sections, so the new crime intelligence section, created with the general crime intelligence operations, was increased. The team 'specialised in gathering information about the activities of certain criminals regarded as potentially dangerous, who their associates were, their habits and their spheres of operation, and their plans for future exploits' (Hatherill, 1971: 32).

During the 1950s, the Flying Squad was expanded from 50 to 100 people, with one team allocated to investigating and proactively targeting pickpockets. The team, in consultation with the Criminal Records Office, produced a pocket-sized index book showing photographs of active pickpockets, called the 'Pickpockets Handbook'. Beveridge (1947) describes an earlier period when thieves who were known to detectives and who knew the detectives, could be arrested at the close quarters engagement required for evidence of 'suspected person loitering with intent'.

Around this time, the Stolen Car Squad was created and then expanded because its activities were soon so successful. There were two kinds of investigator on the squad: detectives and vehicle examiners, the latter being investigative engineers similar to army combat engineers, operating literally at the cutting edge of investigations. The intelligence section at Scotland Yard known as C5(2) grew its own surveillance arm from the early 1960s and with the intelligence sections of the London and Provincial Liaison section (C9) eventually grew into C11 (Laurie, 1970), of which more below, in turn becoming SO11 and finally parts becoming components of the National Criminal Intelligence Service (NCIS) and eventually, the Serious and Organised Crime Agency (SOCA).

The police have long recognised that they had the best potential community intelligence sources of any agency because of the sheer scale of their activity and spread of contacts. This was identified long ago (Vincent, 1881: 202) but formalised into a two-part strategy in the 1960s. Over time, an expanded thieves index was created. This was created from street level tactical activity based on a vehicle identification manual for used car dealers called Glasses Guide. From this, and other research into the coding system for the electrical parts on vehicles, it was possible for a patrolling constable to see whether the index number matched the glass and the electrics. If there was more than a few months difference then the vehicle was a possible ringer: a stolen vehicle with a false identity. Deputy Assistant Commissioner David Powis (of whom more later) developed this first into a mimeographed paper 'Thieves on Wheels' and later into a book *The Signs of Crime* (Powis, 1977). So successful was this expansion of local intelligence collators that the scheme was expanded force wide and copied nationwide.

A group of sergeants based at C11 were used to help a burgeoning group of local collators achieve uniform standards in indexing and local dissemination of criminal intelligence. Intelligence newsletters and summaries began to appear at this time with the arrival of the photocopier and led to higher level targeting. The photocopier's role as intelligence technology has been undervalued as a change agent in intelligence and in the technology of investigation. Incidentally it was a direct result of the 1968 *Criminal Justice Act* (UK) and its requirement for document-based committal proceedings from the lower courts to the Sessions and later to the Crown Court. The 'criminal not the crime' was the motto of C11. Their task was to collect, collate and disseminate, in particular in regard to the major criminals of the capital, a group known as 'the main index men'. On selection boards for the CID in the late 1960s, candidates were asked what information they had passed about local criminals in that category to C11. From *ad hoc* surveillance using privately owned motor vehicles, teams grew and obtained increasingly specialised equipment, skills and training. Advice was obtained from Special Branch and other intelligence agencies, and there was some interchange of personnel (Laurie, 1970; personal experience).

Formalising intelligence systems

Deputy Assistant Commissioner David Powis was operational head of the CID from the late 1970s until the mid-1980s. He was an active police reformer, particularly in regard to the handing of informants, their payment, and their use as participants in criminal activity – all areas of considerable concern at the time (*The Times*, 2001). For decades, the only management of the informer system had been with reward payments, with the courts periodically reviewing the guidance on participation in crime. Powis changed that, initiating detailed instructions regarding personal authorisation and accountability of participation in crime (Kelland, 1986). He also sought the introduction of rewards from outside bodies such as insurance companies. This did not become the force-wide contacts system that his immediate teams employed until later (Billingsley et al, 2001).

From the 1960s, the Central Drug Squad had a card index of reports submitted to the Home Office Drugs Branch. The Home Office maintained their own intelligence index and maintained a counter intelligence anti-corruption relationship with HM Customs using the Home Office Inspectors under the redoubtable Chief Inspector, Bing Spears. Information discovered during visits to chemist shops, doctors' surgeries or during arrests formed the basis of the index. Civilian indexers were employed to keep the index up-to-date and to abstract intelligence from various sources, including Interpol reports.

Following a series of national conferences, not least a particularly acerbic one memorable for a confrontation between police and HM Customs at Morton le Marsh in 1969, a decision was made to make the Central Drug Squad index, parts of C11, and Interpol into a National Index in 1972. The first overseas liaison officer, aside from the Federal Bureau of Investigation (FBI) Legal Attaché, from the Bureau of Narcotics and Dangerous Drugs, was attached to the US Embassy from 1969.

The drive to formalise intelligence systems was also influenced by four important reports; the Baumber report in 1975, the Pearce report (also in 1975), the 1985 Broome Report, the 1986 Ratcliffe report and the Dickens report of 1990. These five important reports by the Association of Chief Police Officers (ACPO) showed that the creation of a Central Drugs and Illegal Immigrant intelligence unit in the early 1970s had not filled the regional nor national voids in the criminal intelligence structures (HMIC, 1997). The reports were influential in leading to the creation of NCIS in 1992 (Howe, 1997). Baumber introduced a standard for each of the 43 (English and Welsh) forces to set up a Force Intelligence Unit; Pearce set up regional groups to coordinate between forces, with centrally directed but regionally based intelligence officers staffing them; Broome applied intelligence thinking to drugs investigations; Ratcliffe ensured that there were field intelligence officers analysing particular problem crimes and developing intelligence; and finally Dickens looked at the intelligence support required for a National Crime Squad (HMIC, 1997).

Among David Powis' reforms was the reorganisation and restructuring of the intelligence process, a move that can be seen as anticipatory of the Ratcliffe and Dickens reports. The restructure conducted by Powis included the removal of the internationally focused (especially American mafia) organised crime desk away from C11 and its reassignment to C5 under his own hand at Portman Square (away from New Scotland Yard). He also staffed it with trusted colleagues from his vice and Notting Hill days. One of the achievements of this group was the introduction of a comprehensive informant daily management system and the early understanding of analysis and open source intelligence (Kelland, 1986; The Times, 2001; Billingsley et al, 2001).

Analytical improvements

The use of tasking and targeting, time lines, event charts, relationship plotting, financial investigation, telecommunication contacts, informant and contact management were all developed under Powis' leadership. The discipline of crime analysis, the employment of civilian analysts and the rights to a commercial system (ANACAPA) all followed. Powis' further contributed to intelligence reform with the introduction to the UK of the FBI discipline of offender (or psychological) profiling. Now known as behavioural profiling, this was trialled following a series of over 25 stranger rapes in London. It was at Powis' instigation that Professor David Canter (then of Surrey University) first met Metropolitan detectives in 1984 (Canter, 1994; Copson, 1995). Subsequently, due to the work of Vancouver Detective Inspector, Dr Kim Rossmo, geographic profiling was also introduced into the UK (Rossmo, 1993; Aitken et al, 1995).

Closely related to these innovations is the child murder database known as 'Catchem'. The system was created independently of the profiling initiative and partly as an answer to some of the failures in investigation identified in the Maxwell, Harper and Hogg child murder cases. The database and more important the analysis arose out of detailed development by Derbyshire Constabulary of the intelligence cell solution to some issues of research, comparison and evidential possibilities proposed following the Peter Sutcliffe serial murder case (Byford, 1981).

While Chief Constable of the Royal Ulster Constabulary (RUC), and before his return to the Metropolitan Police as Commissioner via the Police Staff College, Sir Kenneth Newman had observed from afar the targeting and technical surveillance made possible with Closed Circuit Television (CCTV) in Lewisham, South London, and how it could be used for the arrest of street criminals, robbers and pickpockets. Newman sent RUC officers to see what lessons could be distilled. On his return to the Metropolitan Police Service he formalised the process of coordinating and targeting, analysis, surveillance and arrest for volume crimes, street robbery, burglary, burglary artifice, auto crimes and created four area-based intelligence units (Savage, 2007).

From 1984, Newman's reforms included a planning system for the future CID. Intelligence sits comfortably with management information and project management (Berhardt, 1994; Savage, 2007; Flood and Gaspar, this volume), and indeed many criminal analysis systems derive from them. A force-wide project was created to make intelligence central to crime investigations. At the core of the Force Intelligence Development Steering Committee's (FIDSC) work were the development of 'collection plans' and tiers of coordinating, steering and tasking groups to make use of intelligence assets such as surveillance teams.

Intelligence and community policing are not exclusive. The mobilisation of communities through partnerships started in the UK with the *Police and Criminal Evidence Act 1984* (UK) and has been gaining greater impetus with the *Crime and Disorder Act 1998* (UK). This increase in joint activity with a range of agencies, groups and individuals may be a potentially useful way ahead for policing, with a degree of satisfaction being anecdotally reported with the effectiveness of programs by those involved. Vigorous law enforcement is one contribution to community safety, and intelligence is one part of the overall law enforcement tool bag. The task for intelligence is to provide facts and inferences to support first strategy and policy making, second local strategic crime and disorder decisions and third to form the basis for effective tactical and operational activity. Operations such as 'Bumblebee' (burglary), 'Eagle Eye' and 'Safer Streets' (street crime), 'Trident' and 'Crackdown' (drug dealer and related shootings), 'Strongbox' (a funded targeted policing initiative), and Operation Regis (a combination of street crimes, drugs burglary and handling stolen goods) operated across all levels of the intelligence spectrum.

As has rightly been pointed out, although the more highly organised levels of crime require greater police resources, the fairly chaotic local street end of the crime problem requires just as much skill and probably more patience. The police have less chance of predicting precisely where the crime will occur (Audit Commission, 1993, 1996, 1998; HMIC, 1997). The 1970s had seen the first organised intelligence-led volume crime initiatives by local burglary and robbery squads, though this was not without problems, as demonstrated by the case of Mahonney at the European Court of Human Rights: A burglary and handling stolen goods case which uncovered intelligence assets that had remained undisclosed for two decades. The case opened up a significant debate with regard to privacy and criminal intelligence issues (Wright, 2002).

By 1992, the European Court of Human Rights was well on the way to controlling intelligence activity and would give rise to the *Regulation of Investigative Power Act 2000* (UK) (Neyroud and Beckley, 2001; Wright, 2002). As the Secretary to the Commission wrote; 'there had to be necessity for any interference with human rights, adequate and effective guarantees, and there could be no interference except in the interests of national security, economic well being, prevention of disorder, prevention of crime or the protection of the rights or freedoms of others' (Schengen Agreement, 1985, para 39).

Intelligence and drug violence

The increasing trajectory of challenges at the Court of Appeal over the vulnerability of suspects and the unreliability of some witness testimony was recognised by a small group of police officers and academics. This group began to form a community of ideas which impacted on intelligence-led policing by their identification of the stupidity that had led to some criminal justice disasters (Gudjonsson, 2002). At the same time, the Audit Commission's proposals (1993: particularly Recommendations xi and xii) and their second report in 1996, were to make policing more proactive. This meant more intelligence work, and catching local drug dealers, burglars or street robbers in the act involves not only understanding the whole range of environmental, social, economic and education factors, but had to build on existing best police practice as practised on the streets. A good example of the development of a strategy, driven by threads of street work and intelligence, is drug-related violence.

I want to take the winter of 1993-94 as a case study of the interaction of intelligence and operations. That period followed the murder of Police Constable Pat Dunne and showed the paucity of thinking which had lead to the disbanding of Operation Lucy, an initiative against crack-fuelled violence (Silverman, 1994). In the wake of the Dunne murder, a group of officers – using a public pay phone in the Red Lion public house, a pocket digital personal organiser and a network of contacts across the world – set up an informal coordinating and tasking group to investigate drug shooting and violence. The success of their operations ensured that their activities were made mainstream and incorporated into the intelligence command at SO11 (Small, 1995) when their analysis of the issues was found to match that of an academic (Bean, 2002; Billingsley and Bean, 2001).

From SID via the National Intelligence Model to SOCA

Sir Paul Condon, on appointment as Metropolitan Police Commissioner, said the service must 'develop new professionalisms to do with surveillance, targeting, intelligence, informants and things that will give us a better chance of catching criminals in the act' (interview on BBC *Panorama*, April 1993). The Systems for Investigation and Detection (SID) project began in 1991, and took as its philosophy the catchphrase, 'intelligence is information designed for action' (Sims, 1993) and drove education about intelligence. The project identified commonality of procedures, staffing, roles, an integrated series of levels of activity and responsibility.

The SID categories of subjects, PROMNOM (prominent active local criminal currently targeted), DEVNOM (worthy of consideration as a prominent but being worked up), and AGENCY NOM (a nominal of interest to a particular agency, such as NCIS, for example) were ideal for the criminal histories of the suspects. Intelligence, through SID, was intended to inform all policing strategy, tactics and operations. It was designed through consultation to arrive at shared outcomes rather than shared problems. The police strategy aimed to support partnership, to mobilise society, communities, groups, individuals. The pursuit of terrorists, street robbers, burglars and drugs dealers across the capital and the disruption of their activity and networks were restructured in local partnerships and intelligence informed those partnerships.

A helpful definition of 'proactivity' as 'targeting of specific, criminally-active individuals and monitoring of activities to obtain evidence for successful prosecution, strategic initiatives against particular categories of crime, crime prevention categories and initiatives' was identified by Her Majesty's Inspectorate of Constabulary (HMIC) (1997) in a subsequent review which identified the SID project as a precursor of local best practice. Besides targeted proactive working, other issues identified were the need for projects that were 'sponsored by energetic and enthusiastic leadership', ownership of intelligence at a high level (illustrating perhaps its absence up to then), published communicated intelligence strategies as an integrated structure, including tasking and coordinating meetings and forging partnerships with other agencies (HMIC, 1997). This last item (the forging of partnerships) almost immediately gave rise to obstruction in some quarters with the Data Protection Commissioner called into play as a means of protectionism and parochialism. Fortunately section 116 of the *Crime and Disorder Act 1998* (UK) offered clear legislative support for joint working and sharing of intelligence with relevant agencies working in a crime and disorder local partnership.

As a direct result of various innovations and the finding of intelligence failure in the Stephen Lawrence Inquiry, the Race and Violent Crime Task Force was built around an intelligence cell. The initial assessment was provided by Bowling's work on racist violence (Bowling, 1998) which informed the Intelligence Cell Analytic System (ICAS). ICAS was built in 1998 from the best practice of SID and the development of CRIMINT – a digital criminal intelligence system (Taylor and Tidy, 2000).

The ambition for a top-to-bottom and bottom-to-top integrated intelligence system finally reached its aims with work of Roger Gaspar and Brian Flood in pulling together many of the strands I have described, and putting their own remarkable stamp upon it (Gaspar, 2002; NCIS, 2000; Flood and Gaspar, this volume). The National Intelligence Model, with its tiers of local, cross-border/regional and serious and organised crime, with national and international dimensions is a good example of the flexibility required by Hofstadter (1980) and the aggregation and integration required by HMIC (1997) and identified by Bernhardt (1994). The dedicated specialist staff, 'solely acquiring information', and establishment of Minimum Standards, would be recognisable to the collator sergeants of the 1960s, and by Capstick and Gosling. The tasking and coordinating structure is a highly refined version of that introduced by Sir Kenneth Newman in the wake of the murder of Captain Robert Nairac (McKittick et al, 1999) and introduced by him into the Metropolitan Police through FIDSC. The tactical menu of options is the distillation of vast amounts of street level work collected by regional intelligence officers and demanded by the Pearce and Ratcliffe reports. Its success is, I think, stunning, though the reader should also consider a front-line practitioner view as voiced by Steve Christopher in this volume, as well as some reservations with the ability of national agencies to combat the most serious levels of criminality. One issue that emerged was the increased unrealised potential for dealing with serious and organised crime and from 2007 the government introduced a new agency into the desired closer intelligence/operational nexus at the highest levels in organised international criminality. Thus was born the Serious Organised Crime Agency (SOCA).

Conclusion

In concentrating on a number of local tactical intelligence developments to the exclusion of secret intelligence, covert sources (Billingsley et al, 2001), technology or the history of NCIS, I am aware I have left significant gaps that I hope others will fill. One missing aspect (the development of strategic intelligence within NCIS) will be discussed by Brain Flood and Roger Gaspar in Chapter 4.

Using the ideas of 'intelligence' as 'foreknowledge' (Sun Tzu, 1983), 'orientation' (Gross, 1934) and as 'information designed for action' (Sims, 1993) this chapter has argued for a number of general agendas about the development of police intelligence tactics and operations into strategy. Strategy, particularly intelligence strategy, is tactics given strategic direction and comes from within hearing of the click of the handcuffs and recognising good street-level policing practice. I have argued secondly, that the word intelligence can be reclaimed for communities, used in their service as community impact assessments as part of a wider agenda about policing in the 21st century (Wright, 2002; Metropolitan Police Service, 1998b; Smith, 1996; Hiley, 1997). It has also been argued here that at certain crucial moments in criminal intelligence evolution, individual officers, such as Deputy Assistant Commissioner Powis' henchmen at Portman Square or the Red Lion public house team, all working closely with different communities, provided the strategic direction. As a direct result, contrary to some accounts, I suggest that intelligent-led policing is not derived from a negative (Lowe, 2001), nor as has been interpreted (by some commentators) as a response to the ineffectiveness or failure of patrol (caused by a misreading of Audit Commission reports in 1993 and 1996). Intelligence development has been a positive evolution of street tactics designed to produce evidence in specific cases but also in recognition of the value of routinely gathered information (Travis, 2001; Stanko, 2002; Taylor and Tidy, 2000). Finally, intelligence is about making sense of ambiguities or contradiction and recognising the relative importance of different elements.

At present in the UK, over 130,000 officers are touching all levels of the communities they police, gathering information. They all work with people, creating a million personal contacts a year in London. The potential numbers of intelligence submissions and their contribution to risk and community impact assessment, is staggering; with the latest generation of intelligence tools we now have some of the best processes and technology in the world to collate this information.

References

ACPO, 1975, 'Report of the ACPO Subcommittee on Criminal Intelligence' (Baumber report), Association of Chief Police Officers (UK).

ACPO, 1978, 'Report of the ACPO Working Party on a Structure of Criminal Intelligence Officers' (Pearce report), Association of Chief Police Officers (UK).

ACPO, 1985, 'Report of the ACPO Working Party on Drugs Related Crime' (Broome report), Association of Chief Police Officers (UK).

ACPO, 1986, 'Report of the ACPO Working Party on Operational Intelligence' (Ratcliffe report), Association of Chief Police Officers (UK).

ACPO, 1990, 'Strategic Policy Document: Setting the Standards for Policing: Meeting Community Expectations (Dickens report)', Association of Chief Police Officers (UK).

Aitken, C, Connolly, T, Gammerman, A, Zhang, G, and Oldfield, D, 1995, 'Predicting an Offenders Characteristics: an evaluation of statistical modelling', Police Research Group, Special Interest Series, Paper No 4, Home Office.

Allen, DK, 1980, 'Entrapment and exclusion of evidence', *The Modern Law Review*, vol 43, no 4, 450-456.

Ascoli, D, 1979, *The Queen's Peace*, Hamish Hamilton.

Audit Commission, 1993, *Helping with Enquiries: Tackling Crime Effectively*, Audit Commission.

Audit Commission, 1996, *Tackling Patrol Effectively*, Audit Commission.

Audit Commission, 1998, *Tackling Crime Effectively, Volume 2*, Audit Commission.

Ball, J, Chester, L, and Perrott, R, 1978, *Cops and Robbers*, Penguin.

Bean, P, 2002, *Drugs and Crime*, Willan Publishing.

Bernhardt, DC, 1994, '"I want it fast, factual, actionable" – tailoring competitive intelligence to executives needs', *Long Range Planning*, vol 27, no 1, 12–24.

Beveridge, P, 1947, *Inside the CID*, Pan.

Billingsley, R, and Bean, P, 2001, 'Drugs, crime and informers', in Billingsley et al (eds), *Informers: Policing, Policy, Practice*, Willan Publishing.

Billingsley, R, Nemitz, T, and Bean, P (eds), 2001, *Informers: Policing, Policy, Practice*, Willan Publishing.

Bosworth-Davies, R, and Saltmarsh, G, 1994, *Money Laundering: A Practical Guide to the New Legislation*, Chapman and Hall.

Bowling, B, 1998, *Violent Racism*, Clarendon Studies in Criminology.

Byford, L, 1981, *Report on the Peter Sutcliffe Investigation*, Home Office.

Canter, D, 1994, *Criminal Shadows*, Harper Collins.

Capstick, J, 1960, *Given in Evidence*, John Long.

Cathcart, B, 1999, *The Case of Stephen Lawrence*, Viking.

Clutterbuck, R, 1995, *Drugs Crime and Corruption*, MacMillan Press.

Coates, T, 2003, *The Great Train Robbery. Reprint of 1964 HMI Report*, Coates.

Cobb, B, 1957, *The First Detectives*, Faber.

Copson, G, 1995, 'Coals to Newcastle: Police Use of Offender Profiling', Police Research Group, Special Interest Series, Paper No 7, Home Office.

Critchley, TA, 1967, *A History of Police in England and Wales*, Constable & Co.

Dorn, N, Murji, K, and South, N, 1992, *Traffickers: Drug Markets and Law Enforcement*, Routledge.

Emsley, C, 1991, *The English Police*, Pearson Education.

Ferguson, H, 2004, *Kilo 17*, Bloomsbury.

Fido, M, and Skinner, K, 1999, *The Official Encyclopaedia of Scotland Yard*, Virgin Books.

Fielding, H, 1743, *Jonathan Wild*, Penguin (reprinted 1983).

Fleming, R, and Miller, H, 1994, *Scotland Yard*, Michael Joseph.

Fletcher, I, 1991, *Craufurd's Light Division*, Spellmount.

Flood, B, 2004, 'Strategic aspects of the UK National Intelligence Model', in Ratcliffe, JH (ed), *Strategic Thinking in Criminal Intelligence*, 1st edn, Federation Press, pp 37-52.

Fordham, P, 1965, *The Robbers Tale*, Hodder and Stoughton.

Gaspar, R, 2002, 'Remedies', in De Ruyver, B, Vermuellen, G, and Vander Becken, T, 2002, *Edited Strategies of EU and US in Combating Transnational Crime*, University of Ghent, Maklu.

Gosling, J, 1959, *The Ghost Squad*, W.H. Allen.

Grieve, J, 2008, *Lawfully Audacious: A reflective journey*, in Harfield, C, MacVean, A, Grieve, J, and Phillips, D, *The Handbook of Intelligent Policing*, Oxford University Press.

Gross, H, 1934, *Criminal Investigation*, 3rd edn, Sweet and Maxwell.

Gudjonsson, GH, 2002, *The Psychology of Interrogations and Confessions: A Handbook*, Wiley.

Harfield, C, and Harfield, K, 2006, *Covert Investigation*, Oxford University Press.

Harfield, C, and Harfield, K, 2008, *Intelligence: Investigation, Community and Partnership*, Oxford University Press.

Hatherill, G, 1971, *A Detective's Story*, Andre Deutsch.

Hiley, N, 1997, 'Maggie's Hobby', a review of Smith, M, 1996, *New Cloak, Old Dagger: How Britain's Spies Came In from the Cold* (Gollancz), *London Review of Books*.

HMIC, 1964, 'The Great Train Robbery' (Reprinted by Tim Coates 2003), Her Majesty's Inspectorate of Constabulary, Home Office.

HMIC, 1997, 'Policing With Intelligence, Criminal Intelligence – A Thematic Inspection of Good Practice', Her Majesty's Inspectorate of Constabulary, Home Office.

HMSO, 1974, *Report into the circumstances surrounding the death of Kenneth John Lennon*, Her Majesty's Stationery Office.

Hofstadter, D, 1980, *Godel, Escher, Bach: An eternal golden braid*, Penguin.

Home Office Instruction 35/1986, *Use of Informants*, Home Office.

Home Office Instruction 97/1965, *Use of Informants*, Home Office.

Honeycombe, G, 1974, *Adams Tale*, Hutchinson.

Howe, S, 1997, 'Cross Border Intelligence', *Police Review*, 5 December 1997.

John, T, and Maguire, M, 2007, *Criminal Intelligence and the National Intelligence Model*, in Newburn, T, Williamson, T, and Wright, A, 2007, *Handbook of Investigation*, Willan Publishing, pp 199-295.

Kelland, G, 1986, *Crime in London*, Bodley Head.

Laurie, P, 1970, *Scotland Yard*, Holt, Rinehart and Winston.

Lee, D, and Pratt, C, 1978, *Operation Julie*, WH Allen.

Lowe, D, 2001, 'Shifting Focus', *Police Review*, 30 March 2001.

Macpherson of Cluny, SW, 1999, *The Stephen Lawrence Enquiry*, HMSO.

Mason, G, 2004, *The Official History of the Metropolitan Police*, Carlton Publishing.

McCafferty, J, 1975, *Mac, I've Got a Murder*, Arthur Barker.

McIntosh, M, 1971, *Changes in the Organisation of Thieving*, in Cohen, S (ed), 1971, *Images of Deviance*, Penguin.

McKittrick, D, Kelter, S, Feeney, B, and Thornton, C, 1999, *Lost Lives*, Mainstream Publishing.

McShane, Y, 1980, *Daughter of Evil*, WH Allen.

Metropolitan Police Service, 1994, 'Cracking Crime the High Tech Way', *The Job* (Metropolitan Police Service Newspaper), June 1994.

Metropolitan Police Service, 1998a, 'Delivering Information for Action: Strategies for Information and Communications Systems in the Metropolitan Police Service', *The Job* (Metropolitan Police Service Newspaper), March 1998.

Metropolitan Police Service, 1998b, 'Informant Working Group Report. Informing the Community: Developing Informant Risk Assessment to Reflect Community Concerns', *The Job* (Metropolitan Police Service Newspaper), July 1998.

NCIS, 2000, *The National Intelligence Model*, UK National Criminal Intelligence Service.

Neyroud, P, and Beckley, A, 2001, *Policing, Ethics and Human Rights*, Willan Publishing.

O'Callaghan, S, 1978, *The Triads*, WH Allen.

Pearson, W, 2006, *Death Warrant*, Orion Publishing.

Pedder, K, 2001, *The Rachel Papers*, John Blake.

PONI, 2007, *Operation Bastion*, Police Ombudsman for Northern Ireland, Northern Ireland Office.

Powis, D, 1977, *The Signs of Crime*, McGraw-Hill.

Ratcliffe, JH, 2008, *Intelligence-Led Policing*, Willan Publishing.

Read, L, and Morton, J, 1991, *Nipper*, MacDonald.

Reiner, R, 2000, *Politics of the Police*, 3rd edn, Oxford University Press.

Robertson, G, 1976, *Reluctant Judas*, Temple Smith.

Rossmo, DK, 1993, 'Multivariate Spatial Profiles as a tool in crime investigation', Workshop on Crime Analysis, Chicago, Il.

Rumbelow, D, 1971, *I Spy Blue*, Macmillan.

Savage, S, 2007, *Police Reform*, Oxford University Press.

Schengen Agreement, 1985, The Schengen acquis- Agreement between the Governments of the States of the Benelux Economic Union, the Federal Republic of Germany and the French Republic on the gradual abolition of checks at their common boarders. *Official Journal*, L 239, 22/09/2000 P. 0013-0018. http://eurolex.europa.eu/LexUriServ.do?uri=CELEX: 42000A 0922(01):EN:HTML

Silverman, J, 1994, *Crack of Doom*, Headline.

Sims, J, 1993, 'What is Intelligence?', in Shulsky, A, and Sims, J, *What is Intelligence? Working Group on Intelligence Reform*, Consortium for the Study of Intelligence, Georgetown University.

Small, G, 1995, *Ruthless*, Warner.

Smith, M, 1996, *New Cloak, Old Dagger: How Britain's Spies Came In from the Cold*, Gollancz.

Stagg, C, and Hynds, T, 2007, *Pariah: Colin Stagg*, Pennant Books.

Stanko, B, 2002, *Taking Stock. What do we know about interpersonal violence?*, UK Economic and Social Research Council report.

Sun Tzu, 1983, *The Art of War*, edited and with a foreword by James Clavell, Delacorte Press.

Travis, A, 2001, 'Partners in Crime: Policemen and Academics', *The Edge: The Journal of Economic and Social Research Council and Policy Forum for Executive Action*, Issue 8, November 2001.

Taylor, M, and Tidy, J, 2000, *Policing objectives obtained through targeted information*, Metropolitan Police Service Technology Futures Group, London, unpublished.

The Times, 2001, 'Obituary of David Powis', London, 5 January 2001.

The Times, 2008, 'Obituary of Bertie Smalls', London, 27 February 2008.

Vincent, CEH, 1881, *Police Code. Manual of the Criminal Law*, Cassell.

Wright, A, 2002, *Policing: An introduction to concepts and practice*, Willan Publishing.

Appendix: Towards a history of police intelligence in the UK

Date and Intelligence Event	Notes	References
1725 Jonathan Wild, organised criminal, and use of informers.	Thieftakers, trading justices, corruption and rewards for information.	Rumbelow (1971: 60–75) Fielding (1743) Emsley (1991: 18)
1749 onwards Henry and Sir John Fielding at Bow Street.	Bow Street Runners; Police Office at Courts and elsewhere; collecting information.	Rumbelow (1971: 79) Emsley (1991: 18-20)
1805 – 1829 Sir Charles Rowan, Sir Richard Mayne; joint Commissioners of the Metropolitan Police.	Rowan was one of 1st Commissioners trained by Sir John Moore and Black Bob Craufurd in military intelligence roles.	Fletcher (1991) Ascoli (1979: 80 onwards) Critchley (1967: 51-57) Cobb (1957)
1833 Sergeant William Popay unauthorised undercover role.	Alleged to have exceeded instructions of his Superintendent to observe public meeting in plain clothes and acted as a provocateur; Public Inquiry.	Emsley (1991: 29) Ascoli (1979: 104-106)
1840 Times newspaper calls for detective force.	'Active intelligent officers' employed sometimes in plain clothes; used to trace receivers of stolen goods and stolen property on each London division.	Cobb (1957: 170-182)
1878 – 1883 Howard Vincent.	Vincent (ex-Army officer) emphasises the importance of information from everyone; reforms CID.	Vincent (1881: 202)
1880 Undercover case against abortionist Thomas Titley.	Use of plain clothes sergeant and woman searcher draws judicial and public criticism.	Emsley (1991: 73)
1883 Special Irish Branch.	Unit set up by the Metropolitan Police; later called 'Special Branch'.	Mason (2004)
1918 onwards Flying Squad; Pickpockets Index and Handbook.	Work of the DI/DS Dance Brothers as undercover buyers. Squibs' Dance; 'Find the "run in" then you won't have to waste time following thieves'.	Capstick (1960: 52 onwards)
1945 Special Duty Squad; Ghost Squad (Metropolitan Police).	'Squibs' Dance used as role model for new units.	Capstick (1960: 91-97) Gosling (1959)
1950 onwards Responses to the rise of organised and project crime.	Groups of skilled, prolific pickpockets or armed robbers in particular but also others (for example, lorry hijackers, or protection gangs) as organised crime groups.	McIntosh (1971: 116-130) Hatherill (1971: 32)
1954 C5(2) Intelligence Section formed (Metropolitan Police).	Intelligence section as specialist officers to target the above organised crime groups.	Hatherill (1971: 32)

1960 C11 Centrally directed surveillance and collator system; career criminals. surveillance.	Focus turns to 'criminal not the crime'; collect, collate, disseminate.	Fido and Skinner (1999) Laurie (1970) Fleming and Miller (1994)
1960 onwards Stolen Car Squad; Glass's index; 'ringers'; Vehicle examiners.	Technology developments in recovering obliterated engine marks and uncovering false vehicle identities.	McCafferty (1975: 115) Fido and Skinner (1999)
1963 Great Train Robbery.	Knowledge of existing criminal networks used for crime investigation.	HMIC (1964) reprinted as Coates (2003) Fordham (1965) MacIntosh (1971)
1963 onwards The intelligence response to drugs and trafficking.	Greater use of criminal intelligence employed.	Honeycombe (1974) O'Callaghan (1978) Small (1995)
1964 Krays and Richardson gang investigations.	Major surveillance operation and intelligence operation involving sources; counterintelligence employed to avoid corruption.	Read and Morton (1991: 86)
1967 Regional Crime Squads created.	Emphasis on criminal intelligence.	Read and Morton (1991: 287)
1969 Home Office issues Guidelines on Informants and Agent Provocateur; related case law.	Within limits, informant identity needs to be protected but limit participation in crime, cannot counsel, incite or procure commission of an offence, nor embark upon a course which will constrain prosecution; cannot withhold information/mislead a court in order to protect; supervision of senior experienced officer required.	Home Office Instruction 97/69 R v Birtles (1965) 1 WLR 1047
1972 Central Drugs Illegal Immigrants Intelligence Unit formed.	National unit, later to become the National Drug Intelligence Unit.	Silverman (1994)
1969 – 2007 Terrorism, intelligence and the lessons from Northern Ireland.	The lessons here are numerous. This learning could be bookended by the cases of Kenneth John Lennon (1974) but originating allegedly in 1969; and the Report into Operation Bastion by the Police Ombudsman for Northern Ireland in 2007 concerned about informers.	HMSO (1974) Robertson (1976) PONI (2007) Savage (2007)
1972 Wembley Bank robbery.	Robbery Squad information-led approach set up. Use of *supergrasses* in prosecutions.	Ball, Chester, and Perry (1978) Times Newspaper (Obituary of Smalls, 2008)
1973 Court rules on entrapment.	Court rules that there is no defence of entrapment, being informed on one of the known risks of criminality; Three criteria for suspect suitability: the position of the accused, the nature of the investigation, the gravity or otherwise of the suspected offence.	R v McEvilly and Lee (1973) 60 CrAppR 150. Allen (1980)

1975 Association of Chief Police Officers (ACPO) Baumber Report.	Recommends creation of Force Intelligence Bureaus.	ACPO (1975)
1977 Lewisham 21 Defence Committee set up after arrest of black males.	First use of CCTV in street thefts cases, dedicated surveillance team, community impact assessments.	However, see http://en.wikipedia.org/wiki/Battle_of_Lewisham
1977 McShane case.	First use of concealed CCTV in premises in assisted suicide case.	McShane (1980)
1977 – 1984 Reforms of David Powis and others.	Influence of FBI at Quantico and John Jay College New York; Psychology, analysis and informants; Special intelligence section; ANACAPA and other analytic systems using contacts, open source, time lines, event charts, relationships, telecommunications.	Kelland (1986: 173-217) *The Times* (1997)
1978 Association of Chief Police Officers (ACPO) Pearce Report.	Recommends Regional Criminal Intelligence Units.	ACPO (1978)
1979 Malone case and onwards.	European Commission on Human Rights addresses interception of postal and telephone communications; release of information obtained from 'metering' of telephones.	Malone v the United Kingdom, ECHR judgment of 2 August 1984, Series A no 82, §84.
1980 Operation Julie.	Long-term undercover and surveillance operation into LSD trafficking.	R v Cuthbertson (1980) 2 All ER 401 Lee and Pratt (1978)
1980 Hodgson Committee asked to look at Profits of crime and their recovery; Confiscation of the Proceeds of Drug Trafficking Act, achieved Royal Assent in 1986.	Rise of the role of Intelligence Analyst; UK acknowledged the role of money in criminal activity; strategy to link drugs, money and people. The legislation identified new offences, powers, restraint orders, confiscatory fines and international dimensions.	Drug Trafficking Offences Act 1986, consolidated into Drug Trafficking Act 1994 Bosworth-Davies and Saltmarsh (1994) Dorn, Murji and South (1992)
1983 Greater international collaboration.	UK posts National Drugs Intelligence Unit Officer to Amsterdam; a Customs Officer posted to Karachi.	Dorn, Murji and South (1992)
1983 Developments in planning and intelligence management.	The contribution of Sir Kenneth Newman combines lessons from Northern Ireland with police, project management and business theory into surveillance, analysis, undercover work, informants, tasking, coordination and targets.	Savage (2007)
1983 Brinks-Mat Robbery investigation.	Highly significant organised/project crime; applied intelligence; joint Flying Squad and C11 Intelligence teams. Note also 1985 murder of Intelligence Officer DC John Fordham.	Pearson (2006) Bosworth-Davies and Saltmarsh (1994)
1984 ACPO Broome Committee.	Financial and regional drugs proactive information-led investigations and specialists.	Dorn, Murji and South (1992: 206-227) ACPO (1985)

1984 PACE.	Wide-ranging legislative framework for police powers in England and Wales.	The Police and Criminal Evidence Act 1984 (PACE)
1984 onwards Force Intelligence Development Steering Committees (FIDSC).	Number of working groups covering informants, collection coordinating and tasking.	Savage (2007)
1985 Interception of Communications Act.	Laid out system of warrants to permit legal interception of communications.	Harfield and Harfield (2006)
1986 Association of Chief Police Officers (ACPO) Ratcliffe Report.	Field Intelligence Officers and National Drugs Intelligence Unit.	ACPO (1986)
1986 More Home Office Guidance on informants who take part in crime.	Reiterates earlier instructions not to counsel, incite or procure.	Home Office Instructions 35/1986
1987 – 1989 Operation Lucy.	Crack-related violence information-led operations. Forerunner of Operation Trident.	Dorn, Murji and South (1992) Bosworth-Davies and Saltmarsh (1994)
1990 Association of Chief Police Officers (ACPO) Dickens Report.	Report that recommended the creation of a national intelligence organisation, which would become the National Criminal Intelligence Service.	ACPO (1990)
1991 – 1999 The rise of intelligence-led policing; SID and Kent Police.	SID –Systems for Investigation and Detection partly derived from FIDSC partly from development of quality, rigour and effectiveness in policing in Plus program; CRIMINT – Windows application, minimum staffing, roles, responsibilities, procedures, commonality; Promnoms, Devnoms and Agencynoms. Kent Police force-wide intelligence model at all levels, dissemination using new briefing/debriefing model, permanent briefing officer, debriefing prisoner interviews.	Clutterbuck (1995) Grieve (2008) John and Maguire (2007)
1992 National Criminal Intelligence Service.	Combines NDIU, Football intelligence, Customs (CEDRIC), Organised Crime (C11), International Liaison Officers posted UK and abroad. Prepares threat assessments.	Ferguson (2004)
1993 Winter, murder of PC Pat Dunne and other shootings; Drug Related Violence Intelligence Unit; Operation Trident created.	Red Lion PH Model (see main text); intervention by street officers, following the failure of joined up use of information at most senior level (1987-1989 successful Operation Lucy wound up). Arrangements formalised.	Silverman (1994)
1993 Audit Commission.	'Helping with Enquiries: Tackling Crime Effectively' published.	Audit Commission (1993)

1994 Undercover evidence in the murder of Rachel Nickell ruled inadmissible.	Undercover operation advised by lawyers and psychologist ruled inadmissible by trial judge as manipulating the innocent accused.	Pedder (2001: 386-401) Stagg and Hynds (2007)
1994 Europol begin limited operations.	European Police Office established by the 1992 Maastricht Treaty.	http://en.wikipedia.org/wiki/Europol
1997 HMIC publish 'Policing with Intelligence'.	Adds significant weight to the push for intelligence-led policing; leadership needed in intelligence 'energetic and enthusiastic'; Force Director of Intelligence, ownership, published strategy, integrated and communicated, dedicated training and particularly partnerships.	HMIC (1997)
1998 Human Rights Act published.	Proportionate, legal accountable, and necessary; acting on best information in intelligence operations impacting on rights of others.	Human Rights Act 1998 (c. 42)
1998 Crime and Disorder Act published.	Local authorities involved in intelligence led plans and partnerships. Some local authority intelligence and mapping units.	Crime and Disorder Act 1998 (c. 37)
1999 Stephen Lawrence Public Inquiry reports.	Criticism of local intelligence arrangements in Stephen Lawrence Inquiry.	Macpherson of Cluny (1999) Cathcart (1999) Grieve (2008) Ratcliffe (2008)
2000 RIPA published.	Wide-ranging law that regulates and overhauls surveillance and interception of communications legislation; Surveillance Commissioners appointed; covert human intelligence sources (CHIS) introduced.	Regulation of Investigatory Powers Act 2000 (c. 23)
2000 – 2007 National Intelligence Model and Serious Organised Crime Agency.	Development of intelligence-led policing through the National Intelligence Model, and the growth of SOCA.	Flood (2004) John and Maguire (2007) Flood and Gaspar (this volume)

CHAPTER 4

Strategic aspects of the UK National Intelligence Model

Brian Flood and Roger Gaspar

On a long and difficult journey the starting point, sooner or later, begins to look more attractive than the destination. That is how it has been for over 30 years for the police forces of the United Kingdom (UK) as they have tried to redefine their role in modern life. It has been a journey of adaptation: from the lingering, attractive certainties of the pre- and post-war years to the uncertain, information rich, intelligence-led, 21st century world of multi-agency law enforcement. This chapter briefly charts that journey and explains how a sharp understanding both of the realities of the nature of the modern criminal justice system and of the world of the criminals themselves has led to the acceptance of a new doctrine for policing.

Departure: An era of change and innovation

We can mark three eras in policing within the UK (Gaspar 2008): the first era of the patrolling uniformed officer with the single goal of prevention, the second of the patrolling officer and the reactive investigation, and, by the turn of the second millennium, the third era comprised patrol for prevention and immediate response, reactive investigation and proactivity in reduction, prevention and enforcement. The first era of the patrolling constable as the solution to crime was only sustainable until 1842 with the first detective establishment. In the second era, the Police Service developed an infrastructure to support the two functions of visible patrol and reactive investigation.

The development of the third era has some indistinct origins; however what can be said is that in the 1960s, for reasons that are still the subject of politically charged debate, a long established consensus fell apart. The consensus was that the constable on foot patrol was the keystone of law and order, with the detective catching those criminals that persisted in the life of crime. Whatever the merits of the contemporary arguments about the need to modernise the police and their methods,[1] or, indeed, the accuracy of the traditional image of the

---

1   For a polemical account of the issues see Hitchens (2003).

patrolling constable as a strong but avuncular figure dispensing wisdom and summary justice in equal proportions, for about a hundred years both police and public had shared a more or less workable view of what policing was supposed to be about. A big part of the perceived value of the 'Bobby on the beat' was his (they were, with few exceptions, men) familiarity with his principal clients: the local troublemakers and their potential victims. The policeman's lot was to deter the one and reassure the other. If that lot was not always a happy one it nevertheless had the great merit of clarity and was grounded in two principles of strategic importance: that the primary purpose of the police is to deter trouble rather than to clear up the mess afterwards, and that prevention of crime and other sorts of trouble is critically dependent upon the availability of the right kind of information about wrongdoers and their actual or potential victims. It was not until the mid-1990s that those truths came together again to enable the re-emergence of something like a common policing doctrine, albeit against a background of procedural changes in the criminal justice system and a change in concepts of punishment that, arguably, weakened the deterrent potential of individual police officers.

From the early 1960s, innovation was encouraged in many areas of public service. A number of different 'styles' of policing emerged in the succeeding 30 years, each accompanied by claims as to success and numbers of converts. 'Team Policing', 'Unit Beat Policing', 'Policing by Objectives', 'Sector Policing', 'Community Policing', 'Problem Oriented Policing', and currently 'Neighbourhood Policing' – the variety of labels underlines the gravity of the loss of what was an almost instinctive social accord about how to police most effectively. The plain fact is that until the 1960s there had really been only one way of policing; it therefore hardly needed a label, notwithstanding the gradual emergence of specialists in crime investigation and traffic patrol.

Progress at the strategic level was slow and it was not until 1975 that the Association of Chief Police Officers of England and Wales (ACPO) unequivocally endorsed the establishment of a force intelligence bureau in each police force as a vital part of the armoury that would help to overcome, inter alia, the problems that an essentially locally based national policing structure was bound to experience in tackling cross border criminality in the modern era of greater criminal mobility. This endorsement came through the Baumber report (1975), produced by the Association of Chief Police Officers of England and Wales (ACPO) Subcommittee on Criminal Intelligence (ACPO 1975). The growing power of information technology was quickly perceived as offering opportunities to enhance information flows and operational collaboration between police forces, although many years were to elapse before the vital, practical importance of common standards for recording and dissemination of intelligence material would be fully recognised. This finally happened with the introduction in 1999 of a voluntary code of practice for the Recording and Dissemination of Intelligence Material. Nevertheless, the 1975 recommendations were shortly followed by another ACPO report (the 1978 'Pearce' report) that emphasised the need to improve regional, or inter-force, criminal intelligence capability (ACPO 1978).

The process of rapid change and development was in large measure driven by an apparently relentless increase in levels of reported crime and disorder, much of which was interwoven with the increasingly ubiquitous drugs trade. Great efforts were made in the 1980s to manage better the response to reported crime. Crime management units appeared in many police forces. They put into effect schemes for 'grading' the police response to crime, which included sifting 'detectable' from 'non-detectable' crime, and they offered more support to victims. In reality, much of the 'management' effort of many crime management units was devoted to coping with the explosion in paperwork associated with reported crime rather than with the phenomenon of criminal activity itself.

Against this background, police strength grew from about 75,000 officers in 1961 to around 125,000 in 1991. Although support staff numbers had also grown, the increases did not keep pace with rising crime levels and it was clear by the early 1990s that substantial increases in police numbers were not to be expected. The 'demand gap' began to dominate thinking on future strategy. Table 4.1 below shows the gulf between changes in police strength and recorded crime across the UK, a gulf that demanded a re-establishment of the once universally accepted priority for preventive activity together with the intimate knowledge of criminals and their victims that had been at the heart of the traditional beat officer's role.

Figure 4.1 The 'demand gap' between recorded crime and police strength in the UK, 1970 to 2004

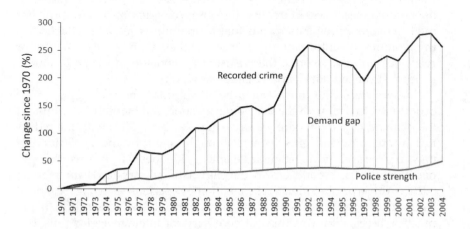

Source: Ratcliffe, JH (2008) 'Intelligence-Led Policing', Willan Publishing, p 19. Reproduced with permission.

By 1990, however, there was no longer any possibility of a return to the supposed golden age of policing as represented by the Bobby on the beat. Public attitudes to the police, the nature of calls on police time, including those emanating from an ever more demanding and seemingly eristic criminal justice system, a burgeoning 'rights culture' and increasingly resourceful and resilient criminals had effectively removed routine foot patrols from centre stage. One feature of the police response to complexity was to create more specialist units, which, notwithstanding any individual effectiveness in targeting areas of criminality such as drug dealing, had the unintended effect of splintering the policing effort at a time when the total available resources were considered to be less than those required to meet the demand.

As the Baumber and Pearce reports had implied, police force activity needed to be better co-ordinated, both internally and externally. That would only be achieved by making smarter use of available information and intelligence in order to deploy police officers to best effect. Neither of these reports, however, led immediately to a dramatic improvement in either intelligence processes or capacity. The explanation for that is twofold: first, most police forces were too busy investigating committed crime to devote significant resources to the development of intelligence systems, and, second, too great an act of faith was required, for there was no history of police intelligence gathering and intelligence exploitation, in a formal sense, outside of the work of the Special Branch and the maintenance of nominal indices by some specialist crime units (Chapter 3 by John Grieve describes these times in more detail). By and large, intelligence gathering from the 1960s onwards was more art than science with most collection capability consisting of the use of informants whose exploitation was usually immediate and sometimes dependent upon the personal insights, priorities and determination of the informant handlers. Intelligence activity in most police forces had exclusively short-term operational objectives. Moreover, the absence of any means to formalise intelligence requirements meant that a premium was often attached to the volume of information recorded rather than to its quality or relevance. In other words, there existed no coherent doctrine of intelligence that spelled out clearly what it was all for.

Where was the infrastructure to support the development of proactivity, to deal with the new sophistication and mobility of criminals, the demand gap and – dare we say – the changes to deal with the reduction in our previous 'effectiveness' brought about by the application of new procedural laws, standards and guidelines? If it was thought necessary in the second era to develop national standards for matters such as fingerprint evidence, the creation of specialists such as Scenes of Crime and Scientific Officers and to search for best practice in many practical areas, why was this not necessary for intelligence-led policing? Of course it was.

Arrival: Learning from the experience of change

The 'demand gap' was real enough though and, as it showed no sign of diminishing, a small number of police commanders began to attach crucial importance to the gaining of a proper understanding of what exactly was going on, at least in the areas for which they were responsible. With the recognition that better information, obtained in a more disciplined fashion, was becoming an increasingly urgent and fundamental requirement, intelligence-led policing was born and, for the first time in the modern era, some police forces began to take a more genuinely strategic approach to the management of their business, an approach grounded in a more precise knowledge and understanding of the problems they faced. Furthermore, the signposts from Baumber and Pearce were still standing, pointing to the wider context for intelligence activity and suggesting that a whole national intelligence structure would be greater than the sum of its parts. In short, the framework for a national doctrine of law enforcement intelligence work was coming together.

The UK's National Intelligence Model (NIM) is the direct descendant of those early developments in intelligence-led policing. The first models were produced in 1993 and 1994 and received a timely boost from the Audit Commission (1993) which drew particular attention to the apparent cost-effectiveness of intelligence, especially that derived from informants, as a means of identifying active offenders and bringing them to justice. The attempts to introduce intelligence-led policing effectively acknowledged, however, that the emphasis in police work had shifted from a doomed effort to detect all the perpetrators of greatly increased volumes of committed crime to a direct attempt to reduce the crime rate and incidences of disorder. There was, however, no centrally driven coordination of effort and progress relied on piecemeal development. In the first edition of this book, Steve Christopher in his otherwise accurate assessment of the NIM after its introduction makes one error in asserting that the National Criminal Intelligence Service (NCIS) 'were commissioned by ACPO to construct a model that would galvanise the service into standardisation of process, the intention being to situate the model as the defining paradigm for contemporary policing' (Christopher, 2004: 184). Alas there was no such commission; indeed there was silence and from many quarters assumptions that all that 'intelligence business' could be left to the then newly created NCIS. The originators of the NIM (primarily the authors of this chapter) had to form their own ideas, consult, seek buy-in and then persuade a policing community itself under pressure from the various dynamics taking place within UK policing at the time.

One specific dynamic was the enormous pressure on NCIS to deliver following its independence from the Home Office on 1 April 1998. Once the post-creation honeymoon was over, the organisation was required to deliver something of use: it had to have sources of information or it would fail. While NCIS was able to do good work on targets in association with local forces, the National Crime Squad and other agencies, the production of the UK Threat Assessment was a particular vulnerability. At an early stage, strong support was obtained from the Organised Crime Strategy Group (OCSG) for the Threat Assessment. This group, chaired by the Home Office and attended by all agencies involved in any way in law enforcement agreed that the NCIS-produced Threat Assessment would be the principal stake in the ground for the creation of the National Organised Crime Strategy. This drove demands for information from forces which many were ill-equipped to supply. Either the information was not there, was not in a retrievable form or comparison was difficult because of differing methodology and standards.

It was clear that the production process behind the writing of the first threat assessment could not be sustained; too much effort was going into the collection of data leaving inadequate time to think about what the data were saying. In a climate where production to a timetable pushed all other considerations aside, the evolution of objective processes for assessment were unlikely to be created without some specific initiative. The situation was that NCIS was in a corner. By dint of its own intention that the Threat Assessment would not just be another document set in a bookrack, but used to help set the national strategy and lead to priorities for prevention, enforcement and intelligence, NCIS had proposed the pivotal role of the Threat Assessment to the OCSG: NCIS now had to deliver.

While NCIS could (and did) issue an intelligence requirement, it was clear that guidance was needed to create the infrastructure throughout the Service that enabled forces to answer the question. It was also clear that such an infrastructure should not be separate from that necessary to make intelligence-led policing a reality at local levels.

At all events, by 1999 enough experience had been gained in individual police forces for the NCIS to attempt to pull the lessons together and produce a single doctrine for tackling crime and disorder on an intelligence-led basis at local and regional levels and for tackling the organised criminality that generally operates in the national and international arenas. The NIM, released in May 2000 in booklet and CD-ROM formats was the result.

The nature of the modern problem

A need to manage the structure of law enforcement better

It will not escape the critical reader that the approach described above, while seeking to integrate activity at the three described levels, nevertheless departs from the conventional 'single stream' view of the need for intelligence to meet strategic, tactical and operational requirements. The NIM is essentially designed to support intelligence-led proactivity in the 43 police forces of England and Wales (in Scotland the Association of Chief Police Officers (Scotland) has also been an enthu- siastic supporter) and it therefore acknowledges the structure of UK policing. The UK policing structure is one in which resources are allocated primarily to local business, which has led to a significant gap in police ability to operate across police force boundaries and in which specialist resources are dedicated to the pursuit of serious and organised crime. While the NIM does indeed describe a process by which national strategy may impact on local policing priorities, it also acknowledges the fact that local police commanders are likely to have priorities of their own that are equally important strategic drivers for their business. In NIM terminology, therefore, 'strategic' is not a term related to exclusively national or whole law enforcement perspectives but is one that is applied to the process of business planning and resource allocation at each of the structural levels within UK policing.

The starting point for successful planning and resource allocation in law enforcement, as in any other undertaking, is 'knowing the business'. The NIM attempts to provide a means by which police commanders in particular, and law enforcement policy leaders in general, can confi- dently approach the problems they face by using a methodology that enables them to devise properly prioritised strategies (for there are never enough resources to do everything) and to execute tactical options with a good chance of success. It provides a framework, too, for integrating better the activities of individual units within police forces (and, as experience shows, between police and non-police agencies) in support of the common strategy and, indeed, for measuring performance against strategic objectives. Its procedures, based as they are on knowledge, are sufficiently sensitive to take quickly into account the emergencies and unforeseen demands that frustrate the steady pursuit of strategic objectives in the generally chaotic day-to-day world of law enforcement.

NIM as a policing business model?

A question that is seldom asked is 'if the role of the model was intended to be the central paradigm for modern police business, why was it called an "Intelligence" Model and not the UK Policing Business Model?' This seemingly simple question is perhaps of more importance than it looks.

It was the view of those in NCIS in 2000 that it would not have been acceptable for NCIS to produce a UK 'Policing Business' Model even if that is what it was. The product was the same whatever the title but consideration had to be given to the acceptability of its presentation. NCIS had set off on a path towards achieving a multi-agency organi- sation (by 2002, the majority of its members were not police officers) and it was not regarded as mainstream policing. This may be regarded as a lack of confidence, but context is everything. At best, delay was seen as inevitable if NCIS had tried to promote a business model; at worst it might have been outright rejected. So the ruse of the title of Intelligence Model was adopted.

There were two dangers in this approach. The first, and this may have been realised, was that the Police Service would not make the shift of paradigm and place the model central to day-to-day business. Second was that ACPO and the Home Office – with their predilection for 'initiatives', 'crackdowns' and other headline-catching exercises – would come to regard the proposals for installation of a modern approach to intelligence across the police world as just another option in styles of policing alongside Neighbourhood Policing or Problem Oriented Policing. The aim was the introduction of a common system that would ubiquitously and continuously run quietly in the background to ensure that all command areas had the best available picture of the problems they faced, and that they could communicate their information to partners in a mutually comprehensible language. In that kind of a world there would be no sudden, politically driven demands for 'crackdowns' because it would long since have been apparent to responsible law enforcement leaders that something needed to be done. As two of the architects of the NIM, we knew that the intelligence model was in fact an ideal model for the whole business of policing that would enable police commanders to understand and anticipate risks and threats across the public safety domain.

The fundamental problem is how to make sense of all the threats and opportunities that exist, so that some sort of coherent choice can be made, and the crime or disorder be rendered more difficult to commit the next time around. There the NIM offers some solutions that are based on pragmatism, a recognition of what works, and on some techniques that help reduce complexity to manageable, if imperfect order.

A need to manage risk in the law enforcement environment

It is helpful, even if somewhat artificial, to view the problem for law enforcement in two parts. The first concerns the nature, demands and risks of the law enforcement environment itself, which includes the criminal justice system. The second concerns the nature of the criminal environment, where the criminals are incessantly active and inventive, cooperating with each other and victimising the rest of society. The job for the intelligence professional in law enforcement is to provide the best possible view of the critical issues in each of these environments. Let us start with a consideration of the law enforcement environment.

One of the less happy realities of life for managers in law enforcement agencies is the extent to which their professional judgments and decisions are hedged about with risk. This is perhaps the most profound change in law enforcement to have occurred in the last 20 years. There is almost no area of activity where it is not necessary to guard against the need to account for decisions made, perhaps many years after the event. A lot of police time is devoted to the defensibility of: strategy; operational decisions; resource management decisions; information handling policy and practices; measures taken for the protection of sensitive techniques, and measures taken to preserve confidentiality and meet duties of care, to name but a few.

Some of the increased effort put into risk management merely reflects the litigious nature of modern society. In the face of an established social trend that seems to disallow honest mistakes, apportions blame and makes sure that someone 'pays' whenever misfortune strikes, it is nothing more than common sense to ensure that police actions should be based, wherever possible, on rigorously evaluated intelligence of known provenance rather than on intuition, even where the latter may have its roots in long experience.

Many of the risks that need to be managed are, however, much more specific than the mere threat of litigation in response to mistakes. They derive from a wealth of legislation on criminal justice and social issues introduced in the past few years. Perhaps the most fundamental step taken by government to have impacted on the culture of the law enforcement agencies was the incorporation of the European Convention on Human Rights (ECHR) into domestic legislation. Articles 6 and 8 of the Convention guarantee rights to fair trial and privacy respectively and their incorporation has widened risks of exposure of intelligence sources and techniques in the courts. Authorisation procedures for intrusive surveillance of all sorts have become highly formalised and are now subject to independent scrutiny by the Office of Surveillance Commissioners, following the passage of the ECHR-inspired *Regulation of Investigatory Powers Act 2001* (UK).

The upshot of all this is a requirement for intelligence processes and intelligence products that have a sufficient degree of integrity both to justify intrusive operations and to withstand the scrutiny of trial judges. In major cases, where intelligence may be derived from a number of sources, as well as from different police forces or even from different units within a single law enforcement agency, the chances of securing judicial protection for intelligence techniques and material may be damaged if common standards are not seen to apply to all the relevant intelligence products and collection processes.

A connected legal issue concerns police duties of care to human intelligence sources, to victims or potential victims of crime and, indeed, to police employees themselves. Aside from the implications of health and safety legislation in respect of law enforcement staff employed on hazardous work, police have become sensitised to the question of duties of care as a result of decisions in the courts. In particular, these decisions raise, in certain circumstances, the prospect of civil claims.[2] The mitigation of these risks plainly demands a comprehensive intelligence picture

---

2   See the cases of *Swinney v Chief Constable of Northumbria* [1996] 3 All ER 449, for the issue of protection of confidentiality of sources, and *Osman v UK* (1998) 29 EHRR 245, for the issue of duty of care in respect of possession of information that may indicate the existence of a threat to life.

of the threats to sources, and a level of capability in information systems and analysis that does not permit serious threats to individuals to remain submerged in a sea of superficially unremarkable data.

In common with most public services, the police and other law enforcement agencies have come under pressure in recent years to demonstrate value for money. A local police command area budget may amount to tens of millions of pounds each year and a commander needs to be able to show that the money has been efficiently and wisely spent in pursuit of improved performance within a coherent strategy. Exactly what a coherent, actionable strategy should contain is a far from easy question for commanders to answer. It will certainly need to take into account objectives and priorities set by government, potentially conflicting demands from local authorities and pressure groups, the realities of current criminal threats and threats of disorder, the nature of community relations and tensions as well as the reality of varying levels of capability on the part of neighbours and partners who may be essential to delivery on strategic objectives. While there are no wholly correct answers for any command area it is clear that avoidance of too many wrong answers is easier if reliable intelligence is available in the form of intelligence products that support the setting of priorities.

At the national level, in tackling serious and organised crime and delineating national strategies that enable the law enforcement agencies to act in concert, the questions are no less difficult. The delivery of strategy is dependent upon a consensus between government departments, the police and other law enforcement agencies about what the priorities actually are and whether a viable tactical response program can be put together. Capability in intelligence and operational response varies significantly at this level, just as it does in local law enforcement. Operations and trials are much more likely to carry a high risk of exposure to sources and techniques, trials are more likely to be hard-fought and performance is more difficult to manage and explain. Complications are likely to arise from engagement with foreign jurisdictions, security demands are more acute and maintaining the unity of purpose of agencies with different cultures, internal pressures and ambitions can be difficult, but is vital. The point is that without intelligence the required case for cooperation cannot be adequately made in the first place, the priorities cannot be identified, the threats cannot be tackled, the most impactive [opportunities cannot be seized, the activities of agencies cannot be coordinated to best effect and, above all, we cannot know how well we are doing.

The procedures and products of the NIM were designed to enable the better management of the risks in the difficult law enforcement environment on the basis of enhanced knowledge and more formalised decision-making. Although that risk management capability is essential it is nevertheless more about defensibility of decisions than about taking the practice of law enforcement forward. To see how the NIM does that we need to turn to a consideration of the criminal environment.

A need to manage complexity in the criminal environment

The key issues in the criminal environment are its extent, its complexity and the fact that criminals are not passive but seek constantly to get better at what they do and make it more profitable. Of course, some of the problems of disorder that make people's lives a misery, which the intelligence disciplines of the NIM are also designed to help tackle, are occasioned by drunkenness or self indulgence that may not necessarily arise from any enduring evil intent. The following observations are, however, primarily concerned with the problem of managing criminality.

The great difficulty we face is in trying to visualise the criminal environment. It seems chaotic, overpopulated, complex and constantly changing in character and impact. Yet some things in it are stable and endure and it is in pinning down a description of those things that we come to a sufficient understanding of the environment so as to enable meaningful strategies and tactical responses to emerge. This all sounds rather theoretical but is rooted in a simple proposition: if a police commander were able to describe or chart all the criminal problems in a command unit, he or she would have the basis for a highly impactive strategy. The tactical execution of the strategy would inevitably depend on the extent and capability of the resources that could be deployed but 'knowing the business', that is 'painting the picture' of crime, gets one off to a very good start. Similar considerations, though with some difference of emphasis in the content of the 'picture', apply to the problem of tackling crime at a cross border or regional level and for the national agencies in their challenge to organised criminals' trafficking of drugs and people.

Naturally, any such holistic picture of criminality must be over-whelmingly large but, as has already been argued, there are some enduring features in the criminal environment that give us a starting point for reducing it to something much more manageable, for putting it all on 'one page'. The settling of this fundamental taxonomy permits identification of the prominent features and patterns that in turn enable the identification of enforcement priorities and the application, through well informed decision-making fora, of a 'tactical menu' to deliver against the priorities. This is what the NIM attempts to do.

Victims: the first consideration

Victims comprise the first element of the picture. In any crime strategy a primary ambition will be to reduce numbers of crime victims. For a crime strategy to be impactive therefore, it needs to be based on knowledge of how people, especially the young and vulnerable, and business and finan-cial institutions are victimised, how systems are abused or circumvented, who has become a victim, what the connection may be between particular victims and what the patterns of victimisation look like geographically and temporally. There also needs to be some predictive capability in the intelligence process as well as sufficient sophistication to translate all this knowledge into target hardening opportunities to reduce the likelihood of future victimisation and to capitalise on successful investigations.

Volume crime: the core of 'core business'

Volume crime comprises the second element of the picture. The NIM recognises that volume crime – burglary, theft, vehicle crime, street robbery and the like – is so extensive and of such overwhelming importance to the day-to-day lives of police commanders that it needs to be made susceptible to a knowledge-based attack if there is to be any hope of bringing it under control. It has long been acknowledged that it is impossible to investigate every committed crime. Some criminals are, however, 'high risk' offenders responsible for disproportionate numbers of crimes (Audit Commission, 1993), and some are more dangerous than others. The key to management of this aspect of criminality lies chiefly in understanding its patterns: the crime scenes that are connected by *modus operandi*, time or other features and which therefore form 'crime series', the geographical areas that constitute crime and disorder 'hot spots', the identity of the high risk and repeat offenders and, these days, the connections between drug addiction and acquisitive crimes. The management of volume crime through discovering the patterns is, at least in part, a matter of securing best value from police operations: it is cheaper to investigate fifty burglaries as a single series than to investigate them individually, and the more data there is in the pot the greater the chance of suspects emerging. This approach assumes, of course, the existence of a significant tactical capability that can respond to the identification of 'crime series' and 'hot spots' and can target the right offenders.

Criminal specialists: a challenge to law enforcement

The third element of the picture concerns the criminal specialists. These are the people who are good at what they do. In some cases they understand better their criminal business than do the law enforcement officers who are trying to stop them. These people are sensitive to the environments in which they operate, exploit market opportunities, build extensive links with suppliers and supporters, often exercise a measure of influence over the volume criminals and serve as role models for the up and coming young villain. They specialise in drugs supply, in fraud, in ringing stolen high value motor cars, they provide security (including the penetration of law enforcement) and money laundering facilities for other criminals, they provide safe outlets for stolen property, they specialise in the provision of transport for traffickers. They are the forgery experts and credit card manufacturers and they exploit fully the opportunities offered by the disclosure rules of the criminal justice system to learn how the police threaten their criminal activities. Aside from the obvious requirement to know who these people are, the key to tackling criminal specialists lies in understanding how they are networked and how their criminal businesses operate. The analysis of criminal business informs the investigators' work and gives a practical shape to crime prevention initiatives.

Criminal leaders: a challenge to the entire criminal justice system

The fourth element of the picture is closely connected to the area of specialist criminality. It is not necessary to identify formality of hierarchy and structure in criminal relationships in order to acknowledge the existence of criminals who exercise a high degree of control and direction over others. Their ascendancy may be built on the length of their experience, on their family connections, on their reputation for extreme violence and their readiness to prove the validity of that reputation, on their tribal influence within an ethnic group or on simply being the nastiest person in the neighbourhood. Whatever the explanation, they cannot be tackled on the basis of a conventional investigation and they cannot be brought to book without intelligence processes and products of the highest calibre and integrity. These are the people who corrupt public officials and members of law enforcement agencies. They may have millions of pounds worth of difficult-to-trace assets with which to support and develop criminal lifestyles and spread corruption. They run legitimate businesses as fronts for criminal activity and know how to exploit the difficulties faced by investigators operating in the international arena. They are masters of their trade and come to grief rarely. When under threat they take steps to protect themselves: they may attempt to sow discord between agencies, they may bring in lawyers to challenge investigations at an early stage and may attempt to penetrate law enforcement agencies with informants tasked to cultivate and corrupt law enforcement officers. There are not so many criminals of this calibre but they constitute a challenge to the very foundations of the criminal justice system that must be answered. Investigations against criminals of this type cost millions of pounds, often end in failure and thereby tarnish the reputation of the whole criminal justice system.

On the other hand, the very sophistication and complexity of their business activities makes them vulnerable to a high quality intelligence attack. They need sources of supply, access to markets and the ability to exploit systems. They need good communications with suppliers, conspirators and others. They need transport, finance and the services of middle men. They need to build and sustain a reputation and they need to be able to manage risk, not just that posed by the criminal justice system but also threats from criminal competitors. The effort to understand how all these things work and to penetrate the business relationships is central to law enforcement's prospects for success.

All of these components (victims, volume crime, criminal specialists and criminal leaders) demand an intelligence response of the highest calibre. Such a response is possible.

Solutions to the modern problem

Aligning business processes with the problem

If we accept these four elements in the picture of criminality we have a workable basis on which to build some strategies and from which to launch a tactical response. The NIM attempts to serve both ends. Its doctrine describes methods for identifying priorities, methods for managerial decision-making at strategic, tactical and operational levels, standards in intelligence activity and the range of assets and intelligence products that enable all these things to be done. In short, the NIM puts intelligence and intelligence-related processes at the very heart of law enforcement business and demands a tactical response capability focused, at least so far as crime is concerned, on the four elements of the picture of crime and criminality described above.

At the heart of business management in the NIM is a tasking and coordination process that depends upon the delivery to managers of a range of intelligence products. That tasking and coordination process operates at both strategic and tactical levels. The model describes four intelligence products: strategic assessments, tactical assessments, problem profiles and target profiles[3] that individually or collectively support the setting of strategy, the application and monitoring of a menu of tactical options and the conduct of operations that deliver against the 'tactical menu'.

The NIM's emphasis is deliberately on formal intelligence products. Intelligence process in law enforcement cannot be merely a voyage of discovery but demands predictability in the delivery and content of intelligence products for managers' decision-making.

The charge of complexity is often levelled against the NIM. It is true that there are a lot of words written within the model but it can be stated quite succinctly. The heart of the process is the Tasking and Coordination process chaired by the head of the command structure and comprising the people in charge of the deployable resources within the command. They receive one or more of four intelligence products to help them make decisions. Those intelligence products differ depending upon whether the group has a strategic or tactical responsibility.

If strategic, the group works on the Strategic (or Threat) Assessment and sets and resources the Control Strategy identifying the priorities for prevention, enforcement and intelligence. If tactical, following the dictates of the Control Strategy, the group works from the *tactical assessment*, the *problem profiles* and *target profiles* to determine deployments of the tactical menu.

Within this system comes the mechanics: analysts prepare the intelligence products using a number of analytical products – techniques – which are nationally agreed and taught to national standards. In resolving any issue, managers must be aware of the four intelligence assets necessary

---

3   In some jurisdictions, the term *subject profile* has replaced *target profile*.

for success: *sources* (of information), *people* (to collect and make sense of information), *system products* (to enable efficient handling of information) and *knowledge products* (to ensure best practice and standards).

That is it! It can be applied at a national level, a regional level, force level or at the local level. And since it is a business model, it can be applied outside of law enforcement. We explain the thinking behind these concepts below.

Aligning strategy to the problems

From the strategic tasking and coordination process should flow a 'control strategy' that sets the priorities for intelligence, enforcement and prevention. This is now a feature of local, regional and, indeed, national law enforcement business, although with currently varying levels of effectiveness that reflect the ongoing process of implementation of the NIM. At the national level, the United Kingdom Threat Assessment from Serious and Organised Crime (SOCA, 2008) is the principal strategic assessment that supports law enforcement activity. Similar threat assessments at the regional level are designed to support the setting of regional control strategies that take into account specifically regional priorities but also incorporate the regional and local implications of the national inter-agency strategies on serious and organised crime.

The setting of a control strategy within a strategic tasking and coordination forum that brings together relevant units and law enforcement partners is described in the model as the prelude to application of the 'tactical menu' under the aegis of a similarly constructed tactical tasking and coordination group.

Aligning tactics to the strategy

The 'tactical menu' is, again, derived from experience. Its content has sought to bring as much clarity and simplicity to the description of the core of intelligence-led policing as possible. There are essentially four things that can be done to manage criminal activity as it was described in the discussion on the criminal environment set out above:

- the **targeting** of individual criminals or criminal groups and networks;
- the identification and management of crime and disorder '**hot spots**';
- the identification and investigation of '**crime series**'; and
- the application of a range of **preventive measures**, which may include everything from requirements for legislative and policy changes, neighbourhood watch schemes, Closed Circuit Television (CCTV) systems and directed patrols, to innovations such as 'restorative justice' programs.

All four options are likely to be pursued at the local level of law enforcement. At the regional and national levels target work is certain to be of more significance but the contention holds good that the described 'tactical menu' represents the full range of options that require consideration. Of course, the secret of both medium- and long-term success lies in securing synergy between the areas of activity so that lessons learned and intelligence gleaned from 'crime series' investigations, 'hot spot' management and target operations are absorbed and used to inform new tactical choices or consolidate the gains through well-informed preventive work.

The tactical assessment is the primary intelligence product supporting the tactical tasking and coordination group's business. At the local or regional level the tactical assessment addresses the current options for targeting, the knowledge of current and emerging crime series together with the requirements for their investigation, the emergence of crime hot spots, other trends and opportunities and requirements for preventive initiatives. It also gives an account of progress made on previously launched operations and identifies new resourcing issues that may impact on performance. The job of the tasking and coordination group is to ensure that the progress on previously agreed plans is being maintained, that new proposals fit the business priorities and, above all, that the assets needed for their delivery are in place. The key to success in the tasking and coordination group's business is the care taken in preparation of the assessment: if the assessment is well prepared the debate will be less about whether proposed initiatives should be launched than how to sustain the allocation of resources to their execution.

Aligning operational intelligence products to the 'tactical menu'

The two operationally focused products, problem and target profiles, are the means by which the analytical work leads to opportunities for action within the 'tactical menu'. Problem profiles describe connected criminal acts ('series' crimes), the nature of 'hot spot' problems and criminal business methodologies. They describe trends and criminal market phenomena within particular areas of criminality or, indeed, geographically. Again, the key to success in intelligence-led policing is the synergy between its components. Problem profiles should routinely lead to the creation of target profiles. They enable investigators and policy makers to tackle the criminals responsible for the trouble analysed in the problem profiles and to link preventive initiatives to the described reality of where and exactly how the criminals are doing their business. The NIM provides techniques for both gaining the upper hand over criminals and keeping it.

This connectivity between assessments and problem and target profiles is no less important in tackling organised crime. Both target work and preventive initiatives are of primary importance to the interagency strategies for managing organised crime. But the scale of the problem (be it international drug trafficking or people smuggling, for example) is often so extensive that a generic exercise to look for targeting and preventive opportunities, for 'series' of evidently connected events or geographical 'hot spots' of criminal activity is too random to strike at the heart of the matter. Nor, as a consequence, does it offer any real opportunity to assess with confidence the 'overall' impact of what is being done: it is necessary to break the problem up into manageable chunks. So the national interagency response to the hard drugs trade, for example, defines 'theatres of operations' in which targeting and preventive work is to take place. The scope of the 'theatres' is based on both common sense and the knowledge provided by drugs related problem profiles. 'Theatres of operation' in trafficking crimes might include overland transit routes, points of entry, abuse of legitimate systems, criminal financing, the role of the 'middle market' dealers in sustaining the trafficking networks, and so on. In a regime such as this the connectivity between problem profiles and target profiles enables performance, that is, the impact of the law enforcement effort, to be assessed with some confidence that the results reflect the extent to which real damage is being done to the criminals and criminal businesses.

Although things seem more complex at some levels of the model, the fundamental process is, in fact, the same: the strategic assessment enables the strategic tasking and coordination group to set the priorities. Through tactical tasking and coordination, problem profiles are commissioned to illuminate opportunities for tactical response and the best means of effecting it. Problem profiles lead to target profiles and assets are lined up to enable investigation and disruption of those criminals and criminal groups chiefly responsible for the criminality described in the problem profile. There is thus a direct link between the strategic assessment and the law enforcement work actually carried out, a linkage that offers a pragmatic basis for performance management.

Looking back and looking ahead

The UK wide implementation of the NIM is a manifestation of the regained consensus about the primarily preventive purpose of policing. As discussed at the beginning of this chapter, that purpose was explicit in the role of the highly visible, traditional, patrolling constable and was, in large part, a function of the constable's knowledge of the problems on his or her beat and of the people who caused them. Nowadays, prevention is a more complex undertaking but it remains grounded in the requirement to 'know the business'. There is nothing new in the desire to get ahead of the criminal. What is new is the formalisation of the strategic knowledge base through the compilation of assessments and problem profiles, and its exploitation through tasking and coordination disciplines. This process is increasingly well understood. Nevertheless some significant challenges remain.

As regards the NIM, there are perhaps some mixed messages about the damage caused by the decision to promote an intelligence model rather than a business model. On one hand, patterns of criminal behaviour still take some in law enforcement by surprise, and within some of the recent initiatives there seems to be little evidence of under-standing of the nature of problems. This is evident when the responses have the traditional look of specialised teams and names such as 'Task Force'. In training, the Intelligence Model still retains that title and is delivered as a way to tackle crime and not police business. This suggests little progress on the central issue.

On the other hand, early on Home Office required police forces to adopt the National Intelligence Model and it is firmly embedded in the National Police Plan (Home Office, 2005). Subsequently, the International Division of Home Office ensured that the UK Presidency of the EU was used as an opportunity to press for a European Intelligence Model. This now features in the EU Strategy for tackling organised crime (Europa, 2005).

There are at least two main issues. The first flows from the necessary deception in the title of the NIM (as explained earlier) and attempts to situate the model as the defining paradigm for contemporary policing. Many have not been sufficiently convinced of the realisable benefits of an intelligence/information rich environment. The result is that there is not much evidence that information management, as opposed to information collection, is really at the heart of UK law enforcement, either in policy or routine policing practice. The problem may be intrinsic to the political relationship between government and the police in so far as governments that live by headlines and spin do not necessarily want a long term, considered assessment of crime and disorder problems; their survival depends upon their being seen to be doing something. Criminal intel-ligence brings bad news along with the good, and the structure of politics can no longer cope with warnings of impending failure in social policy. So there is only a limited resolve to invest in information management – just enough to keep out of trouble.

The second issue is closely allied to the first and that is to appreciate that we have stepped into a new era and that an investment in infra-structure and the development of understanding is vitally important. Intelligence-led policing is not about using more informants or more specialist surveillance teams. It is about understanding crime and disorder problems and using that knowledge to pursue remedies. Information and assessments are the cornerstone of that understanding and achieving excellence in those areas requires just as much effort as went into learning how to interview vulnerable witnesses, find latent marks at scenes of crime or develop DNA profiles. This will be an incre-mental process; there will be mistakes made and misunderstandings. The design of the National Intelligence Model was not the conclusion of this work; merely the beginning.

References

ACPO, 1975, 'Report of the ACPO Subcommittee on Criminal Intelligence' (Baumber report), Association of Chief Police Officers (UK).

ACPO, 1978, 'Report of the ACPO Working Party on a Structure of Criminal Intelligence Officers' (Pearce report), Association of Chief Police Officers (UK).

Audit Commission, 1993, 'Tackling Crime Effectively', HMSO.

Christopher, S, 2004, 'A practitioner's perspective of UK strategic intelligence', in Ratcliffe, JH (ed), *Strategic Thinking in Criminal Intelligence*, 1st edn, Federation Press, pp 176-192.

Europa, 2005, Commission Communication to the Council and the European Parliament of 2 June 2005, 'Developing a strategic concept on tackling organised crime', COM(2005) 232.

Gaspar, R, 2008, 'Tackling International Crime: Forward into the third era', in Brown, SD (ed), *Combating International Crime: The Longer Arm of the Law*, Routledge.

Hitchens, P 2003, *A Brief History of Crime*, Atlantic Books.

Home Office, 2005, 'National Policing Plan, 2005-2008'.

SOCA, 2008, 'UK Threat Assessment of Serious Organised Crime 2008/9', Serious Organised Crime Agency (UK).

CHAPTER 5

Task definition

Jonathan Nicholl

Seven years after first considering the concept of task definition, knowing why an intelligence assessment is required and how it will be used remains a deceptively simple proposition. The basic principles of task definition remain relationship management, refining the question and maintaining analytical integrity; however, new factors have come into play including agency and product context, multiple 'anonymous' clients and intelligence product as a quantitative and qualitative measure of individual and agency performance.

It is not, on face value, overly different to similar work undertaken by law enforcement agencies. For example, if a policy officer is asked to write a briefing paper they will know why it has been requested (as a result of an event or an issue), what it will be used for (to position the agency and influence the event) and the officer will generally receive feedback on the utility of their work to determine if it assisted to position the agency appropriately.

Why then is this concept seemingly so complex for the intelligence producer? Many intelligence reports curiously suffer from a fundamental misunderstanding of what was originally asked. This is often the case even when the intelligence analysts producing the reports are qualified and skilled in the field, and their clients qualified and skilled in theirs. At times like these, the disconnect between expectation and delivery is stark. While the glib response might be that this failure to deliver the right product is simply attributable to poor management, it nonetheless suggests an important part of the intelligence process is either not understood or missing altogether.

From the intelligence professional's perspective, identifying the client and what they want and need is the leverage on which quality work depends. Defining the task and understanding the client, because it is the first consideration in the intelligence cycle, determines whether the product succeeds or fails. Client conviction that the product they receive answers the question asked and proves to be of utility to them, is the most desirable end goal for the analyst.

From a client's perspective, intelligence can often remain an unknown quantity or a frustration; 'Why can't they tell me what I need to know?' or 'I ask a simple question and the answer is neither simple nor accessible'. Of course, a frustrated or ignorant client is not necessarily the fault of the intelligence producer. If clients are unfamiliar with intelligence or under considerable pressure their demands can be unreasonable and their expectations of what the intelligence product can do for them unrealistic. However the key point for the analyst to remember is that the net effect of such a client, left unhappy, is the same – product produced for an unreceptive audience is likely at best to receive minimal attention or at worst face a concerted effort to destroy it.

To overcome the disconnect between producer and client, intelligence analysts need to embrace the concept of 'task definition'.

Task definition is the process by which intelligence professionals ensure that the product requested is the product created. Successful task definition can be summarised as both the intelligence analyst understanding what the client wants and working to that aim, and also the client understanding and embracing what will be produced, how the product can be used and the product's limitations.

To achieve that goal I will outline a number of concepts that can be used to guide the intelligence practitioner in defining a task with their client. These can be loosely grouped under the following categories: *managing the client*, *refining the question* and *maintaining analytical integrity*.

Managing the client explores why the relationship between analyst and client is critical and examines the role of the analyst as a 'relationship manager'. This section will also underscore the importance of clearly identifying the client and the business they do, as well as how to manage client expectations. It will also explore the concept of ongoing engagement with key clients. When *refining the question*, the analyst should work with the client to define and refine the tasking question. This section considers how to clarify what is really wanted by the client and what to do if the intelligence producer discovers the client's question is not realistic to answer. While the process of task definition is essentially one of negotiation, it is also necessary to *maintain analytical integrity*. Strategic intelligence analysis must have credibility and integrity as intelligence, yet a common error among intelligence specialists is to forget that there is a basic difference between policy and intelligence. This section will explore where that difference lies and how to avoid making the error. Ensuring integrity is maintained in an increasingly politicised work place and in the face of deadlines and ever increasing demands is not easy, but I suggest that it is possible.

Traditionally the skill set of the strategic intelligence professional has largely been assessed on the individual's ability to analyse intelligence. In this context a premium is often placed on the 'technical' skills of the profession, specifically the ability to:

- consume and understand broad or specific data from multiple sources;
- interpret medium- and longer-term issues; and
- produce insights.

While these skills are integral to the success of an analyst there is also an attendant danger in this approach. It ignores the *process* of interaction between analyst and client that is vital to ensuring proper input to the process of task definition, analysis and the creation of a valued intelligence product. The processes of *managing the client, refining the question* and *maintaining analytical integrity* will be examined in the following sections. We begin with the client-analyst relationship.

Managing the client

As intelligence practice and capability has matured within law enforcement, the analytical community has improved in terms of both depth and sophistication. However distrust and ignorance of intelligence and its practitioners remain.

Intelligence has traditionally been perceived by law enforcement agencies as being a support function, designed principally to serve the core operational capability of the organisation. As late as 2002, the then National Crime Authority, Australia's national body charged with fighting organised crime, described the intelligence function (its number one organisational output) in these terms (National Crime Authority, 2002: 18).

Within Australia this situation has changed substantially. State and Federal governments established the Australian Crime Commission in 2003 as the country's first national criminal intelligence agency with an investigative capacity and access to coercive powers. Concurrently, State and federal police forces also invested much in developing their intelligence capabilities. Intelligence as a discipline is therefore no longer new, but is not quite fully integrated into organisations either.

The role of criminal intelligence, particularly at the operational and strategic levels was historically limited to the reactive analysis of events after they had occurred. Similarly operational commanders still regularly decide to target a particular crime type in an area and intelligence is asked to provide advice on this decision *after* it has been made. This, even when the intelligence analysis probably played a significant role in first indicating the growth in a particular crime type in the local area. Contrast this with the defence and national security spheres where intelligence is often relied on to take a lead role to inform decisions as yet unmade. This contrast is attributable to a number of factors, the most crucial being that these intelligence systems are mature, understanding (and expectation) of what they can deliver is high and its practitioners have developed credibility and expertise over a considerable period of time.

The relative immaturity of the intelligence discipline within law enforcement environments means that the profession is still evolving. Often this finds manifestation in unreasonable expectations on the part of both the analyst and the client. Users often expect intelligence to be served up to them on demand, but fail to understand, or show scant appreciation of the reality of the time and effort that is often required (McDowell, 1994: 7).

Intelligence producers (and their clients) often work under considerable pressure with a natural tendency to look for shortcuts in processes to achieve a result. The more experienced we are, the more powerful this urge in turn can become as we grow more confident in our own abilities to produce intelligence. We also like to believe our understanding of client needs is beyond reproach.

It is worth noting that a refinement of the task is made harder by an inexperienced client. If the client's experience in dealing with intelligence as a decision-making tool is rudimentary and unsophisticated, the pressure on the analyst is accentuated. In this case, the client will generally be unsympathetic to even reasonable requests for more information, more time or a response indicating the question posed cannot be directly answered. This last problem will require the task to be refined as will be discussed in the next section.

As has been discussed in general terms so far, task definition relies on a 'producer-client' model used to describe a process to be followed by the analyst and client. This process has a number of elements:

1. relating to the client;
2. knowing your client's business;
3. recognising multiple clients; and
4. managing client expectations.

Before examining the elements of the model we should consider a significant change in understanding the intelligence producer's role – the concept of the intelligence producer as a relationship manager. This concept underpins and informs the other elements of the task definition process.

Relating to the client

Strategic intelligence officers increasingly operate in support of multiple clients ranging from internal executive leadership to external clients at varying levels. They are responsible for providing a broad range of strategically focused analyses which feed into executive decision-making processes within their own agencies and in other agencies at the centre of government. For example a task force run by the Australian Crime Commission may routinely have its strategic intelligence product read and acted upon by clients ranging from Local Area Commanders in jurisdictional police forces to senior policy makers in central government departments. Often a single intelligence product is read by a range of clients each for their own purposes. The variety of expectations inherent in writing for multiple clients makes the importance of relating to clients of intelligence products even more critical.

In meeting these responsibilities the intelligence officer needs to work closely and in unison with the client who the product is aimed principally for in negotiating the focus of the strategic intelligence product, while at the same time reporting to the intelligence manager. This balancing requires excellent communication and relationship building skills – it is no longer enough for an analyst to rely *solely* on good conceptual and analytical abilities.

McDowell suggests that intelligence managers are the link between two distinctly separate realities, that of corporate expectations and agendas, and the skills and professionalism of strategic intelligence operators (1997: 21). However, the separation between these two realities is no longer so distinct. While it is outside the responsibilities and generally the skills and experience of the analyst to negotiate on corporate direction or focus of an agency, the strategic analyst needs to liaise *directly* with the executive to gain knowledge of those activities relevant to the intelligence topic. The advantage in this approach is that the intelligence officer:

- has the opportunity to tease out the specifics and details of the tasking;
- can ensure that the tasking directive does not get confused in the translation from one person to another; and
- provides them with an opportunity to have input into the tasking directive.

This approach can be divided into two key strategies – the explicit and implicit engagement with a client. In explicit engagement, the analyst is able to meet with the client and ascertain directly what is wanted, why it is wanted and what are the time frames. This results in a clear direction for a particular piece of intelligence product. Implicit engagement has its basis in knowing the client's business to the extent that the analyst is able to intuitively understand the type of intelligence products they will be interested in and will be of most value to their work.

Neither implicit nor explicit engagement works in isolation. The problem with explicit engagement alone is that it is inherently reactive as it relies on the client knowing that they want or need an intelligence product, and will usually only occur after a problem which needs analysis has been identified. Likewise implicit engagement can give rise to the analyst who claims to know their client from afar, reliant on publications, open information sources and their own views in determining what intelligence product is required.

The answer lies in the combination of the two strategies; explicitly engaging with a client on a regular basis to inform the implicit understanding of what the client is doing, their priorities and the intelligence product they require. This is not easy as it requires the analyst to have a broader knowledge than previously expected and necessitates looking beyond the confines (and comfort zone) of their own work. Using this model the analyst needs to be aware of client needs, policy considerations and agency context, and proactively manage their intelligence product to suit.

While engagement is occurring between analyst and client directly or indirectly, it is also important for the analyst to keep their direct line manager in the loop as to how the relationship is progressing. As McDowell (1997: 21) notes:

> Throughout each strategic intelligence project activity, management overview must be maintained on the progress being made and the directions being taken as the project evolves through the acquisition of data and its subsequent analysis. It is important, too, for the nexus between the intelligence problem and its contextual setting within corporate goals to be maintained; it is the manager's role to ensure that awareness of corporate activities (relevant to the intelligence topic) is kept up to the intelligence officers working on the project.

To gain a comprehensive and first hand knowledge of what is being requested of the analyst it is often best to negotiate directly with the client rather than solely relying on an intelligence manager for direction. Of course this requires the delicate balancing of keeping the intelligence manager well informed while dealing directly with senior executives. Direct contact will enable the analyst to gain insights into what the executive require. It will also work to the benefit of the line manager, ensuring that their section and staff are producing a valued product while at the same time empowering those staff working for them. Law enforcement agencies have progressed this approach in recent years and it has become routine in the Task Force I currently lead for intelligence staff to engage directly with stakeholders from multiple agencies, while keeping me appraised of key developments and issues which may require my intervention.

In utilising direct contact the analyst needs to elucidate from the client exactly what it is that they want, why they want it and how the analysis will feed into, or impact on, the decision-making process. At the same time it is also the responsibility of the analyst to inform the client of the intelligence perspective, capability and limitations. To achieve this balance, strategic intelligence analysts should strive to be effective in their verbal communication as well as written skills. Effective communication with stakeholders, particularly those at senior levels, requires the analyst to combine diplomacy and tact with strength and conviction in their ability and analysis.

The client may be very specific about what is required or may only have a vague notion of what is needed. In either case it is the responsibility of the analyst to ensure discussions with the client translate into a tasking definition reflective of the client's needs (and the analyst's capability). Most importantly the analyst needs to have a thorough understanding of what is required as opposed to what they *think* is needed. Depending on the work being undertaken, the process of defining the task may develop as the work progresses and the analysis reveals itself, or it may be specific and unchanging throughout the life of the project.

There are a number of strategies which can be used in defining the task and they all rely on a level of intuition by the analyst and whether the task is being prepared as a result of direct or indirect engagement between analyst and client.

Under the direct engagement strategy, a task may first be defined through a verbal agreement with the client. This approach is often subject to the vagaries of interpretation and is usually only really effective when the client is very specific in detailing what is required and the analyst is confident they understand that requirement. A safer and more credible approach (time permitting) involves written documentation. This can either be in the form of a minute or a detailed project plan signed off by the analyst, their clients and managers. In time-critical situations an email confirmation from analyst to client as to what is to be undertaken can suffice.

At this early stage it is imperative to clarify clear directions on what is required. Factors which an analyst generally needs to know in order to gain a comprehensive understanding of the tasking directive include:

- what process is the analysis to feed into?
- why is it required?
- when is it needed?
- how will it be used?
- what will it be used for?
- what format is required?
- what level of detail is required?

The last point is particularly significant, as products can range from an in-depth picture to a short snappy synopsis of the criminal environment. This range of basic information is not always provided to analysts. As Peterson (1994: 16) points out:

> The 'failure' of intelligence assessments cannot always be lain at the door of analysts or intelligence officers. Another former CIA manager ... commented that 'Policy makers rarely spend much time detailing to intelligence producers what they need or want to know ...' Thus, the lack of direction may lead to incomplete information-gathering or analysis.

The indirect engagement strategy relies on many of the principles outlined above but also relies on the analyst having a greater knowledge and understanding of the client's business to produce a product.

Knowing your client's business

At this stage the analyst is also generally able to provide preliminary advice to the executive of the feasibility of approaches based on their expertise and knowledge of the subject area. The context of the task impacts on the focus of the analysis and needs to be clearly discussed and delineated. The operating environment of the client agency is therefore paramount in the analysis. For example, the factors to be considered when providing advice on a legislative matter have a different bent to analysis focusing on predictive environmental findings, where a range of perspectives need to be brought into play when analysing intelligence. The important factor is that the client's environment is identified upfront, and that it provides a context within which the analyst conducts the analytical phase.

An analyst who is aware of the client's knowledge base will be better placed to determine the level at which the analysis and language should be pitched. For example, the use of technical terms may be inappropriate or may need to be defined according to the client's level of understanding. A pitfall can be the oversimplification of a topic leaving the client concerned with the level of analytical knowledge or commitment.

Recognising multiple clients

Attempting to deal directly with a primary client may be complicated by the involvement of multiple clients. In this situation, more than any, it is vital that communication with clients remains open and honest. It is important to bring the clients together at the project planning phase and throughout critical stages of the project. Direct engagement strategies include:

- video or telephone conferences; or
- getting the clients physically together in a meeting room; or
- having the analyst individually meet each client then presenting a unison of views in a detailed project plan, requesting that each client sign off on the plan once they are happy with the approach.

The first two strategies are potentially risky. Video or teleconferencing can be stilted with people less likely to give a full account of their desires and needs, especially with other clients, potentially viewed as 'competitors', present. The same concern can apply with physical meetings, although there is perhaps a greater opportunity for the analyst to fill the role of 'honest broker' in these circumstances.

On balance the last strategy offers the most advantages – it allows the analyst to manage the process of ascertaining differing requirements, provides time for the analyst to weigh and balance the needs and provides a clear written record which can form the tasking directive upon which the clients agree, and to which the analyst will work.

These strategies are really only applicable in direct engagement. Where the analyst is required to engage indirectly with clients, a different strategy must be used. Direct meetings with the clients may not be possible or very limited and in these cases the analyst's knowledge of the clients' business will be essential in tailoring a product which meets in full or in part their needs.

The issue of multiple clients not only has the potential to complicate the direction and content of the strategic analysis but also the form of the finalised product. This is further complicated by the nature of information or intelligence used by the analyst and their security clearance level. This is an important factor that must be carefully considered when working to a range of clients. Different clients may also want different end products and this must be clarified with each client upfront, taking into account the time frame for the project and the resources available.

There are several options available to the analyst when managing this issue, and they require the analyst to consider the circumstances before them. It involves the ability to manage time, consideration of the acceptable number of different versions within the project time, appropriateness of formats, the range of different audiences, and the security clearances required. In some circumstances it may be necessary to tailor the intelligence product to meet the different characteristics of each client. In many cases, with time a pressing concern, it may be inappropriate, based on the intelligence used, to have a range of different products and the final product has to meet a compromise in content and format. The central issues here are identification of the constraints and the degree of flexibility possible within the identified restrictions.

It remains up to the analyst to negotiate an outcome that is workable for both them and their clients – again underlining the importance of analysts being assertive and having excellent interpersonal skills. Usually a product accompanied by an executive summary will satisfy the needs of a client requiring a high level of detail as well as a client who can only focus on the key issues presented. In other cases, a 'sanitised' version of the product may need to be produced in order for the product to be used by a particular client who either does not have the appropriate security clearances for the original product or (and this can happen frequently) wants to use the intelligence in a forum or environment where the same level of protection cannot be afforded the product.

Managing client expectations

Negotiating with the client will involve clarification of the magnitude of the task. This involves (among other things) communicating the complexity of the task, availability of intelligence/information, collection plan and a feasible time frame for completion. It is also the optimum time to manage the client's expectations regarding outcomes. In managing expectations it is often useful to be proactive in your advice, while listening to what is required. Pragmatism and realism in advice and approach are essential characteristics at this stage of negotiations. If the client is kept abreast of the characteristics of the task's components and has an understanding of what is required in order to provide the analysis they need, they are brought into the process and have a degree of ownership and involvement. This can only be truly achieved when the analyst has a good liaison process established with the client and can exchange views in an honest and straightforward manner.

Ownership and involvement in the tasking process goes a long way to ensuring client satisfaction with the end product. On the basis of this it is important to keep the client informed at critical stages of the project, from information collection to analysis and the writing up of your findings. The benefit of this is that each stage of the project could reveal a need to shift direction, or the client's perspective may change during the process. Either way these shifts need to be communicated. Bringing the client into the process encourages active participation, and also acts as a safeguard, ensuring the client agrees with the path you are heading down and is aware of all alternatives.

The final advantage is the relationship building benefits which flow on from this consultative approach. The client not only feels part of the process, but feels ownership of the project. The result is increased endorsement and support for the end product. This goes a long way in ensuring continued support for the role of strategic intelligence in the executive decision-making process, and reinforces intelligence analysis as an integral part of the agency's operations.

Refining the question

In this section we will combine the client relationship issues with the need to refine the question using a hypothetical example with mainly indirect client engagement possible.

Let us imagine that the analyst is working on a task force formed for a limited period of time by government to tackle corruption in publicly funded non-government organisations (NGOs). The task force has four broad objectives it must meet over the two-year period of its life. These objectives are:

- understand the nature and extent of corruption in publicly funded non-government organisations nationally;

- identify information sharing impediments to the prevention, detection and countering of corruption in publicly funded NGOs; and

- identify best practice strategies in the prevention and detection of corruption in publicly funded NGOs.

There is no other direct tasking of the analyst working on the task force. Their context is three broad objectives and pressure from task force managers and clients to 'produce some intelligence'. What should the analyst do?

From the section already covered, it is clear the intelligence analyst should develop an understanding of who are the key clients of the task force. In this case while policing agencies will naturally be interested in intelligence on this topic, the key stakeholders will be those responsible for administering the funding of NGOs – government departments involved in health, community services, sports and the like. It's critical to understand what these clients' main concerns are and what they are expecting from the task force. If possible, meetings with key representatives from each agency should be pursued but the analyst needs to be prepared to move forward on the basis of indirect engagement only or (at best) limited contact with stakeholders.

In this example the analyst decides what products to produce in consultation with internal managers, informed by the objectives of the task force and the key functions of the client agencies. Where possible, contact should be made with key areas within the client agencies to advise of the proposed product and seek support. If the analyst and their managers have done the groundwork, such consultation should be a simple and painless process – the analyst will be proposing a product that the client will readily support. An indirect benefit of this approach is a client being approached pro-actively and requiring minimal input.

The process of question refinement can be iterative, with shifts in focus required as more information is revealed during the collection and analytical phases or as circumstances change for the client. While it is important to define the task upfront, flexibility in the project's direction is at times inevitable, particularly when dealing with an agency execu-tive, and often depends on the nature of the request.

Periodically revisiting the tasking ensures all the bases are covered, especially if new information reveals that a different approach is required. Ongoing revision and refinement of the task also ensures focused analysis and prevents 'mission creep' – the gradual extension of analysis beyond the task required. It is a safeguard from straying away from what the client wants to know as opposed to what the analyst thinks the clients should be told. This element of the analytical process requires a good level of intuition and discipline. While the analyst needs to ensure the analysis is focused and hits the mark by reflecting what the client wants, the analyst also needs to judge whether additional infor-mation is helpful or will ensure the client is aware of every aspect of the subject area.

A question may need refinement not only because of changing client requirements but also because of a changing awareness on the part of the analyst. As Mathams (1988: 8) indicates:

> It is often the case that the desk officer has a wider understanding of a problem and its context than the decision-maker ... In such cases the desk officer may well propose changes to the definition of the task or at least ensure that the decision-maker is aware of the additional relevant information.

Question refinement not only gives the analyst the opportunity to seek greater clarification and understanding, but it also allows the client to better appreciate the complexity and the breadth of the issue. From this process, the question may be further narrowed or widened to ensure the client's requirements are met.

Returning to the hypothetical question, after undergoing a process of internal deliberation and consideration with managers of the task force's objectives and the client(s) needs, and preliminary research – in short understanding the context in which the question has been posed – it would not be unreasonable to expect the analyst to have refined the broad operating environment into a task similar to the following:

Box 5.1 Refined task

'To what extent does corruption exist in federally funded non-government organisations in this country?'
 A short, classified, briefing paper of no more than 10 pages, including an executive summary, is to be produced for Deputy Chiefs of the Federal Departments of Health, Families and Communities. A secondary audience will be jurisdictional police intelligence commanders. The deadline is 12 weeks from today and the paper will inform multi-agency responses to this problem.

Thus far we have examined the mechanics of defining a task, but ultimately we need to consider how to apply the individual elements of client understanding, management, liaison, question refinement and feedback effectively and consistently. As has been discussed, the application of task definition processes is critical to developing ongoing credibility with the client and for individual products.

The possibilities for the application of the task definition process are potentially endless, dependent on each intelligence officer's personal approach to their work. Some will choose a largely verbal approach with client and manager while others may favour a formalised project management approach using modern project management software and techniques. The correct approach is the one that best suits the individual work environment, the level of client and analyst understanding of the process and the intelligence producer's skill set. Often it will be a case of trial and error until the correct approach is settled, however the emphasis should be on the analyst to tailor *their* style and approach to best suit the style and requirements *of the client*.

There are a number of different tools that can be used to define the task and the following form is one such example. It has its origins within the Strategic Intelligence Unit of the former National Crime Authority and has been refined over some years and is now used more widely. It is by no means a ground-breaking document: it draws on well established project management and client feedback principles.

The form consists of a series of questions that should initially be answered by the intelligence producer. Each question has explanatory sub-questions which are designed to assist in refining that particular item more tightly. The document also provides the basis for consultation and forms the start point for liaison between client and producer. As is the case with client-analyst consultation, the document may appear in several drafts before finalisation is achieved. Crucially the document calls for sign-off on the planned product by client(s) *and* producer *and* line manager. Having formal sign-off on the question to be answered and the approach to be taken is highly desirable. In the event that the question needs redefining because of a change in circumstances (as discussed previously), the signed-off plan can be a useful reference to understanding what was originally requested and what aspects need to be modified in order to meet the new or altered question.

The following hypothetical example represents a compromise between a purely informal verbal approach to task definition and the ongoing management of the project, and the highly formalised approach called for in true project management systems. For our purposes here, the example country is Australia, and the example State is New South Wales.

Box 5.2 Intelligence Product Proposal

PROJECT TITLE **Extent of corruption in publicly-funded non-government organisations**	DATE TO COMMENCE: 1 March 2008
PROJECT MANAGER/S: Jonathan Nicholl	DATE DUE: 31 May 2008
SECURITY CLASSIFICATION (PLEASE BOLD): Unclassified In-Confidence **Protected** Highly-Protected	PRIORITY (Please Bold): Low Medium **High**

Background How was the need for the task identified? Who requested the task?	1. The Australian Government is concerned at the potential for poor administration and corrupt practices in publicly funded Non-Government Organisations (NGOs). 2. In response, a Task Force has been established to examine this problem further, with the primary objectives listed below. 3. The Task Force requires a baseline intelligence assessment to provide an understanding of the nature and extent of corruption in publicly funded NGOs.
Task Force Objectives	1. Understand the extent of corruption in publicly funded non-government organisations nationally; 2. Identify information sharing impediments to the prevention, detection and countering of corruption in publicly funded NGOs; and 3. Identify best practice strategies in the prevention and detection of corruption in publicly funded NGOs. *... cont*

Proposed Outcomes *Please indicate which objective the outcome will meet. Please directly relate each proposed outcome to the objective.*	• **Meets Task Force Objectives 1, and contributes to 2.** • An intelligence assessment of the current nature and extent of corruption in publicly funded non-government organisations. • In providing an assessment of the nature and extent, the product is expected to illustrate information sharing impediments to the detection and countering of corruption in publicly funded NGOs.
Length	No more than 10 pages inclusive of executive summary.
Proposed activities relating to outcomes *What will you do to deliver the proposed outcomes?*	• Liaise with jurisdictional police and relevant federal agencies to ascertain existing relevant data holdings. • Open Source Intelligence search and search of existing internal data holdings. • Analyse all collected intelligence to produce assessment.
Project Risks *List possible organisational exposure, failure to meet deadline, inability to meet other organisational priorities etc.*	• Delays in accessing and receiving relevant information • Willingness of other agencies to share information • Competing tasks and availability of resources through life of project.
Resources	1 X Senior Analyst– 50% 1 X Intelligence Analyst – 100%
Critical Time Frames *Include progress briefings, submission of first drafts and final document/output*	12 week time frame. • Progress reporting to Task Force leadership Group at scheduled VIDCONs and meetings • Initial liaison with stakeholder agencies – weeks 1 – 4 • Collection and analysis of data – weeks 1 – 6 • Preparation of draft assessment – weeks 6 – 8 • Distribution of draft to key stakeholders for feedback and review – weeks 9 – 10 • Incorporation of final changes, finalisation and distribution of assessment – weeks 10 – 12.

... cont

Information/Data Collection *List information/data sources and how information will be gathered, eg, reports, surveys, etc.*	• Police reports, data and intelligence • Justice / Correctional Services data • Open Source records • Other agency records • Interviews with identified key individuals and agencies. *Attach separate Information Collection Plan if appropriate*
Draft Consultation Process *Who should comment on draft products? What is the proposed time frame for comments?*	1. Identified senior representatives from Departments of Justice, Health, and Families. 2. A sample group of senior representatives from jurisdictional police services. 3. Appropriate peer and internal management review.
Dissemination Strategy *Specify dissemination targets and form of dissemination (electronic, paper, briefings, workshops etc)*	• The assessment will be disseminated in hard copy to the Departments of Justice, Health and Families. • An electronic copy will be made available nationally via the national Australian Law Enforcement Intelligence Net (ALIEN). • The assessment will be presented to a senior stakeholders group from client agencies at a date to be identified.
Project Evaluation *Time frame for evaluation, format, team, key performance indicators.*	• Assessment is completed and disseminated in timely fashion. • Assessment provides a nuanced understanding of the extent of corruption in NGOs. • Case Study informs the basis of operational and/or strategic responses by client agencies.

Approved by	Team Leader	Manager	Endorsed by
Signature			
Date			Date

Maintaining analytical integrity

Much of the conflict and confirmation experienced between intelligence professionals and decision-makers can be attributed to a lack of under-standing of respective roles. In the past, the intelligence community has tended to attribute this lack of mutual understanding to an unwillingness or inability by policy makers to understand the nature of intelligence work. A purist, almost arrogant, approach pervaded this thinking, based on the false notion that intelligence is a pure, objective discipline that should be respected only in its own right and critically could not be considered sub-servient to any other discipline within the agency.

In modern organisations, particularly those where the prime role and function is not intelligence production (such as a law enforcement agency), this approach is fundamentally flawed. It is the responsibility of the intelligence officer to understand the decision-maker's goals and objectives, even more so than the responsibility for the decision-maker to understand the role of the intelligence professional.

Mathams (1988: 14) states; 'Intelligence is not produced for its own sake nor to provide intellectual satisfaction for the analyst. Assessments of intentions and estimates of capabilities are prepared as advice to policy makers'. Matham hints at the necessary divide between the stra-tegic intelligence producer and the consumer. The intelligence producer deals with information. They assemble information, assess the quality of the data and provide analysis or assessment as the result. The policy maker on the other hand deals with action and events, either to minimise the impact of an event or to ensure it is fully exploited to achieve organi-sational aims and objectives. The traditional divide between producer and client outlined above ignores the symbiotic nature of the intelligence – policy maker relationship. One is partially blind without the interplay with the other. In this model, the intelligence producer is interested only in facts while the policy maker is interested only in consequences.

While strategic intelligence producers should never allow policy convictions (either their own or their client's) to colour their analysis, they must be implicitly and explicitly sympathetic to it. In the example of NGO corruption used earlier, it is of little use producing an intelligence assessment focusing on a specific NGO corruption activity being encoun-tered by the Police Service if the current focus of the policy maker is the real or perceived growth in other aspects of NGO corruption. Knowing and understanding the client's current focus is an essential element of ensuring the work produced is welcomed by a receptive client as a relevant and timely contribution. Most critically, client understanding maximises the chance that the intelligence will be utilised and have a positive impact on the criminal environment.

This approach to intelligence production is markedly different to the traditional model of intelligence as a static but objective tool. In an era of shrinking resources relative to organisational responsibilities, many organisations cannot afford the luxury of purely objective general intelligence advice. Instead, they seek intelligence to guide and support specific strategic goals from in-house resources, and seek wider, general intelligence from other specialist intelligence agencies or from open sources. In this way an effective police service will typically possess an intelligence arm focused on providing intelligence advice on specific areas of interest, and the intelligence will be tailored to support the particular aims and directions of the organisation. The service may draw upon wider and more general intelligence and information from specialist agencies such as the Australian Crime Commission or the Australian Institute of Criminology in Australia, and from the Home Office and the Serious Organised Crime Agency in the United Kingdom. The limit of this wider collaboration is, more often than not, only in so far as it supports organisational direction and goals.

The above scenario does not mean that in-house intelligence produced under this model is 'tainted', however the tailoring process does mean that in-house intelligence producers should be sensitive to client needs and approach the gathering, collation, assessment and dissemination phases of the intelligence process with this in mind. While this may be an anathema to the traditional intelligence practitioner, particularly in the more mature intelligence systems of national security and defence, it is nonetheless the current reality within the strategic criminal intelligence environment. For intelligence to flourish it must prove to be useful and be seen to support the decision-maker. It cannot do this if it is not serving the decision-maker's needs.

Examining the hypothetical example, it would be inappropriate for the NGO corruption paper to recommend a specific course of action to be implemented to combat the threat posed by NGO corruption (if any) uncovered by the project. The task did not request options. Equally however, it would be particularly useful for the paper to canvass strategies that have been used successfully elsewhere in similar policing and social contexts and present these as options worthy of further consideration. Such recommendations would also prove valuable if they can identify emerging or potential issues of concern as yet unconsidered by the client's agency, and in doing so provide valuable lead time for the development of an organisational response.

In the event that the paper finds that NGO corruption is of little concern at present, it could helpfully point to potential indicators and warnings that could be used to alert the Police Service to the emergence of NGO corruption as a localised threat.

In applying this approach the analyst is straying from the purist approach to intelligence but they are not producing policy or advocating a single course of action. They are however ensuring that the client is provided with a relevant and context-specific product and in doing so increasing the credibility and relevance of the work.

Conclusion

This chapter has examined the fundamentals of the task definition cycle; managing the client, refining the question and maintaining analytical integrity. All of these elements are crucial to the process but the emphasis upon the analyst-client relationship has been deliberate. Of all the elements this is the most important.

The analyst-client relationship is critical for a number of reasons. It provides the basis on which subsequent parts of the definition process can grow. Refining the question, managing the project through its life cycle, convincing others of the credibility of the product and ensuring it is used: all of these stages will be for naught if the client-analyst relationship is not strong, open and honest. A poor analyst-client relationship has implications beyond the task definition process. The whole of the intelligence cycle is adversely affected with ill-focused research and analysis, inappropriate reporting style, content and format, minimal interest in the published product and either poor or completely absent feedback processes.

As mentioned previously, the emphasis on relationship management represents a new dynamic for most intelligence analysts; it places new and a sometimes difficult responsibility on their shoulders and in some cases engages them with internal agency processes more than they might wish.

The growing emphasis on relationship management within the analytical community has significant implications for law enforcement agencies with an intelligence capability. An exclusive focus on recruiting only those people with high-order technical skills is as flawed as a focus on recruiting only those with excellent interpersonal and diplomatic skills. A balance needs to be struck.

Different emphasis in recruitment programs is required to identify those with the right mix of skills. Agencies and individuals should consider training opportunities to develop communication skills and client relationship techniques. Emphasis should also be placed on continuing to educate clients as to what intelligence can provide within a law enforcement agency. Over time this educational osmosis will contribute to a higher level of client understanding of the intelligence capability and a maturation of the law enforcement intelligence systems generally.

To avoid the responsibility to foster the client-analyst relationship will not make it any less important. A failure to act will contribute significantly to ensuring that intelligence product and its practitioners continue to be misunderstood, misused and misrepresented.

References

Mathams, RH, 1988, *The Intelligence Analyst's Notebook*, Australian National University Strategic and Defence Studies Centre, Canberra.

McDowell, D, 1994, 'Law Enforcement Decision-Making: The Pivotal Role of Strategic Analysis', *Journal of the International Association of Law Enforcement Intelligence Analysts*, vol 8, no 2, 1-9.

McDowell, D, 1997, 'Strategic Intelligence & Analysis. Guidelines on Methodology & Application', The Intelligence Study Centre, Wollongong, Australia.

National Crime Authority, 2002, *Annual Report 2001-2002*, Commonwealth of Australia, Canberra.

Peterson, MB, 1994, 'Analysis, Intelligence and Policy', *Journal of the Australian Institute of Professional Intelligence Officers,* vol 3, no 2, 5-21.

CHAPTER 6

The theory and practice of intelligence collection

Oliver Higgins[*]

There are known knowns. There are things we know that we know. There are known unknowns. That is to say there are things that we now know we don't know. But there are also unknown unknowns. There are things we do not know we don't know.

Donald Rumsfeld, US Secretary for Defense, 12 February 2002

Introduction

Donald Rumsfeld famous quote exemplifies the challenge for intelligence collectors in three parts. Clarifying what is already known is a sensible starting point but this is not straightforward. Individual knowledge is not always reflected in corporate understanding. Meanwhile, focusing solely on what is known is unwise because this would lead to the intelligence picture becoming a self-fulfilling prophecy. Therefore the second element of the challenge, finding out more about gaps in knowledge that are recognised – 'known unknowns', is generally accepted as a core purpose of intelligence collection.

The third part of maxim, the notion that we can confront 'unknown unknowns', was received with a mixture of humour and incredulity, in the aftermath of Rumsfeld's comments. On the face of it, the concept of an 'unknown unknown' is a logical fallacy. And yet there is a sense in which the concept of 'unknown unknowns' has value in practice. Law enforcement has encountered emerging threats which it did not anticipate nor recognise as a knowledge gap until the problem had become established; for example, the exponential rise in wholesale supply and consumption of 'designer drugs' such as ecstasy. The challenge is to recognise this type of emerging threat at the time that, as far as law enforcement is concerned, it is an unknown unknown. The task is summed up by the words of Albert Szent-Györgyi; 'Research is to

---

[*]   The author would like to acknowledge the contribution of a number of people to his thinking and to earlier drafts of this chapter, including; David Bolt, Norman MacSween, Chris Borges, Mark Tyrrell-Smith, Mike Forster, Rob Boyett, Don McDowell and the 'diaspora' who are too numerous to name.

see what everybody else has seen, and to think what nobody else has thought'.[1]

This chapter aims to assist intelligence professionals meet the collection challenge in all three of the guises posed by Mr Rumsfeld. The first step is to recognise that there are distinct perspectives about how intelligence collection should be conducted. Each makes a series of different assumptions about how to conduct intelligence collection effectively. The existence of competing approaches or doctrines is rarely acknowledged and the various strengths and weaknesses seldom debated. The chapter seeks to generate such a debate by setting out a typology of the models and offering practical insights about how to apply them.

Four theoretical approaches to collection

At one end of the spectrum is the *bottom-up approach* reflected in the British policing tradition. This school of thought characterises intelligence being produced by a vast array of enforcement and community interactions across the entire range of policing activity. This includes intelligence gained from patrolling, from members of the public, from stopping a member of the public and asking them to account for their actions, the more intrusive power to stop and search, traffic stops, the execution of search warrants, and forensic evidence. As such, the process of intelligence collection is essentially passive. Where proactive activity does occur this tends to be with an enforcement objective in mind and any resulting intelligence that is of strategic value is an adjunct or secondary benefit.

The bottom-up approach is summed up, in polemical terms, by John Grieve's contention that 'strategic direction comes from within hearing the click of the handcuffs' (Grieve, 2004: 26). The United Kingdom's National Intelligence Model (NIM) takes a slightly more qualified approach. The model does make reference to the issuing of strategic intelligence requirements at the national level which hints at a more 'top-down' approach. However, the core proposition underpinning the model is that opportunity intelligence collected throughout everyday policing is collated and assessed in the form of analytical products (see Chapter 4 in this book).

The *top-down approach* is reflected in some of the contributions to the previous edition of this book (by Christopher, Heldon, and Higgins in Ratcliffe, 2004) and updated herein, including Chapters 6, 8 and 14. Broadly there are three different strands or versions which maintain distinctive characteristics while sharing a core proposition. The unifying thread is that intelligence collection is an active process which is driven by some form of agreed data or intelligence requirement. At the far side

---

1   Quoted in Good, IJ (ed), 1962, *The Scientist Speculates: An Anthology of Partly-baked Ideas*, Basic Books.

of the spectrum is social science research which is the use of the scientific method to produce evidence which can be relied upon as an accurate and consistent representation of reality (Ratcliffe, 2004: 89). The research may use qualitative or quantitative techniques or some combination. The fact that the standard process is used means that the research can be replicated by others and the results tested.

A second strand of the top-down approach may be termed the *classical model*. This draws on long established practices in the military and national security spheres. In essence the start point is an intelligence requirement which sets out the gaps in understanding to be filled. Examples include the intelligence requirements that the Joint Intelligence Committee (JIC) issues to the intelligence agencies in the United Kingdom (UK).[2] A further example is the National Intelligence Requirement (NIR) which acts as a guide to law enforcement agencies that collect intelligence relevant to serious and organised crime. The NIR is produced in line with the *Serious Organised Crime Control Strategy*, the UK's multi-agency response to the UK Threat Assessment. Both these documents are wide ranging in scope containing generic, 'high level' questions. The expectation is that the collectors take a proactive approach to meet the requirements resulting in a regular flow of intelligence. Customer needs determine the timing and scope of assessments based on the available intelligence although sometimes intelligence producers will initiate an assessment where an opportunity arises to throw new light on questions contained in the requirement.

The third strand may be termed *intelligence research* or *phenomena research*. McDowell (1998) advocates an intelligence collection process which has affinity with aspects of the classical approach and social science research. McDowell's version of the intelligence cycle is geared to researching and putting broad phenomena, like 'the drugs problem in London', in context. McDowell emphasises the drawing of inferences in order to understand crime problems or trends rather than the purely deductive method integral to empirical research, and stresses the importance of anecdote in order to provide context (though this conflicts with the disciplined use of a structured research instrument that is central to the scientific method). Where McDowell departs from the classical approach is that the collection process is subject-specific, and tailored to parameters defined in terms of reference for a study required by a specific client.

Figure 6.1 provides a typology of the various approaches to intelligence collection and research. The aim is to compare and contrast the strengths and weaknesses of the different traditions to aid the discussion which follows.

---

2   See *Joint Intelligence Committee Terms of Reference* at <www.intelligence. gov.uk>.

Figure 6.1 Typology of collection models

Category	TOP-DOWN			BOTTOM-UP
Version	Social science research	Phenomena research	Classical model	Traditional/ NIM
Characteristics	Use of the scientific method, a standard, structured process that actively collects data to test hypotheses. Deductive.	Use of a standard process to actively research intelligence or secondary data about a specific topic. Either deductive or inductive.	A generic and open-ended process whereby collection assets are actively directed to fill gaps in knowledge. Inductive.	A passive process based on collation of information produced by everyday policing and from tactical collection plans. Inductive.
Strengths	Tests validity of anecdote, perception and conventional wisdom. Can be replicated elsewhere enabling comparative studies. Suited to understanding cause and effect.	A rigorous approach enabling full exploitation of non-law enforcement data sources. Suited to gaining a broad understanding of a topic – provides context. Optimises understanding of what is known.	More dynamic and therefore timely. Able to throw light on unknowns. Provides answers to the 'why' questions, not just inferences.	The quickest results by collating what is known rather than collecting anything new. Provides insights about emerging trends on the ground, possibly including unknowns.
Weaknesses	A closed process restricted to points in time. Less suited to gaining a broad understanding of a wide-ranging topic. No answer to the assumption that there are inevitable gaps in data and uncertainties about the covert aspects of criminality.	Findings may be historic or quickly dated. Use of secondary data and anecdote means that validity of evidence can be questioned. Less suited to advancing understanding of unknowns.	Findings may lack validity due to lack of context and empirical content. Risk that the process may be self-fulfilling, collecting intelligence against a static set of requirements.	Risk that the process maybe self-fulfilling – not suited to advancing understanding of known unknowns.

... cont

When to use?	In depth knowledge of the impact of criminal behaviours and law enforcement activity on society and the economy.	The context in which the enemy operates – 'social' trends, opportunities and market demand.	Criminals' activity (including market indicators such as price), associations, attitude and capability (for example, knowledge, power, financial assets and other resources). Filling known unknowns. Identifying unknown unknowns.	To gain community intelligence or intelligence about prices in illegal markets at street level, new or changing popularity of criminal methods, suspects whose profile and impact are growing, criminals' assets. Establishing known knowns and identifying unknown unknowns.

Intelligence collection in practice

Know your client

The collection of intelligence is central to the delivery of assessments that are valued. Unless relevant data and intelligence is known to the author, it is possible that the end product will miss the point or misdiagnose the threat. In turn, effective intelligence collection relies on three criteria being met; the output must be *reliable*, *valid*, and *timely*.

- **Reliable**. It is essential to convince the client that they can rely on the data which underpins the conclusions that are presented to them. That means that the process should be sufficiently comprehensive to convince the client that all of the appropriate collection requirements, or questions, have been pursued and intelligence from all relevant sources gathered.[3]

- **Valid**. The collected data and intelligence may reliably reflect what is known but does this amount to a true or full understanding of the topic? An intelligence collection process becomes a self-fulfilling prophecy unless an attempt is made to fill gaps in knowledge and is misleading unless any limits on the capability to fill such gaps are acknowledged. A key element is the ability to recognise and place in context a single fragment of intelligence that provides insight and a vast array of data that does not.

---

3   It is also important that the client is assured that the reliability of any intelligence that is delivered has been critically evaluated. But this concerns the evaluation and assessment of intelligence which are outside the scope of this chapter.

- **Timely**. Even if an assessment is well founded it is of little use to decision-makers if it is not available at the time that a decision is required.

The required standards can be achieved by following a five stage process. The steps logically follow each other, therefore missing one or more puts the quality of the end product at risk. The process follows the traditional intelligence cycle (see Chapter 1 in this book) including an additional step that bridges 'direction' and 'collation' ('the collection strategy'). The classical 'collection' stage is split into three supporting phases ('ask the right questions', 'targeting sources' and 'non law enforcement sources of information'). As such, the process outlined below is broadly recognised by each of the top-down approaches. A purist interpretation of the bottom-up model is at odds with the notion of proactively collecting intelligence but in practice this happens in policing today, although tactical aspects sometimes dominate.

Select collection model(s) to follow

Making an explicit choice about the type of data or intelligence collection to be pursued overcomes the risk of unthinking attachment to one of the models. This can be achieved by considering the purpose of the task in view of the strengths and weaknesses of the models and the available time. This step in the process is just as applicable to covert or operationally focused collection tasks as the delivery of 'strategic studies'. For example, an operational manager may benefit from empirical techniques (even if this is outsourced) in order to gauge the impact of operational activity. Similarly, phenomena research may inform an operational plan by establishing a clearer picture of the wider context. To illustrate the process for selecting collection models in more detail, consider the example in Jonathan Nicholl's chapter in the first edition (Nicholl, 2004). The task was to examine, within one month, the extent to which Former Soviet Union Organised Crime (FSUOC) exists in Australia and the specific impact on New South Wales.

The bottom-up model

This approach is well suited to the task given the shortage of available time. Given that the client has acknowledged a lack of awareness of the topic (Nicholl, 2004: 60) the bottom-up approach may add value by revealing tactical strands of intelligence that have not previously come to the attention of the Deputy Commissioner (the client) and placing these in context.

Phenomena research

Potentially this approach could add value by providing a rich context. For example, describing the structures and methods used by FSUOC elsewhere and the social, political and economic conditions associated with the emergence of such groups. Some additional progress may be possible in the available time beyond the commitment to interview community leaders already stated in the terms of reference (Nicholl, 2004:64). For example, liaison with overseas counterparts to access existing knowledge and obtaining population and immigration statistics. However, two months is unlikely to be sufficient to complete a comprehensive collection process.

More could, of course, be achieved if additional resource is allocated to the task or if follow-up work is agreed. Additional data collection might include obtaining employment data by sector, relevant details of company registration, structures and capital flows, collection and analysis of suspicious activity data (relating to laundering of criminal proceeds), consultation of other law enforcement agencies and public bodies including the probation service, consultation of private sector organisations which may see evidence of an emerging threat such as the stock exchange, banks, equivalent of land registry and consultation of non-government bodies including those involved in the treatment of drug addicts and the support of 'trafficked women'.

Social science research

There is limited scope to use this technique in the time available although there is scope to do more should follow-up work be agreed. To support the immediate task, it would be possible to structure the interviews that are conducted so that a consistent set of questions is asked. Following this up by coding the responses, that is, categorising them in a way that is comparable, would enable measurable conclusions to be reached based on the interviews.

The benefits of structured interviewing should be considered against the costs and risks while formulating the collection strategy. Coming up with a structured interview plan and coding the responses, in particular, is time consuming. A more informal approach is sometimes better suited to situations where the interviewee may be uncomfortable with authority. Similarly there may be occasions where the interviewer decides that a flexible method is best. For example, if they can not easily predict the ground that an interviewee is going to cover and the interviewer wants to explore an interesting or unexpected point in some depth. While the results of an unstructured interview can still be coded, the extent which results can be reliably compared becomes questionable the more that a standard structure is not followed.

If more time is granted for follow-up work, it may be possible to conduct an empirical analysis of the conditions that may facilitate and/ or indicate the impact of FSUOC in New South Wales. This may be possible by analysing the experience elsewhere and formulating a series of measures that reflect that experience. Data could then be collected in New South Wales against the same measures. Examples might include immigration statistics, the degree of penetration into the property market of FSU nationals, prison statistics, suspicious activity data relating to criminal proceeds and company registration statistics. The reason that this type of data collection is likely to be time consuming is that it depends on prior research to establish possible indictors and subsequent enquiries to establish if comparable data is available in New South Wales and from the other locations. Finally, it is worth stressing that while empirical analysis can bring rigour to a collection process, the conclusions rely on context. For example, there maybe entirely legitimate reasons why large volumes of cash imports to New South Wales may be innocent whereas elsewhere this is indicative of penetration by organised crime.

The Classical Model

Although there is no explicit mention in the terms of reference about filling gaps in knowledge, clients often expect this. The classical top-down model is well suited to this but there will not be sufficient time to re-position covert assets. It may be worth stating this in the terms of reference in order to manage the client's expectations.

The entry in the table below summarises the choice of collection models based on the preceding discussion. The text could be included in the terms of reference published by Nicholl (2004: 63) or to an 'Intelligence Product Proposal' (Nicholl, 2009: 14-15).

Collection Explain which research and intelligence collection models are to be used and how this impacts on the Project Aim, Objectives and Timeframe.	The emphasis will be on collating and analysing existing knowledge as this is the only viable approach in the available time. Basic empirical analysis will be delivered based on interviews. No predictions will be included. Future options include, <ul><li>More in depth empirical and phenomena (contextual) research, over six months, to evaluate whether the conditions associated with FSUOC in other countries are present in NSW;</li><li>A predictive element could be included in the above;</li><li>Proactive collection to intelligence fill gaps would report in 2-4 months after the current deadline.</li></ul>

Know what we know

The Chief Executive Officer of a blue chip company once told his staff that 'we do not know what we know'! The route of the paradox is, of course, that the knowledge held by individuals or within units of the company was not assimilated and understood at the corporate level. Overcoming this challenge is the next step in the collection process. The underpinning rationale is simple: Clarifying what is already known is a prerequisite to defining what further intelligence is needed.

Assimilating what is currently known has an obvious affinity with the bottom-up model. In years gone by, intelligence staff in police forces were known as 'collators' since the challenge was to organise the volumes of opportunity intelligence that were being received. While processes have been modernised and roles have been refined, the challenge remains. In fact, 'knowing what we know' is integral to each of the models included in the typology. Framing standard research questions, as part of an empirical approach, requires some prior knowledge. So too does generating hypotheses as part of phenomena research. Meanwhile, proactive collection of intelligence in line with the classical model is dependant on first defining the 'unknowns' or gaps intelligence which need to be filled.

Assimilating existing intelligence: some guidance

The start point for the assimilation of knowledge is the tasking document that commissioned the collection process. This may be an operational plan or a terms reference for a strategic study. The objectives of the collection process form the framework for initial research, which should involve a handful of simple steps. Researching previous assessments and academic or other reports on the subject is a good way of gathering background information and context. Meanwhile, researching the agency's own intelligence databases should be routine, although this is not always undertaken as thoroughly as it should be. Sometimes officers may not have the required systems access and the risk of data overload can be off-putting. Ultimately though, the research of internal systems is part of the hard graft that enables further collection of intelligence to be directed with confidence.

When interrogating intelligence databases it is worth bearing in mind some basic pointers. Spelling mistakes complicate database retrieval and law enforcement agencies sometimes use different operational names for the same investigation. Above all, the absence of data standards hampers searching. One comprehensive analysis revealed 45 different terms referring to roles and responsibilities in organised criminal networks facilitating illegal immigration to the UK. This included nine different terms for the leader of a network and five different ways of describing a person responsible for the finances (Jarvis, 2003).

A further critical limitation is that law enforcement intelligence systems are often incomplete. Even valuable knowledge which exists in documentary form within the agency is often held separately. This may seem strange to the uninitiated. None the less, the causes tend to be fairly entrenched and include the existence of separate case handling systems and management processes, the preference of investigating officers to save case papers on local directories so that they can control and account for the scheduling and circulation of these and the sheer volume of documentation which can be obtained by investigations.

The upshot is that analysts and intelligence officers should take a pragmatic approach and learn to navigate their own organisation, unlocking internal sources of knowledge. Two useful sources in the UK context are the case summaries that are compiled for prosecutors of the evidence gathered during a criminal investigation and, at an earlier stage, the summaries submitted by case officers to management for review. Both documents provide a useful summary of the knowledge gained during an investigation but are rarely recorded on an intelligence database.

A helpful way of identifying relevant investigations, case documents and other information sources is to network with subject matter experts. This includes the client (where applicable) and anyone with a similar interest in other law enforcement agencies or a relevant policy interest in government. It is important to stress that the collation and assimilation of organisational knowledge should not be limited by the information held within the agency. Otherwise there is a risk that the collection process will not be sufficiently comprehensive and at worst the outcome may be a self-fulfilling prophecy (Sheptycki and Ratcliffe, 2004: 201, 205). The targeting of external sources of information is discussed in greater depth in a later section.

Organisational considerations

The assimilation of knowledge should not be limited to historic information. Opportunity intelligence, that is to say unsolicited information or intelligence that arises as a by-product of a collection task, can make a significant contribution to organisational knowledge. This kind of intelligence may throw light on 'known knowns', 'known unknowns' or even 'unknown unknowns' outside of an agencies current operations and priorities. How can law enforcement agencies ensure that they capitalise on rather than overlook such intelligence?

Making best use of opportunity intelligence raises questions of organisational culture, design, resources and systems. Crucial intelligence may be a fragment of information, contained in a single report and yet the volume of information received by law enforcement makes setting people aside to read every piece of information impractical. There are two complementary solutions. The first is to set up systems to monitor known patterns. For example, to identify whether a person who is assessed to be a prolific offender features in any newly received intelligence report.

The second approach can assist law enforcement identify 'unknown unknowns' from newly received intelligence. The trick is to ensure that those reporting new intelligence are sensitised to recognise intelligence that is unusual. This approach is sometimes referred to as the 'push model'. The advantage of the push model is that the originator of the intelligence highlights and disseminates significant intelligence to those charged with evaluating and acting on such knowledge. Merely submitting the intelligence to a central organisational database, rather than drawing it to the attention of a human being, runs the risk that those responsible for intelligence analysis will miss something potentially significant.

Some intelligence collectors will know intuitively or from experience when new intelligence is exceptional. Others will need briefing and support to comprehend the status quo, or the baseline intelligence picture, as a benchmark to compare new intelligence against. A briefing or coaching aide is to quote examples of events or developments that were recognised as 'known unknowns' or, with the benefit of hindsight, should have been. For instance, in relation to the emergence of ecstasy consumption, various indicator might have been spotted, including attempts by criminals to source pill-making equipment, intelligence about attitudes and user demand within the burgeoning club scene reflected and discussed amongst the criminal fraternity, drug production trends in Belgium and the Netherlands and pronounced shifts in the demand for particular precursor chemicals.

Ask the right questions

Using a purely deductive or empirical method alone is not sufficient to understand criminal markets and behaviour. The scale and dynamic nature of serious organised crime alongside the efforts by criminals and the consumers of illegal products and services to conceal their activity mean that there will always be gaps in law enforcement knowledge.

The requirements that drive the collection process are simply pertinent questions about gaps in intelligence or that are intended to test an officer's existing conceptual knowledge. A good starting point is the classic questions: who, what, when, where, why and how? The following section describes some techniques for generating more specific collection questions and for prioritising these.

The role of hypotheses

A well known technique to drive understanding about a problem or topic is to develop hypotheses which are speculative questions that can be based on deductive or inductive logic. The hypothesis technique is discussed in depth elsewhere in this volume and the previous edition. Hypotheses can be used as part of a structured, systematic process to define the research questions in empirical or phenomena research or to generate scenarios as part of predictive analysis (Ratcliffe, 2004; McDowell, 1998; Heldon, 2004; Quarmby, 2004). Alternatively, hypotheses can be used in a slightly looser way to inform collection planning by fleshing out intelligence requirements.

In the Methamphetamine example that follows, four broad alternatives about the future direction are defined. The construction of a range of scenarios is important because the data and intelligence that would confirm or deny the various possibilities may differ. Without defining the alternative scenarios, the collection process may not gather all of the relevant data and as a consequence the validity of the end product is threatened. Hypotheses are generated by drawing on knowledge about the topic, general knowledge about criminal behaviour and/ or common sense in order to form a speculative idea. The resulting ideas do not need to be defended or justified at this stage since they are consciously speculative. In fact it is sometimes the most speculative ideas that challenge conventional thinking and nudge the process towards unknown or at least less familiar territory.

Box 6.1 Example hypotheses

Project

Threat to the UK from Methamphetamine

Background

Methamphetamine is a synthetic drug which is highly addictive and damaging to users' health (SOCA, 2008b: 34). There is widespread abuse of the drug in the United States (US), south east Asia and elsewhere, although the UK has not been similarly affected. This suggests the question 'What is the threat to the UK from the distribution and consumption of Methamphetamine'?

The following hypotheses highlight a number of potential scenarios in order to direct the collection effort.

Hypothesis 1 (H_1): A limited increase in consumption, primarily linked to communities that are major consumers of the drug elsewhere.

Hypothesis 2 (H_2): A substantial increase in consumption driven by the production of the drug in laboratories located in the European continent.

Hypothesis 3 (H_3): A substantial increase in consumption driven by the production of the drug in laboratories located in the UK.

Null Hypothesis (H_0): No discernible increase in consumption as the price of cocaine and ecstasy remain low denying the opportunity for a new market to develop.

Focus

Once the hypothesis technique has been used to generate plenty of potential questions the next step is to prioritise these. After all, collectors' time is precious. It is therefore important to focus their efforts on addressing the questions that matter most. And, of course, there is a risk that if collectors are faced with a vast wish list they may make their own judgments about the priorities. Or, their goodwill may be challenged and given the pressure that they frequently face for tactical results they may play lip service to the strategic collection task. Two short questions help to tease out the key issues: 'Why?', and 'So what?'.

It is critical that collectors and analysts planning collection keep the 'Why' question at the forefront of their mind. Interpreting and attempting to explain criminal markets, attitudes and behaviour can tease out the facilitating conditions or underlying causes and, in turn, provide pointers about possible interventions. A good example concerns the strategy that reduced the spree of street robberies in the UK a few years ago when large numbers of people were mugged for their mobile phones. The volume of offences meant that reducing the problem through enforcement was not feasible. However, the knowledge was built that the crime wave was facilitated by the ease with which stolen phones could be re-chipped for the stolen goods market. Intelligence collection highlighted that as a result of the criminal opportunity provided by re-chipping, a plethora of semi-legitimate businesses had grown, offering this service and as a consequence, fuelling the crime wave on the streets. Based on this knowledge, a preventative strategy was put in place, similar to the successful strategy that reduced mobile phone theft in the US (Clarke et al, 2001).

Despite the importance of the 'why' question, it is rarely prominent in collection processes. Intelligence collection tends to have a tactical focus in law enforcement concentrating on delivering criminal justice outcomes. And to achieve tactical outcomes it is rarely necessary to interpret or explain the underlying problem. Investigating the latest mobile phone theft on high street will not be assisted by speculating about why so many related incidents are occurring. Therefore a big challenge for collectors is to ask themselves the 'why' question despite the fact that this may not be second nature to them and there may be pressure to focus on who, what, when, where and how?

As the purpose of collection is to improve understanding in order to influence a client or customers' decision-making, the 'So what?' question is essential to focus on questions which have most relevance to decision-makers. It can be phrased in numerous ways; 'Do I need to act?', 'If so against which aspect(s) of the problem?', 'What are my options?' and 'How much resource should I assign'?

While decision-makers will naturally wish to concentrate resources on the most significant current problems that they face, they will also want to be alerted to emerging threats so that they have the opportunity to intervene early. A technique that can deliver early warning for decision-makers is known as intelligence indicators.

Intelligence indicators

Intelligence indicators are observable 'clues' or 'signs' that can be collected to meet a particular intelligence requirement. The role of indicators is to enable intelligence professionals to look for and monitor evidence that either supports or challenges a particular scenario (Dearth, 1995). Indicators are generated by taking an intelligence requirement or hypothesis and deducing what events, incidents, actions or patterns of behaviour might signal or point to the scenario underpinning the requirement being realised (McDowell, 1998).

The application of the technique is illustrated by revisiting the scenario about the threat of methamphetamine discussed earlier. Box 6.2 below, takes the hypotheses and defines a series of indicators. Note that the box is for illustrative purposes only and therefore is not intended to be a comprehensive reflection of all of the relevant indicators.

As well as providing early warning, intelligence indicators are a means of oiling the collection process in general. Broad general questions are often difficult to answer since they require the collector to make a series of assumptions and judgments. Instead, it is advisable either to

Box 6.2 Intelligence indicators

Hypothesis 1 (H_1): A limited increase in consumption, primarily linked to communities that are major consumers of the drug elsewhere.

- Possible indicator (a): Increased seizures on persons flying to the UK from the US and south east Asia and increased postal seizures from parcels originating from the same areas.
- Possible indicator (b): Intelligence received from overseas law enforcement that individuals are exporting the drug to the UK on a personal basis.
- Possible indicator (c): Intelligence reporting increased availability within specialist user communities in the UK.
- Possible indicator (d): Street price of methamphetamine remains high. Crack and cocaine markets flourish.

Hypothesis 2 (H_2): A substantial increase in consumption driven by the production of the drug in laboratories located in the European continent.

- Possible indicator (a): Increased seizures at the channel ports in commercial quantities.
- Possible indicator (b): Intelligence received from overseas law enforcement reporting increased seizures in Europe and growing number of methamphetamine labs detected.
- Possible indicator (c): Growth in multi-kilo seizures within the UK as well as increased seizures at street level. 'Meth houses' emerge.
- Possible indicator (d): Street price of methamphetamine drops substantially and becomes comparable to crack and ecstasy. Growing number of addicts found requiring treatment for the symptoms of methamphetamine abuse.

Hypothesis 3 (H_3): A substantial increase in consumption driven by the production of the drug in laboratories located in the UK.

- Possible indicator (a): Seizures of methamphetamine at ports remain static. Increased seizures of the relevant precursor chemicals detected at ports and within the UK.
- Possible indicator (b): Growth in detection of waste from methamphetamine production. Growth in number of individuals referred for hospital treatment arising from chemical burns or toxic gas inhalation or exposure to toxic waste.
- Possible indicator (c): Growth in multi-kilo seizures within the UK as well as increased seizures at street level. 'Meth houses' emerge. Greater numbers of labs detected in the UK.
- Possible indicator (d): Street price of methamphetamine drops substantially and becomes comparable to crack and ecstasy. Signs of conflict between criminals supplying crack/heroin and those offering methamphetamine. Growing number of addicts found requiring or seeking treatment for the symptoms of methamphetamine abuse.

Null hypothesis (H_0): No discernible increase in consumption as the price of cocaine and ecstasy remain low denying the opportunity for a new market to develop.

- Possible indicator (a): No increase in seizures.
- Possible indicator (b): No significant new overseas intelligence and no signs of UK labs.

direct collectors towards observable measures or to pose specific questions that are more refined than merely re-stating a hypothesis.

A number of limitations apply to the analysis of intelligence indicators. The most obvious point is that indicators are not mutually exclusive. For example, an increase in domestic production may be accompanied by an increase in the importation of methamphetamine. Furthermore, one scenario may pave the way for another. A limited increase in the consumption of methamphetamine, linked to small importations by specific communities, may stimulate wider demand and highlight an opportunity to criminal networks which are established suppliers of other drugs.

The limitations of indicator data analysis can be mitigated. One option is to try a technique known as 'triangulation'. In this context, triangulation means considering the range of indicators relevant to each competing hypothesis and evaluating which hypothesis is supported by more indicators. A slightly more sophisticated version of this approach analyses whether one or more indicators stand alone and provides decisive insight.

In practice the analysis should not cease at the point that a tentative conclusion has been reached. Where the potential consequences of an emerging threat are significant, further intelligence collection should be tasked to bear down on the key gaps where the intelligence is patchy or unknown.

The overall use of the indicators and warnings approach carries further health warnings. The technique does not cater for some of the core collection issues including the 'why?' and 'so what?' questions. Intelligence indicators should therefore be used in conjunction with other collection techniques. Meanwhile, collection planners often choose indicators that are observable measures. As such, there is a risk that the analysis merely highlights the visible consequences of a new threat becoming established. This can be mitigated by collecting intelligence which focuses on criminals' intent.

A further potential pitfall is the trade off between value and validity. There is some evidence that acting speedily to control the anticipated emergence of a threat can successfully limit it (NCIS, 2002: 30). The longer law enforcement takes to construct hypotheses, develop indicators, collect data, refine the collection process and deliver an end product, the greater the risk that an opportunity to intervene will be lost. And yet the longer one takes to build knowledge and understanding of the problem, the more valid the resulting indicators are likely to be. As long as this dilemma is recognised, it can be managed on a case by case basis. There is a compromise position whereby intervention is attempted prior to the indicator process delivering confident judgments. Intervention may be necessary in view of the wider context or because the decision-maker believes that the risk of not acting is too great. In this eventuality, the indicator technique will still have a role to play in monitoring what impact is achieved.

Targeting your sources

Once the requirement for intelligence and other data has been defined, the next step is to establish what sources of information may hold the answers. It is common for analysts to launch into a shotgun approach sending a list of each requirement to every possible contributor. This wastes the time of contributors, may undermine goodwill and may deflect analysts from building relationships with those who have most to add. This can be avoided by using an old fashioned collection plan matrix which lists the requirements down the far left column and the potential contributors across the row at the top. Sources of information should then be cross-referenced to requirements where it is judged that the source may have a contribution to make.

A further benefit of this longstanding technique is that the person planning the collection exercise can draw together all of the requirements relevant to a particular source, enabling a consolidated request to be delivered to that contributor. A collection plan remains a sensible approach if the client requirement is for a baseline assessment, precluding an in-depth research effort. In this case, potential sources can simply be struck off the plan to restrict the collection effort given the lack of time. This also provides a transparent basis for clarifying the limitations of the subsequent end product.

Building relationships with covert collectors and operational teams

The list of sources to target should include covert collectors, case officers and senior investigators with something to contribute. Although the ideal approach to collecting intelligence within law enforcement is the 'push model', discussed earlier in the chapter, in reality it remains necessary for those owning collection plans to take a proactive approach. Large volumes of knowledge remain tacit, 'inside officers' heads', rather than recorded in intelligence records which can be shared at the push of a button. This is a consequence of cultural factors, as well as performance and resource pressures, and even sometimes clunky processes and systems. The upshot is that analysts and intelligence officers must learn how to build corporate knowledge by debriefing investigating officers and developing productive relationships with covert collectors.

Debriefing investigators

There are a number of basic pointers for how to debrief effectively. At the outset, the analyst should ensure that individuals are selected for debriefing based on conscious decisions relating to existing intelligence held by the analyst or knowledge of the contributor's role and expertise. This means that the analyst must actively research each operation that they consider may be suitable for debriefing. A key benefit is that the analyst makes efficient use of their own time by concentrating on those who have the most to contribute and avoids wasting the time of others. Good preparation also helps to sell the process to the person being debriefed and to operational managers worried about the abstraction of their staff; 'I am very keen to discuss "x" because this is of great strategic importance'. Meanwhile, the preparation enhances the analyst's credibility. Their standing is enhanced enormously by being able to talk authoritatively about the operation and if they are astute, to massage the investigator's ego about what worked.

Once a decision to proceed has been taken, the analyst should prepare a list of intelligence requirements as 'primers' to ensure that they ask the right questions. This should, of course, be based on a synthesis of knowledge assimilated to date and the analyst's research of the specific operation. The preparation can boost an analyst's confidence and helps the debriefer to focus the conversation on the salient points.

It is also important that the debriefer does not take an unduly formal, structured or rigid approach. Obtaining detailed insights from the contributor rests on establishing rapport and trust. It can be helpful for the debriefer to begin the process by asking about an aspect of the intelligence that they are familiar with, that is not threatening to the contributor and that, ideally, reflects well on the intelligence producer. It is also worth allowing the flow of conversation to answer the questions on the intelligence requirement, asking supplementary questions at convenient times rather than rigidly sticking to a prepared script.

Effective debriefing relies on the quality of the debriefer's listening skills. Contributors sometimes advance opinion or anecdote in the guise of intelligence. A useful technique is to ask the contributor if they can provide evaluated intelligence or evidential material to back up a point that the debriefer perceives to be questionable. This pins the producer down and if the intelligence is provided the debriefer has a more sound basis for judging the veracity of the contributor's claims.

Building relationships with covert collectors

Building sound relationships with covert collectors is a crucial task for analysts and intelligence officers. Covert collectors generally hold the key to answering the 'why question' and 'known unknowns'. Sometimes they can also identify 'unknown unknowns' because of the insights that they gain about criminals' attitudes and intentions as well as actions. They are also busy people and face the dilemma of what intelligence to disseminate to their customers. As customers for their information, analysts can help by providing clear and concise requirements and regular feedback. Not only does the feedback assist collectors prioritise their effort, it can assist them interpret what they are learning, especially as they are rarely experts on most topics or problems faced by law enforcement. This process of engagement also gives the analyst the opportunity to inform the collector whether a new piece of intelligence is unusual or indicative of a new criminal opportunity or emerging threat. Meanwhile, all of the pointers about debriefing investigators also apply to the interaction between an analyst and a covert collector. Ultimately, if analysts can develop relationships on the basis of mutual interest as well as building rapport, they will create goodwill and obtain greater insight from collectors.

Driving strategic thinking in collection: organisational process

Although it is important for analysts to develop productive relationships with collectors, it is important that law enforcement agencies promote strategic thinking in corporate processes. While the bulk of the collection effort operates at the tactical level, it is possible to deliver a unified process that integrates strategic requirements. In practice this means including the definition of outcomes at the outset of an investigation and including the delivery of intelligence and improved knowledge as part of the objectives. There are legal requirements to satisfy in terms of the collection, retention, protection and potential disclosure of such material to defendants. But these points are manageable. In fact, collection of sensitive intelligence has long been a staple of covert investigations. The only refinement is to consciously introduce strategic thinking into the collection process. Ideally this can be achieved through an interactive process whereby the part of the agency responsible for strategic knowledge contributes to the shaping of the investigation's objectives.

An example unified approach to outcome measurement and intelligence collection, in this case relating to the investigation of a suspected methamphetamine production lab, is shown in the following box with commentary in italics.

Box 6.3 Example unified collection plan

Strategic aim

To control the growth of the distribution and consumption of crystal methamphetamine in the UK. The aim is a collective strategy shared by partner agencies across the public sector. The strategy will undertake early intervention, where justified, in the form of enforcement action and will implement policy and other measures, as necessary, based on knowledge of the problem.

(Comment: This strategic aim sits above the objectives of any investigations and other initiatives under the strategy).

Strategic outcomes

- To prevent a substantial drop in the price of meth, benchmarking against the street price for cocaine and ecstasy (subject to independent market developments),

- To reduce direct harms caused by the production and consumption of meth,
- To control violence between rival criminals groups that may be threatened by the spread of the meth market.

(Comment: These outcomes relate to the strategic initiative to control the spread of meth. However, the specific investigation, described below, should be expected to contribute data and learning that will be aggregated to form an overall impact analysis. The analysis of the outcomes will depend on data collection that is independent of (but may be informed by) the progress of supporting investigations. For example, empirical research should be targeted towards the user population. Depending on timing, it may not be feasible to establish a baseline pre-intervention picture. Nonetheless, some qualified conclusions could be drawn from the intelligence and evidence gained as well as the historic experience of relevant drug treatment agencies).

Investigative aim and objectives

To confirm or deny whether John Doe and any currently unidentified associates, are producing and selling crystal methamphetamine, a Class A controlled drug, within the UK.

This aim will be delivered through the following objectives;

- To establish whether an illegal drug production lab has been set up, to identify the location of any such lab and to gain control of the premises in order to protect the public and gain evidence,
- To establish the identity and roles of any criminal associates of John Doe engaged in the production and sale of crystal methamphetamine,
- To establish the modus operandi of any drug production and distribution and any associated money laundering,
- To identify and restrain any assets that are the proceeds of crime in order to prevent and deter any further criminality,
- To produce and share, as appropriate, intelligence that supports the investigation and the prevention or detection of any other serious offences.

(Comment: Note how the objectives explicitly refer to the gathering of intelligence and how the achievement of the investigative objectives will naturally lead to the delivery of knowledge).

Intelligence collection plan

- The scale of production including: volume of any drugs seized, production capacity of any detected lab, nature and volume of any pre-cursor chemicals seized, evidence of previous transactions including chemical orders (including volume and timescale),
- The identity of any supplier of pre-cursor chemicals and customers of any drugs,
- Any indications of production costs, including payment to associates and for production equipment and precursor chemicals,
- Any indications of price charged,

- Any indication of how market demand was established and where the drugs are sold (including open market/ meth house),
- Any indications of conflict experienced or anticipated with other criminal networks engaged in Class A supply,
- Any indication that the subjects under investigation have involvement in the distribution of other Class A drugs, and whether this continued/stopped/ceased once they began to supply meth,
- Any information pointing to the capability of others to fill any production vacuum and the likely response of users to detection of a lab,
- Any indication of what happened to the toxic waste and any evidence of other direct health hazards arising from production.

(Comment: The purpose of this section is to build on the investigative objectives setting out the intelligence requirement for the investigation. Since the collection is intended to provide strategic understanding as well as supporting the investigation, the collection plan may be wider in scope than the investigative objectives. This is, of course, subject to compliance with legal requirements, the capabilities of collectors, and agreement of the senior investigator. On some occasions it may be more appropriate to mount a separate intelligence gathering operation that will sit alongside and be coordinated with the criminal investigation).

Non-law enforcement sources

The collection process should not rely on law enforcement intelligence alone. Data from a range of non-law enforcement sources, including official statistics, can provide pointers about the scale and nature of various threats. However, various factors can limit the value of government figures, at least in the UK experience. Sometimes offences are not recorded and in other instances measurement is inconsistent (AGO, 2006). There is also the widely recognised point that a disputed but potentially sizeable proportion of crime is not reported.

There are numbers of ways to counter-balance the limitations of official statistics in a collection strategy. Surveys can provide a wider perspective than official statistics about the scale and nature of crime. Influential examples include research by government researchers, such as the *British Crime Survey*, which measures the experience of crime encountered by a sample of the British population (see, for example, Nicholas et al, 2007).

A slightly different approach is to think imaginatively about how available government data can be synthesised with other information to provide a fuller picture of the problem. For example, in the UK official figures for the number of registered cocaine and heroin addicts have been multiplied by an authoritative estimate for the annual consumption of the respective drugs to calculate the overall size of the drug market. For those sectors or types of crime for which there is an ongoing collection requirement it may be worth attempting to align government processes in order to provide more useful data for intelligence assessments.

An alternative tactic is to make use of open source information. The assessment of the scale of hi-tech crime is a good example. Hi-tech offences are generally coded under other headings in official reports and are often not reported. However there are a number of academic and private sector bodies that study the scale of the problem and produce regular reports.[4] Another approach is to obtain data from private sector organisations that are either the victims of crime or represent the victims. For example, payment card clearing services and issuers have a useful picture of the size of payment card crime since they track and record the losses.

Private sector organisations can also be useful sources of information about the nature of a criminal threat. Companies that are the victims of crimes which are not a high law enforcement priority can provide details of offences and criminal methods which law enforcement would not otherwise obtain. This applies to the payment card and intellectual property crime fields. Equally, private organisations can often assist the assimilation of data about crimes which *are* law enforcement's priorities by providing a consolidated picture of offences across agency boundaries. A good example in the UK is the British Security Industry Association, which collates information on cash-in-transit robberies.

Meanwhile, there is a range of non-governmental organisations that work with the victims of crime and are in a position to inform law enforcement about trends in criminal markets. Examples include charities and community organisations working with problematic drug users. These include groups that can detect trends about drug supply at street level, and victim support organisations that work with women who have been trafficked for prostitution. Law enforcement needs to operate sensitively to build relationships with non-governmental organisations (NGOs) of this kind given the responsibility that NGOs have to client confidentiality.

Open source information published by news agencies or on the World-Wide Web can provide a broader or fuller perspective than intelligence held by law enforcement agencies. The media and Internet sources contain reports on cases across the world, useful given the global nature of many threats (NCIS, 1999). Beyond this, media and other public sources are often more timely than law enforcement in reporting new cases or incidents such as a shooting which appears to feature in a recent series. In addition, it is worth consulting a range of open sources for demographic or contextual information relevant to a threat. Sites for contextual material include news agencies and the Central Intelligence

---

4   Examples include the Computer Security Institute <www.gocsi.com>, the JANET-CERT <www.ja.net/CERT/JANET-CERT>, and the UK's Audit Commission and Department of Trade and Industry. See NCIS (1999) *Project Trawler: crime on the information highways* (pp 4 and 7) and the UK Threat Assessment (2003) 'Hi-Tech crime'.

Agency's website <www.cia.gov>. There are often a range of open sources that can support specialised or detailed intelligence requirements. For example, tourist boards, local authorities and regional airports all offer general or contextual information on labour market demand or migration flows (Jarvis, 2003).

The ubiquitous nature of open source information means that the risk of data overload is greater than for other types of data. There are simple measures for controlling the risk. The key point is to define specific questions prior to beginning the research. This should ensure that research is focused. If interesting information is encountered that sits outside the objectives this should be ignored or at most parked and only followed up if there is sufficient time. Another tip is to build a list of useful sources so that time is not wasted trying to find or assess the credibility of new contributors or contacts. Finally, it can be worth setting an upper limit to the time made available for open source research. This concentrates the minds of the researchers and means that the open source collection does not gobble up large amounts of time required for collecting information from other types of source.

Conclusion

Rising to the challenge implicit in Donald Rumsfeld's famous phrase is a tough assignment. It is crucial to start with clarity of purpose firmly focused on customers' needs. It is important to recognise the strengths and weaknesses of the four collection models, avoiding unthinking attachment to one or the other. A dose of common sense, sound organisational knowledge, an open mind and breadth of perspective are assets. And it is advisable to use the available techniques wisely and build productive relationships. But individual performance only goes so far. Ultimately, the challenge rests on cultural organisational change that values strategic thinking, transcends the notion that tactical imperatives matter most and learns how to capitalise on tacit knowledge.

References

Attorney General's Office, 2006, *Fraud Review*, <www.islo.gov.uk/fraud_review.htm>.

Christopher, S, 2004, 'A practitioner's perspective of UK strategic intelligence', in Ratcliffe, JH (ed) *Strategic Thinking in Criminal Intelligence*, Federation Press.

Clarke, RV, Kemper, R, and Wyckoff, L, 2001, 'Controlling cell phone fraud in the US: Lessons for the UK "Foresight" Prevention Initiative', *Security Journal*, vol 14, no 1, 7-22.

Dearth, DH, 1995, 'Failure in Intelligence, Decision-Making and War', in Dearth, DH, and Goodden, RT (eds), 1995, *Strategic Intelligence: Theory and Application*, Center for Strategic Leadership and Defense Intelligence Agency, Washington DC.

Grieve J, 2004, 'Developments in UK Criminal Intelligence', in Ratcliffe, JH (ed) *Strategic Thinking in Criminal Intelligence*, Federation Press.

Heldon, CE, 2004, 'Exploratory intelligence tools', in Ratcliffe, JH (ed), *Strategic Thinking in Criminal Intelligence*, Federation Press.

Higgins, O, 2004, 'Rising to the collection challenge', in Ratcliffe, JH (ed) *Strategic Thinking in Criminal Intelligence*, Federation Press.

Jarvis, N, 2003, 'Research tools and techniques', REFLEX Secretariat Workshop, May 2003.

McDowell, D, 1998, *Strategic intelligence: A handbook for practitioners, managers and users*, Istana.

NCIS, 1999, *Project Trawler: Crime on the Information Highways*, National Criminal Intelligence Service.

NCIS, 2002, *United Kingdom Threat Assessment of Serious and Organised Crime 2002*, National Criminal Intelligence Service.

Nicholas, S, Kershaw, C, and Walker, A, 2007, 'Crime in England and Wales 2006/07', Home Office.

Nicholl, J 2004, 'Task definition, in Ratcliffe, JH (ed) *Strategic Thinking in Criminal Intelligence*, Federation Press.

Quarmby, N, 2004, 'Futures work in strategic criminal intelligence', in Ratcliffe, JH (ed), *Strategic Thinking in Criminal Intelligence*, 1st edn, Federation Press.

Ratcliffe, JH, 2004, 'Intelligence Research', in Ratcliffe, JH (ed), *Strategic Thinking in Criminal Intelligence*, 1st edn, Federation Press.

Sheptycki, J, and Ratcliffe, JH, 2004, 'Setting the strategic agenda', in Ratcliffe, JH (ed), *Strategic Thinking in Criminal Intelligence*, 1st edn, Federation Press.

SOCA, 2008a, The National Intelligence Requirement for Serious Organised Crime (2008-9) <www.soca.gov.uk>.

SOCA, 2008b, The United Kingdom Threat Assessment of Serious Organised Crime (2008-9) <www.soca.gov.uk>.

CHAPTER 7

Intelligence research

Jerry Ratcliffe

Good research takes time, and time is usually the one thing that strategic intelligence analysts do not have. This chapter outlines some basic research strategies that can be employed by analysts on a deadline, while at the same time cautioning that the higher level analytical products – explanatory and predictive intelligence assessments – require skill, training and time. Of course, many analysts start the hard way and seek complicated analytical solutions to questions that have already been answered elsewhere. Law enforcement is littered with examples of 'reinventing the wheel'. The chapter therefore begins with some strategies for evaluating the existing body of knowledge in regard to an intelligence task. The chapter also has some inevitable overlaps with approaches to information collection, and this chapter should be read in conjunction with Chapter 6 in this book.

Reviewing the existing literature

Some commentators appear to feel that intelligence has the 'defining characteristic that it is to be adduced from information otherwise denied and likely to be wreathed in deceit – the rest is research' (Phillips 2008: 89).[1] Such an interpretation of intelligence ignores the abundance of insight to be gained from official (and often public) records, the wisdom of colleagues, and the experiences of analysts who have gone before. There is a temptation to believe that in the intelligence arena all sources must be the 'cloak and dagger' variety; however, as McDowell (1992) notes, 'strategic intelligence will always need to look beyond and outside of the agency perimeter, tapping into a wide variety of sources, most of them free of charge'. Before commencing an analytical task, it is thus valuable to conduct a thorough literature review. This may not be necessary if an analyst works in one specialised area all of the time, for example, as a member of a drugs or fraud desk; it would be hoped that analysts in this position would be familiar with the current research. However even then, regularly revisiting the existing body of work will help to maintain a high degree of specialisation and knowledge, and

---

1   Phillips credited this definition to Abram Shulsky in an uncited attribution.

even familiar and well-thumbed works can reveal fresh insights with the passage of time and experience. Research findings can also be a vital starting point for recommendations. For analysts delving into a relatively unknown area, a scan of the existing knowledge is essential.

The term 'literature review' is not actually very helpful. It conjures up images of a high school essay that lists lots of books but doesn't get to the point. A better term would be a 'critical analysis of the existing body of knowledge'. A critical analysis should identify the key pieces of research, extract the main points and implications, and recognise any limitations to the work. In essence, it should identify the good and the bad points of each article examined, and how these points construct a picture of the existing knowledge.

What constitutes 'good' research? Unfortunately there is no guaranteed way to do good research, but there are lots of ways to conduct bad research. Good research is based on professionalism and integrity. The pressure to produce intelligence shouldn't cloud the necessity to be honest about any limitations in a research project, and should not be used as an excuse to cut corners. The Butler Inquiry (2004) into the intelligence surrounding claims that the Iraq Government possessed weapons of mass destruction is a cautionary lesson in the dangers of not recognising and articulating limitations in intelligence research. The consequences were especially significant given the eventual clients included the general public, a group not generally versed or experienced in the uncertain and sometimes unreliable nature of intelligence work.

Good research is thorough, evidence-based and rigorous. In the intelligence arena it is also relevant and persuasive. The value of an evidential base cannot be underestimated, because evidence to support a case will ensure that the intelligence product is robust and can be defended against criticism. Good research also uses the right tool for the job, even if it means the analyst has to learn a new technique. It is a cliché that when all you have is a hammer then every problem looks like a nail, but it is also generally true that many intelligence analysts possess a limited range of analytical tools. Good analysts recognise that a range of different problems ('nails') will each require a different type of hammer; creativity and a willingness to explore new techniques should be an employment requirement.

Unlike pure scientific research, an analyst may not have the luxury of designing the analytical phase based on a thorough and critical combination of the existing literature and a deep grasp of the theoretical constructs behind the processes. Time pressures and access to material may hamper collection efforts. Furthermore, analysts rarely set the agenda. That is the role of the client. However, scoping the existing literature can help to reassure the analyst that they are on the right track in regard to the big issues, and that they haven't missed anything substantial.

Being critical

Information can come to us in a variety of ways. Let us assume here, for simplicity's sake, that everything comes to us in a written format. An analyst may, for example, receive information relevant to an intelligence tasking from academic journal articles, law enforcement magazines, confidential briefings, academic books, government reports, web pages, an exposé article in a national newspaper, and from a strategic intelligence assessment in a related area. The analyst then starts to wade through this information and attempts to assess its value to the tasking. In essence, the analyst is now becoming a consumer of other people's research. This has advantages and disadvantages. Research conducted by others can be a potential short-cut to a successful intelligence product, but it can also leave the analyst relying on the work of others, people who may have their own biases, agendas or limitations. So how should such a critical review be undertaken?

A good starting point is to consider the medium used for the material. The analyst should assess the article to gauge; the intended audience, any particular bias that the author is likely to have, the relevance to the task, and the choice of medium. To take some terms from documentary research processes, the analyst should examine the *authenticity, credibility, representativeness* and *meaning* (May 2001: 189). *Authenticity* relates to confirming that the author or authors are who they say they are, and that the work can be definitely attributed to them. Are they also believable, and can the date of writing or publication be ascertained? The *credibility* of the authors is another matter. Are they qualified to write material that could influence the intelligence handed to a decision-maker? How accurate were the original authors in reporting their findings? Do they have an interest in the research that they have not declared (were they paid or funded by a body they are reviewing, for example)? The *representativeness* of a document relates to a measure of typicality. In other words, is the document an unusual case or an indication of the broad trend in the area? Both types of source can be useful, but it is important for analysts to determine what type of source they are examining. Finally, it is important for the analyst to determine the real *meaning* of the document. For analytical and academic pieces, this can often be the hardest task. It is often useful to summarise a source in two or three sentences. This exercise helps to distil the article down to the key findings and meaning.

The range of possible data sources includes the following list. Academic journal articles tend to be blind peer-reviewed, which means that the articles have been approved for publication by other academics and respected practitioners in the field. This is not a guarantee that the article is accurate and fair, but it does tend to mean that at least the editor and another two or three researchers working in the same field have generally agreed that it should be published. Law enforcement magazines can be a useful method of getting a quick overview of an area, and these can often be found lying around a police station meal room. However, some caution should be exercised, as their aim is usually to entertain as well as inform. The editors will check an article for any language that is libellous but will rarely check to ensure that the author is a recognised expert in their area. An article therefore runs the risk of being either lightweight (due to the short length of most articles) or possibly incorrect (due to a lack of blind peer-review and fact-checking). Academic books can provide quick access to a range of background material to a strategic tasking, if caution is again employed. Academic texts range from the very lightweight pitched at less-than-undergraduate level, to the esoteric which can only be understood by a guru with three PhDs.

Government reports or documents from public sector agencies often provide the solid framework of hard data on which many intelligence assessments sit. In contrast, web pages can range from the truly useful to the truly awful, within one click of the mouse. National newspaper articles can provide an interesting background to an issue, and can also help a decision-maker gauge likely public opinion on a topic. Newspapers are however expected to have an opinion – it is unlikely that the opinion will be an unbiased one. Strategic intelligence assessments from other agencies or previous assessments from the analyst's own agency can provide a wealth of material – if a number of points are addressed. First, if the report is a good one, why has the analyst been tasked with a similar assessment? Is the executive aware of the first assessment? If they are, what do they want that is different or better? Secondly, how relevant is the assessment? How many years old is it, and what has changed in the meantime? Finally, the methodology and data sources should be critically examined. Are improvements possible? A predecessor's techniques are not necessarily appropriate.

Conducting research within time constraints

Time is a significant constraint for an intelligence analyst, and far more so compared to social science researchers. Sissens' (2008) survey of accredited United Kingdom (UK) intelligence analysts found that over half of her respondents lost more than a quarter of their work day to administrative functions, limiting the time available for intelligence analysis. Structured and clearly defined tasks will generally include an expectation of a product by a set deadline (see Chapter 5), and institutional expectations generally run high within the law enforcement arena. There is also a common misconception among policy makers as to how long it takes to conduct quality research and produce a good strategic intelligence assessment. This misconception rarely works in the analyst's favour and deadlines are never generous.

To conduct good research, and to understand how other people have conducted research, it is helpful to have an idea of the standard methodology used by social scientists, termed the scientific method. This is the process by which researchers and scientists try and construct an accurate representation of the world that is reliable and consistent. As Higgins points out (this volume), there are different collection models that analysts can employ. The purpose here is not to advocate for the scientific method as a collection strategy, but rather to explain the method as an aid to understanding the research process employed in many academic studies relevant to crime reduction. The key to the scientific method is the reliance on evidence rather than putting faith in belief, guesswork or hunches. There are some central steps to the scientific method, involving 1) the statement of a question, 2) the formation of a hypothesis, 3) some experimentation, 4) interpretation of the results from which conclusions are drawn, and finally 5) the use of the conclusions to revise the hypothesis. All of this sounds similar to the intelligence cycle, because it is.

Like the intelligence cycle, the scientific method was designed (albeit over many years in an *ad hoc* fashion) to reduce the chance of making errors and to create a process that could be followed, and ideally replicated, by others. There are differences between the work of scientists and intelligence analysts of course, but also a surprising degree of similarity (Prunckun, 1996). Both research approaches require time.

Time management problems with the intelligence cycle can often occur at the collection stage. Data collection can be hugely time-consuming, especially in areas with which the analyst is unfamiliar. The tendency is to collect as much as possible, for fear of missing a vital piece of evidence, and results in a 'naïve empiricism' – the assumption that having more information will inevitably lead to becoming better informed (Gill, 2000: 211). This can result in 'information overload', where the analyst is unable to discern important information due to a glut of low value material that works to confuse rather than enhance the picture. Broad collection strategies can be important, but there is often an emphasis on collecting more, not collecting better. The resulting 'noise' (Sheptycki, 2004) can rise to a symphony ending in 'paralysis by analysis', where everything gets thrown into the equation simply because it has been collected.

If time is a constraint, and a specific question requires an answer, it may be better time management to re-examine the intelligence cycle and think backwards. The aim here is not to become an intelligence heretic, but to consider a more pragmatic approach for time-limited projects. The traditional intelligence cycle has been described as an 'ideal-type' process that will always be subject to the real constraints of time (Gill, 2000: 213). If time is pressing and an answer to a specific question is sought by the client, then it might be valuable to consider the latter stages of the intelligence cycle first. In other words, to answer the question and produce an intelligence product, what analysis would be required? In fact, Juett and colleagues (2008) went a stage further with their study for the Greater London Alcohol and Drug Alliance by outlining the stages and sections of the final report prior to commencement of the work.

By focusing on the analytical technique that would produce the necessary answer, and therefore the substance for a product, the analyst identifies the required technical mechanism that is necessary. Once an analytical technique has been identified, the next stage of the reverse process is to identify the necessary information that would have to be collected in order to conduct the analysis. The 'reverse cycle' model therefore first decides what type of analytical technique is required, and then decides what data would be required to plug into the analytical technique. This dramatically simplifies the data collection phase. Stepping out of the intelligence cycle in this manner is not necessarily heresy, given that some authors prefer to see the practical reality of the intelligence cycle as more of a 'matrix of interconnected, mostly autonomous functions' (Hulnuck, 1991: 84, cited in Gill, 2000).

This 'reverse cycle' model has the advantage that it can still achieve the required answer, but can do so with a more focused collection stage which will hopefully be quicker that the traditional approach. The aim is for a more directed project that seeks to answer a question as quickly as possible. This type of approach is not appropriate for all intelligence taskings, as descriptive tasks will place a greater emphasis on broad collection. There are other disadvantages, in that this approach requires a more expansive range of analytical skills from the analyst. The 'reverse cycle' method here may provide a quick answer to a question, but to complete this requires analysts to construct a clear hypothesis, and to then employ an effective research methodology to extrapolate the answer. For a practitioner perspective of the merits of various collection strategies, the reader is directed to Chapter 6 in this book.

Developing a hypothesis

'People differ enormously in their power to construct useful hypotheses, and it is here that true genius shows itself' (Wilson, 1952: 26). A hypothesis is a testable, trial idea concerning the mechanisms that cause some sort of effect: in a strategic intelligence world, usually a criminal effect. It is a trial idea, because at the hypothesis generation stage the analyst is unlikely to yet be able to say if it is true or not, or if it is a universal fact. A hypothesis should be testable so that at the end of the research the analyst should be able to say something definitive about the question.

For example, an analyst may have a task that explores the relationship between money laundering and banks on a small South Pacific island. From a reading of the literature, discussions with colleagues and conversations with experts in the field, the analyst comes up with a 'tentative guess' (Robson, 1993) as a starting research hypothesis. It may be difficult to explore actual laundering activities directly, so the analyst decides as a starting point to examine if organised crime groups maintain accounts on the island. The research hypothesis becomes:

The majority of organised crime groups in the region conduct financial transactions through banks in Vanuatu.

This is a research hypothesis because the analyst may be able to conduct research and decide if the statement is true or not. This is the first stage to a clearer understanding of the relationship between money laundering and the island. With each hypothesis it is always helpful to explicitly state a null hypothesis, which is usually the opposite state to the research hypothesis. In this case the null hypothesis would be that the majority of organised crime groups do not have a presence on Vanuatu. The research hypothesis and the null hypothesis are not necessarily complete opposites, as in this simple example. There may be a number of competing hypotheses, but it is always helpful to identify one null hypothesis. In testing the null hypothesis, the true answer to the other possibilities may become clear. To take a second example, an analyst may note that when an intelligence-led policing operation was conducted crime appeared to decrease. The analyst is tasked with identifying if and why crime came down, and from this tasking identifies the following hypotheses:

- **Hypothesis 1** (H_1): Crime reduced because of the activities of the police operation.

- **Hypothesis 2** (H_2): Crime reduced, but only because of factors external to the police operation (such as reduced unemployment or an improving economy).

- **Hypothesis 3** (H_3): Crime reduced due to police activity not related to the operation.

  - **Null hypothesis** (H_0): The perceived reduction in crime was due to normal variation in the crime figures and the reduction was not significant.

In tackling the various hypotheses, it may be possible to use time series techniques to determine which of the four hypotheses is most appropriate.

Formulation of good hypotheses is important because without asking the right question, an analyst will rarely get a useful answer. Without an explicit hypothesis the analyst is often left with an unclear strategy for data collection and analysis and ends up collecting too much information – just to be on the safe side. The result is a project that grinds to a halt, dying from 'paralysis by analysis': analysing too much information in the wrong ways and failing to come up with any sort of meaningful result.

Tapping networks

The drive to increase use of partnerships and networks that coordinate security across various scales is a relatively recent shift in policing (Wood and Shearing, 2007). This more inclusive approach introduces new clients to the mix, but also adds to the number of collaborators analysts can draw on for ideas and inspiration when forming hypotheses, seeking out relevant material, drawing conclusions and suggesting recommendations to decision-makers.

Networks of collaborators can involve other analysts and people within the law enforcement environment, but could also include thinkers in the private sector, prosecutorial services, crime prevention, academia, and the military – all of whom bring a different perspective that can help an analyst think in new ways that are often outside the traditions of their individual agency. Every policing organisation has a number of agency-specific accepted wisdoms; some are justified while others are vague, poorly defined, and rooted more in tradition than evidence. The thread that joins them all is usually an absence of supportive evidence combined with a reticence to test these conventional wisdoms. Breaking away from the myths of an agency requires creative thinking and a willingness to challenge convention.

> Creative and innovative thinking involves creating something new and valuable. It goes beyond thinking about events sequentially; it requires a range of cognitive skills including flexibility, originality, fluency, elaboration, imagery, and abstract and allegorical thinking. Innovative thinking is to stimulate inquisitiveness and foster divergence. In addition to requiring knowledge, comprehension, application, synthesis and evaluation, it also includes skills such as comparison, use of analogies, inductive reasoning, judgement, instinctive and intuitive perception-skills regarded as craftlike, or philosophical rather than scientific (MacVean and Harfield, 2008: 98).

MacVean and Harfield articulate quite a tall order for analysts everywhere, and it is through networks of collaborators that analysts can potentially explore creative and innovative thinking that might be initially considered heresy within their own organisations. By drawing in analysts and intelligence experts from other areas, new ideas can be introduced to an organisation by transferring the legitimacy of the other groups. It is sometimes said that you can't be a prophet in your own land; however, the bigger aim is crime reduction and this may be a relatively small price for helping a group of executives think in new and productive ways about a crime problem. Of course, this means that an analyst may have to share some of the glory! At the very least, reaching out to a network of smart people will help an analyst silence that nagging doubt that something obvious is being missed, as well as flag to colleagues in other agencies the nature of the project being addressed. This has the advantage of allowing collaborators to pass on relevant information in the future, and prevent an analytical 'blue on blue' where multiple agencies are working on the same topic, each foundering without the insight that other departments could contribute.

Networks can be formed geographically, by discipline, or virtually; analysts in a city research department could reach out to analysts from other agencies that are based in the city or surrounding jurisdictions, they could seek out other analysts who specialise in their particular area (for example money laundering), or it is possible through electronic mail lists to connect with analysts around the world. Each approach has advantages and disadvantages that analysts should weigh in terms of security, convenience and value. These networks are often informal and are constructed on the basis of connections and trust as a means to overcome agency rivalries (Ratcliffe, 2008). Like any relationship, they must be nurtured and managed, especially given the proclivity for information trading rather than sharing that is common in the criminal intelligence world.

Research methodologies

Many research activities fall into one of two general categories: quantitative and qualitative research. Quantitative research techniques focus on the analysis of empirical data that can be categorised, counted and measured. If data can be categorised then they can be compared and analysed. This can range from the simplest information (such as the gender of arrested persons) to more complex quantitative data (for example the purity and quantity of heroin seizures). Quantitative research will often use tables, graphs and maps to indicate what is occurring, and may use statistical techniques to distinguish significant differences from random variation or fluctuation. Quantitative research is good for answering questions regarding generalisations and aggregation. It can be used to examine a range of descriptive, inferential and evaluative questions.

In contrast, qualitative research is more interested in value, opinions and perceptions. Qualitative research data tend to be analysed by means of logic rather than statistical power. For instance, an analyst might use a Delphi (Loo, 2002) technique to investigate the views of senior intelligence managers regarding the war on drugs.

Qualitative data are often gathered through interviews, surveys and questionnaires. In a minority of studies researchers can use observational work, but the applicability of this at the strategic intelligence level is rare. Content analysis can be a useful way to establish priorities from studies of newspapers, intelligence briefings or a wide range of other documents. Case studies can also be used, either as examples of common behaviour, or to emphasise extreme cases.

The difficulty for strategic analysts is the shear range of techniques available in both of these categories. Few strategic assessments go beyond the mere descriptive. There are a range of both quantitative and qualitative approaches that can address more profound questions that are explanatory or even predictive, but few analysts have these tools at their fingertips. This is not just a problem within strategic law enforcement, but in the broader research community. While university courses will often offer quantitative and qualitative classes, usually separately, few analysts have the training or educational opportunities to take an intelligence assessment to the highest level, for example, a predictive assessment based on quantitative findings. Rarer yet is the assessment that combines qualitative and quantitative analyses.

The gulf between quantitative and qualitative researchers has often been wide. Quantitative analysts considered that a numerical value could be placed on everything and that it was possible to quantify and measure just about anything. In contrast, qualitative researchers found that the number-crunchers missed the complexity and richness of the data, constrained as they were to aggregating and codifying everything. Recently researchers have recognised that both groups are correct to a point, but that quantitative and qualitative research processes can complement each other. Quantitative research can often tell you 'what' is happening, and qualitative research can tell you 'why' it is happening. This notion has parallels with the dichotomy with crime analysis and criminal intelligence, as the two closely-related disciplines are often described. In a simplistic sense, it could be argued that crime analysis provides the 'what' while criminal intelligence fills in the 'why' (Ratcliffe 2008).

The complementary nature of the two can add weight to a study. Consider the case studies in Box 7.1 and Box 7.2. In both cases, the wealth of information in police records would certainly provide a clear picture of what was happening; however, the qualitative research provided 'context and richness' to the narrative (Stanko, 2009: 232).

Box 7.1 Hate crime

Stanko's (2009) research with the Metropolitan Police in London, orchestrated through the Understanding and Responding to Hate Crime project, debunked the commonly held assumption that violence associated with racist, faith-conflict and homophobia is founded in a hatred motivated by 'distance, dissimilarity, and unfamiliarity' (p 232). The research drew on a quantitative analysis of crime records reported to the police. Police records captured victim and offender profiles, crime locations, the nature of the 'hatred', repeat victimisation, and types of weapons involved. The quantitative analysis was supported by a qualitative analysis of crimes that occurred during a single random day, and an in-depth examination of both repeat victimisation and the most serious incidents.

Rather than supporting the myth of distance and dissimilarity as a cause for hate-crimes, the research demonstrated that the police were most commonly contacted in regard to the behaviour of neighbours, work associates and other acquaintances. In this, hate crime shares many similarities with domestic violence, and is a crime that is the result of 'local encounters that are often difficult to avoid'.

The primary difficulty with many of the techniques employed by criminal intelligence analysts is the inherently retrospective nature of the analyses (Gill 2000), essentially resulting in a descriptive product at best. Few of the myriad tools and computer programs that can be found in the typical analyst's office are employed with any real explanatory or predictive power. An intelligence office that functions with a basic suite of, for example, Microsoft Office and a Geographical Information System (GIS) will have little available in their attempt to create higher level intelligence products. As the reader will discover in the later chapters in this volume, exploring the potential for criminality into the future requires a greater emphasis on training and brainpower, rather than computing prowess. The case study in Box 7.2 is illustrative of the challenge. Blending and weighing the merits of a survey of law enforcement organisations with media reports on gang activity and unstructured information gleaned from myriad covert sources is a considerable challenge requiring balance and finesse.

Box 7.2 Violent street gangs

The New Jersey State Police produces a regular Statewide Intelligence Estimate, an assessment of strategic concerns for the east-coast American state (Ratcliffe and Guidetti, 2008). Flowing from one of their regular estimates, a 2004 survey of law enforcement agencies in the state found there were an estimated 148 gangs in the state, and almost 30 gangs with over 100 members (NJSP, nd). These levels of gang membership were obviously considered a significant threat to public safety in the state.

Tasked with the identification of the gang that was most violent and an emerging threat, New Jersey State Police analysts drew on both quantitative and qualitative information. Their analysis included information from 300 intelligence reports, data from 177 municipal police departments, over 50 media articles, and covert information gathered from nearly 100 confidential informants. The research identified a subset of the Bloods gang as a major target, and it was the combination of quantitative measures and qualitative contextual information that persuaded the State Police management to mount a major operation. As a result of Operation Nine-Connect, dozens of gang members were arrested in a major east-coast police operation (NJSP, 2006; Ratcliffe, 2008; Ratcliffe and Guidetti, 2008).

Action research

While there are some research activities in the sciences that simply aim to advance knowledge, these *pure research* activities are of limited value in the criminal intelligence arena. While it might be nice to learn, for example, that pre-natal neurological damage may increase the risk that certain individuals will display criminal tendencies (Lowenstein, 2003), this knowledge is of limited practical, direct, crime prevention benefit. In contrast, *applied research* is oriented towards creating information and intelligence that has a direct relevance to decision-makers and the formulation of policy (Senese, 1997). In the criminal intelligence arena, few areas of research are as policy-specific and applied as action research.

Definitions of action research are difficult to tie down, because the term has been used by different people in different ways (Robson, 1993); however, a general definition is that action research is a methodology that seeks to develop a hypothesis about an issue, test that hypothesis, implement some kind of change on the studied issue, and evaluate and learn from the result. In other words, with action research the aim is to determine the main drivers, cause a change on the subject, and to observe and learn from what has happened.

This type of research appeals to police officers as it has practical qualities. For example, an agency could remove one money laundering opportunity for an organised crime syndicate, perhaps by using financial legislation to close down an overseas bank, and then observe the syndicate's response. In doing so it could be possible to learn how they adapt their behaviour to deal with the new operating environment. It may then be possible to learn new aspects about the syndicate, expand knowledge of their other activities, determine the decision-making structure of the syndicate, how long it takes for them to react, and discover what measures they adopt to restrict the impact of law enforcement on their business model. This type of intelligence may have benefits beyond the syndicate in question, and may be of value in understanding similar organisations.

Both quantitative and qualitative research methodologies can support this type of research. In the example here, an analyst might use financial transaction monitoring to identify changes in the direction and amount of dealings. This would tell the law enforcement agency 'what' has changed in the criminal environment. Electronic and physical surveillance, informants and suspect interviews after arrest may be able to explain 'why' the syndicate chose new operating mechanisms in response to the action undertaken by law enforcement.

By acting on the target research area, action research moves the research agenda from a more passive practice (the remote collation of information) to an active research agenda. This move from the passive to the active does have a price attached to it. Active intelligence gathering requires greater analytical effort to interpret a dynamic and changing environment, especially as the force for change has probably been a law enforcement activity. The intelligence that can be gained from knowledge of how a criminal structure reacts to enforcement efforts may be invaluable.

As Gill (2000: 239) points out, involvement in operations that attempt to understand a criminal network may require analysts to work in more flexible arrangements, and in environments that reduce the cultural distance between targets and analysts. This may require a revision of the traditional hierarchy that typifies many police intelligence units, but will be necessary if disruption of criminal networks becomes a common tactic (Ratcliffe, 2008).

Secondary data analysis

Secondary data analysis involves the examination of data that the analyst was not responsible for collecting, or it examines data that were collected for a different purpose from the one under investigation. There are a number of advantages for the analyst, and this can be a useful tactic for an intelligence analyst short on time. Secondary analysis enables the analyst to capitalise on data already collected, data that might either be too time consuming to collect again, or may be too expensive to collect. Findings should seek to go beyond the first analysis, adding value and not just repetition.

Examples of data that would be far outside the capacity of a strategic intelligence analyst to collect include census data sets. These are collected by national agencies with huge budgets, and have multiple purposes and applications. A strategic analyst may use changes in population demographics in a region to predict new criminal opportunities, such as certain types of activity targeted at an increasingly aging population. An understanding of the ethnic composition of a city, derived from census data, may help an analyst appreciate the potential areas for racial tension or potential growth areas for ethnic-based organised crime groups. The census data were never specifically collected for this type of analysis, but secondary analysis allows for this type of work.

Although large data collections such as census data have clear secondary applications, it is also possible to find secondary benefits from more local sources. For example, a survey of local police intelligence officers by a central unit in an organisation may help determine the data collection needs of local intelligence officers. However, a secondary analysis at a later stage may help answer further questions that were not of concern in the original study. The survey returns may, for example, be used to gather the ranks and experience of the intelligence officers, or help to determine future intelligence training needs for the organisation.

There are some caveats with secondary data analysis. The analyst should always be aware that the original surveys were unlikely to directly address the secondary problem under investigation (Robson, 1993: 282). This means that the wording of questions may not suit the secondary problem, or the data may not be recorded with the same rigour as the data that addressed the main problem of the original study. Furthermore the original data may not be held in the raw form it was gathered in, and may only be available in summarised form. For example, the authors of the biennial Australian Illicit Drug Data Report (IDDR) sensibly include a number of pages at the end of each report detailing the statistical limitations of their work, knowing that they have to rely on data collected by other agencies. As they noted in the 2006-2007 report:

> The lack of consistency between law enforcement agencies in the way they record illicit drug arrests and seizures presents difficulties when data is aggregated and compared. Disparities exist in the level of detail recorded for each offence, the methods used to quantify the seizures, the way offence and seizure data is extracted, and the way counting rules and extraction programs are applied (ACC, 2008: 102).

This does not mean that the data are worthless – on the contrary the IDDR represents one of the best summaries of drug and arrest information in Australia. It simply states that the analysis should be interpreted with caution and an understanding of the limitations of the underlying data.

There is another implication for strategic analysts. Large data sets require a considerable technical ability in order to manipulate and analyse the data. Analytical techniques for large data sets include regression, non-linear and time series techniques that can be used for evaluative and predictive intelligence products, but these approaches are not to be conducted lightly. Few intelligence departments employ large groups of analysts with significant research training; however, while it is still rare for staff (civilian or sworn) to have graduate level research skills, this situation is showing signs of improving. In a recent survey of UK analysts, Sissens found about two-thirds had a tertiary education (Sissens, 2008).

Conclusion

You may be able to see from this chapter that the task definition stage becomes fundamental to a sound project. As Jonathan Nicholl points out (Chapter 5 in this book), it is useful to frame the task in the form of a clear question. If that is not done then the research hypothesis will not be clear, and it is possible that either confusion or 'mission creep' – where the task drifts into areas not considered by the client – can result.

Once the task is proposed and refined, the demands for products coupled with the inevitable time constraints place significant pressures on the intelligence analyst. This is simply the nature of the job, but these constraints mean that few analysts have the option of primary research analysis: there just isn't the time to go out and collect your own data. Many techniques, such as the Delphi method (Loo, 2002), can take months to complete. Some analysts resort to secondary analysis of data already collected. This requires an appreciation and understanding for the method of data capture by the original research, and the method of analysis.

If strategic intelligence analysis is going to seek a place at the head table, then policy makers are likely to expect the same levels of technical sophistication with regard to analytical technique, as they are now expecting from tactical analysts. This places an onus on strategic intelligence personnel to expand the range of methodologies employed, and to develop a broader appreciation for different research methodologies beyond the traditional tools used for descriptive analyses. Clients are demanding explanatory and predictive products. In many strategic intelligence departments, the concern is that the toolbox for these types of analyses appears to be rather bare.

Further information

So where is a good place to begin? It is great if an organisation has a library, but smaller libraries often have limited collections. For broad background pieces in the criminal justice and law enforcement area, the following web sites contain material that can act as a good starting point:

- The US National Criminal Justice Reference Service <www.ncjrs. org> has a huge collection of useful works and an effective search facility. The service contains abstracts of over 170,000 criminal justice publications as well as containing over 7,000 full-text publications that can be downloaded.

- The Home Office Research Development Statistics site <www. homeoffice.gov.uk/rds> contains a wealth of material relating to policing, crime reduction and crime prevention across the UK. Most of the research reports are downloadable.

- The Australian Institute of Criminology <www.aic.gov.au> has an on-line publishing arm, and so like the Home Office in London, most of its publications are available to download from their site. Their *Trends and Issues in Crime and Criminal Justice* can usually be a good place to find background and overview material on a wide range of topics.

- For traditional crime problems such as robbery, burglary, graffiti, car theft, the Center for Problem-Oriented Policing has a large web site with downloadable research findings and examples of projects conducted by police departments from around the world <www.popcenter.org>.

References

ACC, 2008, *Illicit Drug Data Report 2006-07*, Canberra, Australian Crime Commission.

Butler, Lord, 2004, *Review of Intelligence on Weapons of Mass Destruction: Report of a Committee of Privy Counsellors*, HC898, London.

Gill, P, 2000, *Rounding Up the Usual Suspects? Developments in Contemporary Law Enforcement Intelligence*, Ashgate.

Hulnuck, AS, 1991, 'Controlling intelligence estimates', in Hastedt, G (ed), *Controlling Intelligence*, Frank Cass.

Juett, L, Smith, R, and Grieve, JDG, 2008, 'Open source intelligence – A case study (GLADA: London: The Highs and Lows 2003 and 2007)', in Harfield, C, MacVean, A, Grieve, JGD, and Phillips, D (eds), *The Handbook of Intelligent Policing: Consilience, Crime Control, and Community Safety*, Oxford University Press.

Loo, R, 2002, 'The Delphi method: a powerful tool for strategic management', *Policing: An International Journal of Police Strategies and Management*, vol 25, 762-769.

Lowenstein, LF, 2003, 'The genetic aspects of criminality', *Journal of Human Behavior in the Social Environment*, vol 8, 63-78.

MacVean, A, and Harfield, C, 2009, 'Science or sophistry: Issues in managing analysts and their products', in Harfield, C, MacVean, A, Grieve, JGD, and Phillips, D (eds), *The Handbook of Intelligent Policing: Consilience, Crime Control, and Community Safety*, Oxford University Press.

May, T, 2001, *Social Research: Issues, Methods and Practice*, Open University Press.

McDowell, D, 1992, 'Strategic intelligence and law enforcement', *Journal of the Australian Institute of Professional Intelligence Officers*, vol 1, 9-20.

NJSP, 2006, 'State Police lead team of 500 officers to decapitate most violent set of Bloods street gang' (press release), Trenton, NJ: New Jersey State Police.

NJSP, nd, *Gangs in New Jersey: Municipal Law Enforcement Response to the 2004 and 2001 NJSP Gang Surveys*, Trenton, NJ: New Jersey State Police Intelligence Services Section.

Phillips, D, 2008, 'Analysis – Providing a context for intelligence', in Harfield, C, MacVean, A, Grieve, JGD, and Phillips, D (eds), *The Handbook of Intelligent Policing: Consilience, Crime Control, and Community Safety*, Oxford University Press.

Prunckun, JHW, 1996, 'The intelligence analyst as social scientist: A comparison of research methods', *Police Studies*, vol 19, 67-80.

Ratcliffe, JH, 2008, *Intelligence-Led Policing*, Willan Publishing.

Ratcliffe, JH, and Guidetti, RA, 2008, 'State police investigative structure and the adoption of intelligence-led policing', *Policing: An International Journal of Police Strategies and Management*, vol 31, 109-128.

Robson, C, 1993, *Real World Research: A Resource for Social Scientists and Practitioner-Researchers*, Blackwell.

Senese, JD, 1997, *Applied Research Methods in Criminal Justice*, Nelson-Hall.

Sheptycki, J, 2004, 'Organizational pathologies in police intelligence systems: Some contributions to the lexicon of intelligence-led policing', *European Journal of Criminology*, vol 1, no 3, 307-332.

Sissens, J, 2008, 'An evaluation of the role of the intelligence analyst within the National Intelligence Model', in Harfield, C, MacVean, A, Grieve, JGD, and Phillips, D (eds), *The Handbook of Intelligent Policing: Consilience, Crime Control, and Community Safety*, Oxford University Press, pp 121-130.

Stanko, B, 2008, 'Strategic intelligence: Methodologies for understanding what police services already "know" to reduce harm', in Harfield, C, MacVean, A, Grieve, JGD, and Phillips, D (eds), *The Handbook of Intelligent Policing: Consilience, Crime Control, and Community Safety*, Oxford University Press.

Wilson, EB, 1952, *An Introduction to Scientific Research*, McGraw-Hill.

Wood, J, and Shearing, C, 2007, *Imagining Security*, Willan Publishing.

CHAPTER 8

Exploratory analysis tools

Corey E Heldon

Introduction

Analysis is at the heart of the intelligence process. Whether the analyst is providing support to investigators in a patrol environment or assisting decision-makers in the development of policy, analysis is central to their role. Value-adding to information gathered in the intelligence cycle is the function of the analyst and it is where intelligence should provide the edge for law enforcement. While statisticians employ scientific methods, such as statistical analysis, to analyse quantitative data, this chapter will focus on the analysis of qualitative data in an intelligence setting.

Exploratory analysis tools provide to the analyst a range of ways of viewing information and, as the name suggests, exploring the issues beyond what is immediately apparent. The analyst should seek to develop a deeper understanding of the issues to elicit the underpinning meaning behind what is there. These tools can be used to develop key findings, articulate options to decision-makers, and decide the priority level of different issues.

There are a range of exploratory analysis tools that can be used by an analyst depending on the issue and the situation. A number of these tools are complementary and can be used in conjunction with each other to comprehensively explore the issue and develop the understanding required to provide appropriate advice to the decision-maker or client. Each of the techniques has strengths and weaknesses and the analyst may find not all are appropriate for use in each situation. The analyst often has to make a judgment call regarding the type of tool to use and when.

This chapter aims to provide an explanation of a range of techniques and provide examples of how these approaches can be used to analyse an issue. The chapter will also explain how these tools can be used in conjunction with others. The tools discussed in the chapter are by no means the definitive list of exploratory analysis techniques, but are provided as a basic toolkit to stimulate thought and as a starting point for other analytical options.

Before starting, although this chapter focuses on the exploratory analysis tools an analyst can use to probe an issue or problem, it is appropriate to look at the process of thinking and how we approach analytical problems.

Structured thinking

Abram Shulsky (quoted in Lefebvre, 2004) stated; 'it may not be possible to lay down rules that will inevitably guide us to analyse intelligence information correctly, it is nevertheless useful to try to identify intellectual errors or deficiencies that may be characteristic of the analytical process'. Analysts need to be able to think effectively. While this simple statement seems to make sense the process of thinking requires some effort. Much has already been written on the way the human mind works and this chapter is not the vehicle to be covering the same ground. It is, however, useful to consider the way we process information and understand some of the issues that exist with how we do our thinking.

Do many analysts in law enforcement or in national security agencies use structured analytical techniques to process information? Anecdotally and through research the answer to this question appears to be 'no'. Why is this the case? Hulnick (2006) stated that analysts complained that the pressures to produce intelligence reporting did not allow time to learn or use new skills. Unfortunately, in the current law enforcement environment where policing agencies are at the forefront of combating terrorism, transnational crime as well as more 'traditional' community-level offences, understanding and information are critical. Intelligence must be able to support decision-makers to negotiate this environment.

Jones (1998) states that while we are natural problem solvers, structuring analysis is 'at odds with the way the human mind works'. Folker (2000) agrees: His research indicated that most analysts preferred a more intuitive method of analysis and eschewed the prospect of using structured analytical techniques. Unfortunately this intuitive approach can lead to a number of analytical 'sins'. They include:

- beginning analysis by formulating conclusions;
- collecting information that affirms pre-existing beliefs, thus reinforcing them;
- intuitively favouring solutions that are the first ones that appear satisfactory;
- confusing the process of discussing or thinking hard about an issue as being analysis. As Jones (1995) states; 'discussing and thinking can be like pedalling an exercise bike: they expend lots of energy and sweat but go nowhere';
- focusing on the substance (or evidence) of analysis and not on the process of how we are actually *doing* the analysis; and
- lack of familiarisation with the techniques that can be used to structure analysis. It is hard if not impossible to use a tool or technique that is completely foreign.

(adapted from Jones, 1995: 11-12)

Morgan (1998) goes further to list what he considers to be the seven most problematic thinking traits that have adverse effects on the ability to analyse and solve problems. They are:

1. The emotional dimension to almost every thought and decision we make.

2. Mental shortcuts our unconscious minds continuously take influence our conscious thinking.

3. We are driven to view the world around us in terms of patterns.

4. We instinctively rely on, and are susceptible to, biases and assumptions.

5. We feel the need to find explanations for *everything*, regardless of whether the explanations are accurate.

6. Humans have a penchant to seek out and put stock in evidence that supports their beliefs and judgments while eschewing and devaluing evidence that does not.

7. We tend to cling to untrue beliefs in the face of contradictory evidence.

It is important for us to recognise these issues and the potential dangers they present to us when we attempt an analytical task. The next section develops this theme and identifies a number of common fallacies in reasoning that can undermine the analytical process. All the techniques described in this chapter have been selected with a view to providing a range of methods that minimise some of the traits outlined above, minimise bias and provide depth.

Reasoning and logic

The intelligence process is essentially a process of inductive reasoning. The practice of inductive reasoning generally starts with an examination of known facts and progresses to the development of theory of what happened or what the issue is about. Inductive reasoning is therefore about the synthesis of information to develop theories or hypotheses about the event or issue.

The conclusions an analyst reaches in the inductive reasoning process does not always stem from the evaluation of the information obtained. On occasion, the conclusions have to be inferred from the information, as not all data can be obtained or observed by the analyst. It is this inference development that makes the intelligence process inductive.

Reasoned argumentation is vital to the process to ensure credibility. Given that an argument is a connected series of statements to establish a definite proposition, it is with this in mind that an analyst develops an assessment to provide advice and guidance to the decision-makers in the organisation in which they work.

By contrast, research conducted on an issue for the purpose of proving (or disproving) a hypothesis is considered to be deductive reasoning. For example, a scientist may set up an experiment to prove a hypothesis is correct. This is seen as deductive reasoning because research conducted by the scientist is generated by the original hypothesis, not the other way around.

Inductive arguments can be subject to change when new information comes to light. New premises can undermine the strength of an inductive argument whereas with a deductive argument, unless new premises do not refute, change or invalidate the original argument, then the argument remains valid.

While intelligence analysis is primarily inductive there is scope for the use of deductive arguments. An analyst can develop a hypothesis about a problem and conduct research to prove or disprove this theory (deduction) or start with a plethora of information about a subject and from this infer certain things and, from this, develop a hypothesis. The possibility is there and should not be discounted.

Logic is a pattern of systematic thinking with the end in mind to develop an argument. The structure of an argument consists of a series of premises and a conclusion. Unfortunately there are fallacies in logic that can skew the results of the argument, as well as fallacies in the development of premises that constitute the argument itself. These fallacies in logic, if used to form the basis of the argument, can mean that the conclusion reached is fundamentally incorrect.

Logical fallacies

If our argument is flawed or our reasoning is faulty then the best advice cannot be provided to the decision-maker and our credibility is decreased. Awareness of our reasoning processes, as discussed above, is therefore appropriate to ensure we are approaching the argument with clear thinking and a lack of biases. A small number of logical fallacies will be discussed below, as a background to the following description of exploratory tools.

Generalisation is a 'conclusion or assertion about a whole class or category of things' (Holt, 1983). An example of this is 'All Muslims are terrorists' or 'All Asians are drug dealers'. The **over-generalisation fallacy** behind this type of reasoning is that the behaviour or attribute is claimed to be true of a whole class of objects when this is simply incorrect. Generalisation can occur in both types of reasoning: inductive and deductive.

The **false cause fallacy** relates to the relationship of cause and effect. Sometimes arguments are developed based on the idea that simply because an event preceded another the second event was caused by the first. These events may be coincidental but that is not considered when this fallacy in reasoning is used. Often there are many causal relationships that affect complex issues, and to attribute only one cause may also be a fallacy in reasoning.

Ad Hominem is a Latin phrase which means 'against the person'. The *Ad Hominem fallacy* stems from the concept that the argument presented is aimed against a person when, in fact, it should present reasons aimed at a position or viewpoint. For example, if there is argument against the Federal Government's immigration policy any argument against it should be critical of the policy itself rather than at any government minister as a person. It is considered bad reasoning because it is merely a way of diverting attention from the proper issues.

These examples of fallacies in logic are not a definitive list, and there are a number of logic texts that have more in-depth explanations of the range of fallacies. However, they are included here to highlight the range of ways that arguments can be flawed due to biases and faulty reasoning in a strategic intelligence environment. With this out of the way, the chapter proceeds to examine a number of the exploratory analysis tools that an analyst can use to explore strategic criminal intelligence issues.

Systems thinking

When Gandhi said 'there is more to life than increasing its speed', he was talking from a philosophical view point. Systems thinking advocates something similar in a business sense, and is a style of management that was popularised by Peter Senge in his 1990 book *The Fifth Discipline*. What Senge suggests is that we have evolved to a point where we focus too readily on events rather than the underpinning structures that have slowly developed to create the environment we are currently experiencing. As Covey (1989: 232) observed, 'often the problem is in the system, not in the people'. Systems thinking suggests that we must look 'beyond individual mistakes ... to understand important problems. We must look beyond personalities and events. We must look into the underlying structures which shape individual actions' (Senge, 1990: 43). These structures aren't necessarily those traditionally thought of in the sense of being a hierarchical structure or another form of formal arrangement. Rather, these can be anything from the connectivity between population growth, changes in legislation, drought or the onset of civil unrest in a nation state. Figure 8.1 shows a model of the 'iceberg' composition of systems thinking. At the bottom of the iceberg are the structures or causes of the problem. These underpin the entire issue. They are not immediately apparent and often are not obvious or cannot be directly linked to the effects at the tip of the iceberg. The patterns in the middle control the structures. They give an indication of what the causes are and lead to the events or effects.

Events are at the tip of the iceberg. These are the things that are most obvious and can be seen. As an example, consider Operation Anchorage, a short-term intelligence-led policing operation conducted by the Australian Federal Police (AFP), in response to a rise in burglary rates and other property crime in the Australian Capital Territory (ACT). The effect

Figure 8.1 The iceberg composition of systems thinking

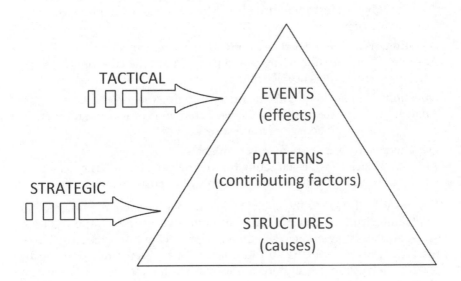

of the operation in the short term was a decrease in the number of burg-laries, yet the pace and commitment to the operation was, in the long term, unsustainable due to cost and limited police numbers.

What the operation didn't address was the underlying issues that brought the situation to that point. There were no dramatic or obvious events that could be directly attributed to the rise in burglary rates; it was gradual: over time the police-to-population ratio had decreased (Rat-cliffe, 2001). There may have been other factors that caused the burglary rate to increase, however, no long-term issues were addressed during the operation. The tactics therefore focused on the targeting and arrest of offenders. However, the causal factors that created the burglary rise in the first instance were not addressed and subsequently a rise in property crime should be expected to take place again.

When considering these types of questions we must remember that problems such as burglary are complex and multi-layered. Indeed deal-ing with these problems is 'notoriously difficult' (Aronson, 1996). If, during Operation Anchorage, the effects of property crime were dealt with (such as locking up offenders), what were the potential causes that created the situation in the first place? In the ACT what structure or system is in place that encourages or allows property crime to become an issue that necessitates a comprehensive operation such as Anchorage? One way of approaching this is simply to ask 'why?' in a question and answer format.

Question: Why are there a large number of property crimes in the ACT?
Answer: One answer could be that statistically, recidivist offenders have a history of drug use. Money is needed to purchase drugs.

Question: Why are the recidivist offenders using drugs?
Answer: They are unemployed and living in a social environment that encourages use of drugs.

Question: Why is this environment encouraging the use of drugs?
Answer: Drugs are readily available. Boredom is prevalent and there is a perceived lack of interesting activities.

Question: Why are drugs readily available?
Answer: Lack of police targeting of drug dealers. Many drug dealers on the streets, all with a supply of the drug wanted.

The answers then lead the analyst towards one possible hypothesis that combating drug dealers may be more effective in reducing burglaries. These answers may not necessarily be the correct ones for the situation in the ACT, however, this is an example of how systems thinking can be used to delve into the underpinning reasons for the rise in crime and other strategic issues. An analyst could ask a range of questions regarding a chosen issue. These questions are 'effects' questions and the answers to them prompt the analyst to understand why.

Systems thinking challenges the analyst to slow down and look beyond the effects of an event or issue, to focus on the underpinning causes and to understand the deeper meaning behind them. Systems thinking is a useful strategic tool that, combined with other exploratory tools, may assist in asking questions that delve into the structures behind the problems and allow us to develop a more robust response to the task. By recognising that the issue has taken a long time to reach the point that it has, that life has not 'increased its speed', we can counter it in a more appropriate and thoughtful manner.

Process mapping

Process mapping is a technique developed for businesses to identify each step in a procedure (Damelio, 1996). The development of the tool occurred when managers wanted a way to identify inefficiencies in industrial processes such as production lines and the manufacture of goods. When the steps are mapped out in their simplest form the breakdowns in the process (if there are any) are readily identifiable and can be dealt with.

This charting technique can be useful in a law enforcement context in assisting the analyst to identify the methodology of criminal groups or the steps taken when a criminal activity is undertaken. By understanding the steps taken by the offenders to carry out the activity, opportunities for law enforcement intervention may become apparent and recommendations can be made to target the weaknesses in the activity.

The process mapping technique uses different symbols to highlight such things as decisions, actions, terminations and inventory. As each of these things is used in each step taken to undertake the activity they are focused on in the development of the chart. The symbols that are commonly used in the process maps have specific meanings and are connected by arrows indicating the flow from one step to another. Ovals indicate both the starting point and the ending point of the process steps, whereas a box represents an individual step or activity in the process. A diamond shows a decision point, such as 'yes or no' or 'go or don't go' decision step (it should be noted that each path emerging from a diamond must be labelled with one of the possible answers). A circle indicates that a particular step is connected to another page, for example an annexure, or part of the process map (and a letter placed in the circle clarifies the continuation), while a triangle shows where an in-process measurement occurs. For process mapping to be used in law enforcement it may necessitate the change or creation of symbols relevant in a law enforcement context. The use of a legend would aid comprehension in this circumstance.

Figure 8.2 below shows many of these stages, using a simple example addressing the process of illegal immigration.

Figure 8.2 An illegal migration example process map

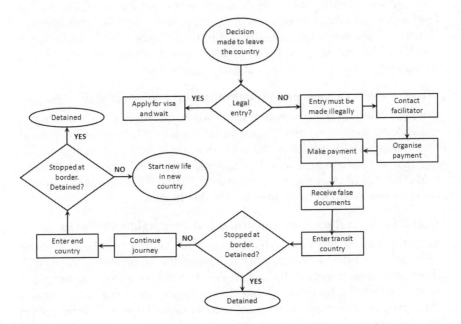

Trend analysis

While a trend can be defined as a 'general tendency', it can more importantly be used to identify those general tendencies in the conduct of criminal activity through the analysis of information and statistics. Trend analysis is used both quantitatively and qualitatively in intelligence analysis and is useful in identifying a range of factors including:

- geographical locations of similar events;
- similarities in methodology used by criminal entities (this could be anything from new communication methods to use of technology to facilitate the activity);
- emergence of a new crime type; and
- emergence of a new criminal structure or type.

The emergence of these issues is often a slow, evolutionary process. As previously discussed in Systems Thinking, the underpinning factors that create a circumstance develop over time. Identifying these trends and the effect they have on the environment are the key factors behind this type of analysis.

Trend analysis often looks at broad developments in the environment that can affect society, technology and the political landscape. These trends have been referred to as 'megatrends' <www.strategy.gov.uk>. Major trends tend to change society and can have other implications and counter-act each other, while some trends may be of a smaller but no less important scale. In other words, they may not have the broader impact of these so-called 'megatrends' but may have a major influence in specific jurisdictions, counties or States. Trend analysis can be used in a four-step process. Here we look at each stage in turn.

Step 1: Develop a conceptual framework of the forces at play

When developing the conceptual framework, the analyst is attempting to understand the key factors that make up the issue. This relies heavily on the analyst's ability to define the issue that has to be analysed and articulate that in a meaningful way. It is this definition of the problem or issue that is pivotal to creating an effective information collection plan that will elicit the required information to undertake the task.

Step 2: Look for theoretical constructs that shed light on those forces

Here the analyst identifies what background knowledge there is about the task and related issues. This identifies the information gaps and, through this examination, the action the analyst can take in the next step to fill the information gaps (what do we know, what don't we know?) through the collection of relevant information. Historical information about previous (similar) trends can be useful in examining the effects of the trends and what prompted them in the first instance.

Step 3: Seek out any relevant information

This part of the process involves examining the information gathered on the issue and analysing it for both its manifest and latent content. This means that the analyst examines the material to see what the facts are and what is inferred from the information contained within it. Once the manifest and latent content of the material have been identified it is then important to further examine the information to determine what, if any, interpretation has been placed on the content by the author. This assists the analyst in determining the credibility and validity of the information.

Step 4: Derive an alternative future implied by the examination of that system

The final part of the process is the development of conclusions based on the information gathered and analysed in the previous steps. These conclusions will be probable at best, drawing on the hypotheses developed by the analyst. It should be possible to forecast future trends based on the past data and the indicators identified during this process.

Trend analysis can be used as part of an early warning indication regime (see next chapter) to observe possible futures and risks, and can also be used as a platform from which the analyst can generate scenarios for the longer term. However, identification of a trend may be difficult. 'Fads' can be mistaken for a trend and can divert attention away from real issues.

Trends often don't occur in isolation. It is possible that one trend may lead to further responses from different areas of society. For example, civil unrest or vilification of ethnic minorities in various nation states may cause a rise in people from those countries seeking asylum. This in turn may lead to a trend in the increase in illegal migration of asylum seekers and the increase in document fraud in transit countries. These trends may affect legislation in the end country and so on.

Delphi technique

The Delphi technique is a method that is used to collect the views and opinions of 'experts' on a given issue or subject (Loo, 2002). The analyst can compare the different views and, through the results of these surveys, get a grasp of a particular issue being researched. The technique is useful if the analyst is looking at an issue where there is a previous body of work involved. It is possible that the research being conducted may have been canvassed previously by one or more of the experts who are providing information. This allows the intelligence analyst to immediately draw on expertise without having to 'reinvent the wheel'.

There are drawbacks to this particular method of gaining information. It can be time consuming in that it can require a lot of effort to formulate the questions, research who would be appropriate experts to canvass and follow up with them to ensure a response. Once collected, the responses require examination and analysis to ensure there isn't any inherent bias inserted by the expert and that it is free from 'conditioning and conformity' (McDowell, 1998: 191). If the issue is complex enough and the analyst has time to explore the views and opinions of others from a range of other organisations or agencies, it may be a beneficial exercise to gain greater insight into the problem.

The surveys are done over several sessions. The process is as follows:

1. Identify the issue and engage the panel of experts to respond.
2. Response to the questionnaire. The experts reply anonymously to the survey. The answers are collated by the analyst who formulates a second questionnaire in order to elicit responses to the comments made in the first one.
3. Create and send second questionnaire. This provides the respondents with the opportunity to refine their first ideas and to identify new ones based on the original replies.
4. Responses to second survey. The surveys are returned to the analyst for collation.
5. Create and send third questionnaire. This questionnaire summarises the ideas from the first two and seeks further clarification as required. Any strengths or weaknesses in the responses are identified at this point.
6. Continuation of process. This stage calls for continued refinement of the preceding steps. At this point the analyst should be able to highlight the consensus in the opinions of the panel of experts.

There are difficulties with this technique. They can be any or all of the following:

- definition of an 'expert' and the method by which the analyst determines their status
- the questions formulated may be biased;
- the technique requires considerable commitment from the analyst and participants; and
- there can be a tendency to force consensus and be 'middle of the road' – extreme views may be discounted because they have not conformed to the more general view.

However, the technique also has a number of advantages, including:

- it allows the sharing of information around the group of participants;
- it can be a reliable indicator of current thinking on the issue being canvassed;
- consulting a range of people can be more beneficial in formulating results than relying on one expert; and
- by using experts in the field it can give the findings authority and legitimacy.

SWOT analysis

SWOT is a useful way of assessing the characteristics of a criminal group or event to identify ways that law enforcement can have an impact on an issue. It is a quick method of taking a 'big picture' view of that issue or group. It can give you an insight into the past activities of the group or the background to the event or issue and, from there, give an indication towards future developments or activities. SWOT is an acronym for Strengths, Weaknesses, Opportunities, Threats. The analyst lists each of these characteristics in an attempt to 'tease' out the key features of the problem, and in order to identify where weaknesses are counteracted by strengths, and opportunities are menaced by threats.

Strengths

This part of the analysis focuses on the attributes of the entity. These strengths may range from the knowledge the criminal entity possesses of the crime to be conducted. For example, have they successfully undertaken the activity before? Do they possess the technical knowledge necessary to be successful at the criminal enterprise? This part of the analysis affords the opportunity to consider the finance they may have to fund the activity (also see Weaknesses), the structure of the entity (close-knit family group, criminal syndicate that has been operating with each other for some time) or even their geographical location (for example, drug syndicates operating from Hong Kong or Burma). There are a diverse range of things that may be considered strengths for the criminal entity. The range and number will depend on the circumstances of the analysis.

Weaknesses

Weaknesses are the entity's liabilities, such as lack of finances, lack of knowledge and lack of opportunity to undertake the activity. One of the more obvious weaknesses in the entity may be that law enforcement is aware of them and their activities. Again, the weaknesses in the entity will entirely depend on the nature of the activity, the analysis task and the entity itself.

Opportunities

Opportunities can be examined in two different ways. Opportunities can be analysed from the criminal entity's point of view and also from the point of view of law enforcement. When observed from an entity perspective, the analyst can look at the opportunities available to them to achieve their criminal endeavours. This may be a change of legislation (or lack of appropriate legislation) or new technology developed that may assist in the success of their activity. When viewed with law enforcement in mind, opportunities may be analysed by identifying ways to interdict the activity, or infiltrate the group or syndicate. This analysis usually stems from the analysis of the weaknesses of the entity.

Threats

Threats are external conditions that act upon the entity or their activity that can prevent the success of their endeavours or cause harm to the entity itself. These threats can be varied but can range from a change in legislation, new competitors in the market, financial transactions becoming difficult to conduct, and the interest from law enforcement in their activities.

SWOT analysis is a way for an analyst to observe the internal and external forces at play relating to a criminal entity or syndicate. The 'strengths and weaknesses are internal characteristics and opportunities and threats are external characteristics' (Kahaner, 1997). Each of these traits contributes to the way in which the criminal group can operate and achieve their outcomes. Through this analysis the analyst can identify them and explore possibilities for exploitation or interdiction by law enforcement.

Ishikawa diagrams

Ishikawa (or fishbone) diagrams are used to explore cause and effect situations. They were developed to identify the underpinning or causal factors that contributed to the success or failure of manufacturing processes.

Ishikawa diagrams were developed in 1950 by Professor Kaoru Ishikawa. Ishikawa was a leading advocate and pioneer of quality control in Japan. He invented the diagram that often bears his name as a simple tool for doing 'root cause' analysis, the search for – and elimination of – the key causes of quality problems that may arise in manufacturing. Within law enforcement, Ishikawa diagrams can be used by intelligence analysts to display key features of the issue being analysed, the causal factors that could potentially lead to the problem and the subordinate factors that underpin the problem. Preparing an Ishikawa diagram is a four-step process:

1. identify the problem or effect to be analysed;
2. identify the causes that lead to this problem or effect;
3. identify the subordinate factors contributing to these causes; and
4. develop recommendations.

Step 1: Identify the problem or effect to be analysed

The first part of the process is to identify the problem that is to be analysed. This is an important part of the process as a defined problem or task is essential in focusing activity and directing the elements of the analysis. To attempt to analyse an issue that is too broad in its scope does not allow for the analyst to delve into the issue too deeply.

For example, if you were asked to analyse property crime in your jurisdiction perhaps the way to do this more effectively is to look at one aspect of the problem. You might identify that there has been an increase over time in the reported property crime rate. The question then may be 'Why has there been an increase in the property crime rate in the last six months?' This gives you parameters to work within and defines your task.

Step 2: Identify the causes that lead to this problem or effect

The next step in the process is to identify contributing factors that may lead to this problem taking place. You may find a brainstorming session effective or you may simply ask yourself, 'What factors could enable this situation to exist?' This process may lead you in a number of different directions. These broader headings then allow you, further on, to explore the subordinate factors that underpin each of the causes you have identified. For example, when analysing an increase in property crime you might identify any of the following:

1. changes in the community demographic;

2. increase in unemployment;

3. supporting other illicit activity;

4. financial stresses in the community;

5. increase in drug use;

6. higher price paid for goods;

7. boredom; or

8. statistical anomalies.

This list is not exhaustive and merely an example, but it gives you a range of factors to explore in more detail.

Step 3: Identify the subordinate factors contributing to these causes

Once we have a number of possible causes, the next task is to identify the subordinate factors. We must ask ourselves, 'What makes these things happen?' or 'What are the contributing factors surrounding these issues?' When we have done that we begin to get to the root causes of the problem. The way to do this is to look at each of the 'fishbones' on the diagram and come up with a list of possible reasons as to why that cause may have taken place. For example, within each category, we might list the subordinate causes. These subordinate causes are listed against the fishbone that relates to the larger category. This is demonstrated in Figure 8.3 where changes to income levels, and changes to the urban population density (infill) are associated with the demographic change cause, and the closing of a factory is associated with the broader issue of increased unemployment.

This is a small example of the types of root causes that stem from the causal factors identified in the initial analysis. This would be done for each of the 'fishbones' that are created in the diagram.

Figure 8.3 Example Ishikawa diagram exploring causes of increased property crime

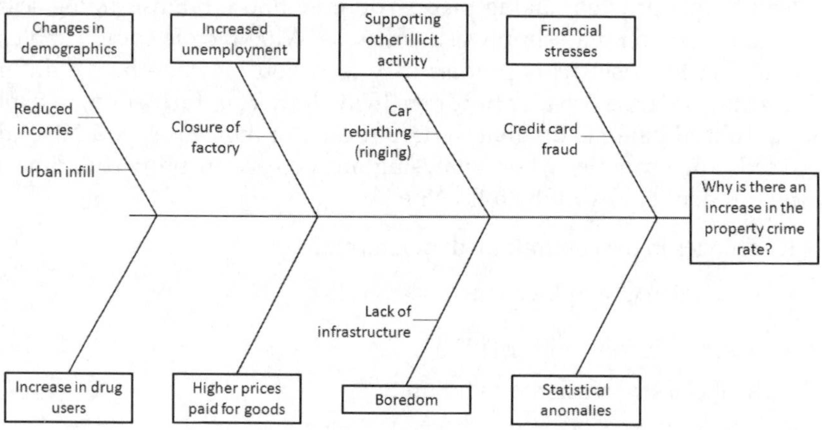

Step 4: Develop recommendations

Once you have canvassed the range of different causes to the problem you should then develop your recommendations. These recommendations should be directly aimed at addressing these causes to either eliminate them or minimise their effects. This may include recommendations such as target hardening of premises to minimise the possibility of victimisation, to involving other government and non-government departments to assist in rectifying the problems that cause the issue to take place.

You may see some similarities between the analytical method of Ishikawa Diagrams and the systems thinking earlier in the chapter. Both are systems-based and are aimed at identifying the underpinning causes of the issue being analysed.

PESTEL analysis

PESTEL (or sometimes PESTLE) is an analytical method that examines a range of external factors that may affect an issue or a problem. These factors cover a range of different aspects that may have some impact on the issue either now or in the future.

The PESTEL factors are:

- Political – political pressures;
- Economic – local, national or international economic impact;
- Sociological – effects of changes in society;
- Technological – new or emerging technology and its impact;
- Environmental – local, national and international environmental issues; and
- Legal – impact of local, national or international law.

As with SWOT analysis, these factors can be looked at in both a positive and negative sense in that these factors can affect the issue in either way and it is important to acknowledge both. By identifying both, the analyst has the opportunity to address all issues. The six factors can be applied to the whole of the issue or just one particular aspect of it. This is done to consider the likely effects of each on the problem.

For example, the importation of illegal drugs has long been an issue for Australian law enforcement. Using the headings we can examine the issue by identifying some of the external factors that can affect the drug importation. These may be current or future factors.

Political:

- change to government policy regarding the interdiction of drugs at the Customs border
- increase in funding to law enforcement agencies to investigate the matter

Economic:

- negative change of fortune for national governments in source countries prompting increased need for funds (licit or illicit)
- upturn in Australian economy (more people have more money to buy drugs – possibly creating increased demand)

Sociological:

- public perception of illegal drugs softens and becomes more liberal
- aging population moves away from the use of illegal drugs

Technological:

- better search methods developed for border protection
- increased effectiveness of analysis techniques for drug analysis

Environmental:

- drought affecting growing conditions in source countries

Legal:

- stricter legislation enacted
- pressure from UN brought to bear on source countries to have stricter enforcement of laws

Following this analysis the analyst should then consider the internal factors at play that may affect the issue. This could be from an organisational viewpoint, considering issues such as resources (financial, human etc) and priorities. PESTEL headings are also suitable as headings for step 2 of an Ishikawa diagram.

Morphological analysis

Morphological analysis is a method used to explore a range of different possible explanations for a number of issues. This tool breaks down the issue into a number of elements and generates explanations as to why the event or issue has taken place. Some of these explanations may not be feasible, however this tool allows the analyst to be lateral in their thinking and cover a range of options that may not have been considered previously. Morphological analysis is displayed in the form of a matrix that shows the different elements of the problem and permits the analyst to visually represent the steps in the analytical process. There are four steps in the analysis process.

Step 1: Break down the problem

In this first stage we look at each of the broad elements that constitute the issue being analysed. It is important to look at each of the elements in this way rather than looking at them too minutely. This analytical tool is not intended to drill down at the issues too deeply. Rather, it can be used to start off the analytical process and give the analyst some direction.

For example, the issue being analysed may be the smuggling of humans seeking asylum. The method in which they attempt to enter the country may be via boat, air or a container loaded on a freighter. These individual elements can all be grouped under the heading 'Method of entry'. If this process is conducted with the full range of elements involved in the problem, the matrix can be created.

Step 2: Create a morphological matrix

Once we have decided upon these elements we can create the matrix. All of the headings go on the left hand side with the elements listed against them on the right hand side. Using another example, a question may be asked regarding what type of threat we may face from terrorism in the next 12 months. We can create a matrix to reflect some possible combinations to explore (Figure 8.4). Features in subsequent rows need not relate to the group above: the important thing is to list all of the important options along a row.

Figure 8.4 An example morphological matrix

Elements of problem				
Group	Religious fundamentalist	Environmental group	'Lone gunman'	Radical element
Type of attack	Bombing	Product tampering	Gas attack	Hijacking
Location	Government building	Transport infrastructure	Iconic location	Military installation
Motivation	Money	Revenge	Anger at government policy	Cultural / religious

Step 3: Develop explanations

The next step in the process is to develop possible outcomes or explanations for the problem. This is done by going down and across the matrix and looking at the range of possible explanations. Not all of them have to be logical at this stage as we will rank them at the end of this part of the process. What this part of the analysis does is open up options to assign attributes to a scenario that may not have been considered before. This can provide the analyst with choices that may not have been explored but are worthy of further work.

Figure 8.5. Example of a morphological matrix

Elements of problem				
Group	Religious fundamentalist	Environmental group	'Lone gunman'	Radical element
Type of attack	Bombing	Product tampering	Gas attack	Hijacking
Location	Government building	Transport infrastructure	Iconic location	Military installation
Motivation	Money	Revenge	Anger at government policy	Cultural / religious

For example, Figure 8.5 indicates the way in which the analyst can generate a range of possible outcomes for the issue. Following one line the outcome is that a religious fundamentalist group undertakes a gas attack on an iconic location because of cultural or religious reasons. Another possible outcome the matrix can generate may be a radical element committing a bombing of a government building for revenge.

Step 4: Rank explanations

Now we have developed a range of possible explanations to the issue we can rank them from most feasible to least feasible. When assessing this stage of the process ask whether or not the explanation you have created is possible, practical and feasible (you may be able to use SWOT to assist with this process). When you have developed explanations for the issue you consider to be realistic in this way, you can then conduct further analysis to better understand the issue and develop recommendations for action, by concentrating on those aspects that are most possible, practical and feasible from a criminal perspective.

Competing hypothesis

Competing hypothesis is an analytical technique used to objectively create a range of possible answers to a question. This technique uses a multi-step technique to explore a range of hypotheses in order to evaluate them and identify the most plausible of the options. This tool encourages creativity by using the information currently available which allows the analyst to recognise that the same information can lead them to a number of different conclusions. It is a valuable tool because it can be used to minimise the 'pet-theory' factor that can develop in a project or operation. The other benefit of this technique is that it can provide the analyst with an audit trail to show what was considered and how a judgment was made. This may be important if the issue analysed is political or sensitive. The process has a number of steps. These are:

1. identify potential hypotheses;

2. list significant evidence;

3. develop the hypotheses matrix;

4. refine matrix;

5. draw tentative conclusions;

6. analyse sensitivity;

7. report conclusions; and

8. identify milestones for future observation (early warning indicators).

The technique is best demonstrated with an example. The following assumes that the analytical task is to examine the reasons why there has been an increase in the trafficking of heroin.

Step 1: Hypothesis identification

Identify possible hypotheses to be considered in the analysis. Brainstorming ideas is an option at this stage of the analysis.

- Hypothesis 1 – increased heroin from existing sources;
- Hypothesis 2 – increased heroin from new sources;
- Hypothesis 3 – increase in demand from users (more users?);
- Hypothesis 4 – switch from cocaine to heroin.

Step 2: Identify evidence

At this stage, it is useful to list significant evidence relating to the issue being analysed. Inclusion of evidence of the absence of things that prove a hypothesis is also important:

- Evidence 1 – heroin seizure statistics up;
- Evidence 2 – international trends indicate switch from heroin to cocaine;
- Evidence 3 – heroin prices down;
- Evidence 4 – scientific analysis of seized heroin (same source?).

Step 3: Create matrix

In this step consider how each item of evidence relates to each of the hypotheses. The hypotheses are placed in the columns of the matrix, the evidence in the rows. The analyst should consider whether each piece of the evidence is 'consistent with, inconsistent with, or irrelevant to each hypothesis' (Heuer, 1999). If an item of evidence is consistent with each hypothesis then it is considered to have no diagnostic value. There is much evidence that will go this way and it may be necessary to delete it to make the matrix manageable and, most importantly, meaningful. If there is an item of evidence that is significantly more likely to be aligned with one hypothesis rather than the rest then this piece of evidence should be placed in the matrix under that hypothesis, indicating that link.

Perhaps the most significant evidence is that which clearly refutes a particular hypothesis. This evidence should be marked in the matrix with a double minus or some other indicator to highlight its importance. By the end of this step the analyst should have matched all evidence against the most relevant of the hypotheses.

For example, in Figure 8.6 evidence that supports a hypothesis is assigned a plus (or two plus signs for strong evidence), while evidence that is inconsistent with a hypothesis is assigned a minus. Evidence that refutes a hypothesis is given a double minus. A question mark indicates evidence that neither supports nor refutes a hypothesis.

Figure 8.6 Example of a Competing Hypothesis matrix

	H1	H2	H3	H4
E1	+	+	+	?
E2	-	-	-	-
E3	+	+	+	+
E4	++	-	?	?

Step 4: Refine the matrix

Now the analyst reviews the evidence and deletes any that have no probative value in the matrix and that do not relate to the hypotheses being considered. There are other issues that the analyst can consider at this point. Are there two or more hypotheses that are so similar they should be combined? Is the wording of each hypothesis appropriate, or is the wording preventing the necessary consideration of evidence against that hypothesis?

Consideration of these issues and that of the evidence should give a clear indication of what can be deleted and what should remain. Any items that are not considered to have any diagnostic value can be deleted from the matrix and set aside. A record should be kept to indicate the consideration of the evidence (E2 in Figure 8.7). In our example the international switch from heroin to cocaine does not appear to have had an impact on the Australian market if seizures have increased, and the switch from cocaine to heroin use (H4) could be combined with H3 (increase in demand) (see Figure 8.7).

Figure 8.7 Revised matrix, once two hypotheses have been combined and one evidence item discarded

	H1	H2	H3	
E1	+	+	+	
E3	+	+	+	
E4	++	-	?	

Step 5: Draw tentative conclusions

In this step the analyst can form tentative conclusions about the likelihood of the each of the hypotheses. This should be done by attempting to refute each of the hypotheses rather than proving them. The matrix should give the analyst a sound indication of the relative strengths and weaknesses of each hypothesis. In previous steps the analyst has spent time considering each piece of evidence and its relationship with the hypotheses. The analyst may not have considered some of these hypotheses seriously before this, and with this stage, a deeper and more critical consideration is forced upon the analyst.

When examining the matrix the analyst should look closely at the number of minuses against each of the hypotheses as this is an indication that the hypotheses may be weak compared to the gathered evidence. These minuses can be a good reason to reject a hypothesis as more unlikely than others. However, many pluses against a particular hypothesis are not necessarily an indicator that it is a more likely hypothesis either, and this can be a trap for an analyst.

Step 6: Conduct sensitivity analysis

In this stage we review the inferences drawn from the evidence that was considered during the analysis. What would be the consequences if the evidence were misinterpreted? Could the inferences be incorrect or misleading?

Step 7: Report conclusions

In this step the analyst discusses the likelihood of each of the hypotheses, not necessarily just the most likely ones. In this way the client is aware of the range of options considered during the analysis.

Step 8: Identify milestones

These milestones are sometimes referred to as indicators or warnings. They are 'flags' for future observations that may indicate the event is taking place or that there is a change in the direction that was expected. If this takes place and the milestones are noted, continued monitoring and analysis of the issue can take place.

Competing hypothesis can be useful for analysts to think in a clear and unbiased way. It forces the analyst to consider the information they have accumulated and assess it individually on its merits. This drives away the 'force it until it fits' mentality that can permeate the thinking of some analysts. It is an effective analytical tool for these purposes.

Combining tools for maximum effect

Sound analysis comes from undertaking robust research and using techniques that elicit considered responses to the task at hand. Analysts have at their fingertips a 'toolbox' of possible analytical techniques that can be used to ensure the analysis is undertaken with little bias and is as substantial as possible. The challenge is to use them effectively.

Combining tools is one way of being certain that the result is a sound piece of analysis. For example, morphological analysis can assist in developing a range of possible scenarios for a particular question or issue. Once the feasible scenarios are rated, process mapping can show how an event could eventuate. Once the analyst has this understanding they can develop recommendations to put in place early warning indicators to flag when these possible events could be taking place. In another case trend analysis can be used to consider the changes in circumstances over time. Once these trends are identified the analyst can consider the underpinning causes using Ishikawa diagrams. Through exploring the use of a combination of tools in the analysts 'toolbox' the analyst is able to display a deeper understanding of the issues and develop a sound research and analysis regime that can withstand greater scrutiny.

Analysis is all about understanding: understanding issues, questions posed, the environment we live in. Analysis is at the core of the intelligence process. By utilising and combining robust and sound analytical techniques the analyst can play their part in guiding decision-makers through the difficult task of choosing the right path for law enforcement.

References

Aronson, D, 2003, *Introduction to Systems Thinking*, Accessed online at <www.thinking.net>.

Covey, SR, 1989, *The 7 Habits of Highly Effective People*, The Business Library.

Damelio, R, 1996, *The Basics of Process Mapping*, Productivity Inc.

Folker Jr, RD, 2000, *Intelligence Analysis in Theatre Joint Intelligence Centres: An Experiment in Applying Structured Methods*, Joint Military Intelligence College, Washington DC, Occasional Paper No. 7.

Heuer, RJ, 1999, *Psychology of Intelligence Analysis*, Central Intelligence Agency Publications.

Holt, RF, 1983, *A short course in everyday logic*, MCAE, Bathurst, Australia.

Hulnick, AS, 2006, 'US Intelligence Reform: Problems and Prospects', *International Journal of Intelligence and CounterIntelligence*, vol 19, 302-315.

Jones, MD, 1995, *The Thinker's Toolkit*, Three Rivers Press.

Kahaner, L, 1997, *Competitive intelligence: how to gather, analyse and use information to move your business to the top*, Touchstone.

Lefebvre, S, 2004, 'A Look at Intelligence Analysis', *International Journal of Intelligence and CounterIntelligence*, vol 17, 231-264.

Loo, R, 2002, 'The Delphi method: a powerful tool for strategic management', *Policing: An International Journal of Police Strategies and Management*, vol 5, no 4, 762-769.

McDowell, D, 1998, *Strategic Intelligence: A handbook for practitioners, managers and users*, Istana Enterprises.

Morgan, MD, 1998, *The Thinker's Toolkit: 14 Powerful Techniques for Problem Solving*, Three Rivers Press.

Ratcliffe, JH, 2001, 'Policing Urban Burglary', *Trends and Issues in Crime and Criminal Justice*, No 213, Australian Institute of Criminology.

Senge, P, 1990, *The Fifth Discipline*, Random House.

CHAPTER 9

Threat and risk assessments

Natasha Tusikov and Robert C Fahlman

Introduction

Law enforcement agencies around the world differ widely in how they identify, assess and prioritise threats and risks posed by various crimes and criminal groups. Analytical methods within crime intelligence are typically divided into two broadly overlapping categories – qualitative and quantitative techniques. 'Hard' quantitative techniques are sometimes preferred over 'soft' qualitative as having more rigour with numerically measurable outcomes. However, qualitative analysis can, and often should, encompass structured methodologies to logically assess problems in a systematic way. There is value to the integration of both qualitative and quantitative techniques into a structured approach to assess threats and risks.

Given the necessity of interagency (and often international) cooperation in addressing crime (see Chapter 13 in this book), it's essential to discuss fundamental principles that can facilitate a systematic approach to threat and risk assessments (TRAs) that are applicable to a variety of different needs or clients. There is no single TRA model that will serve the diverse needs of all law enforcement agencies; however, the establishment of a common framework for TRAs can ensure that analyses can be compared between different agencies, jurisdictions and countries.

In advancement of this goal, in this chapter we propose certain key ingredients:

- a common TRA framework must be flexible enough to encompass threat and risk assessments that have different requirements;
- the underlying analytical principles must be simple enough to be applied by analysts and understood by clients;
- the analyst may choose to enhance readability through the inclusion of relevant charts, diagrams and illustrations; and finally,
- the TRA must be consistent in the use of terminology that is clearly defined and commonly used.

This chapter is meant to be a practical guide for practitioners of criminal intelligence to undertake a TRA. It details the basic terminology, concepts and components within threat and risk assessments. The sequential steps for undertaking a TRA are outlined with an emphasis on maintaining methodological rigour. Throughout the chapter, there is a focus on useful processes to facilitate consistency in identifying, assessing and prioritising threat and risk in the production of TRAs.

Building a Threat and Risk Assessment

Threat and *risk* are terms often incorrectly used interchangeably. A threat assessment examines the nature and magnitude of specific threats that can pose harm. On the other side of the TRA equation, risk is the probability that an adverse event may occur and the impact of that event in terms of extent and severity. Some intelligence assessments are incorrectly identified as risk assessments when they lack a risk component and are more properly threat assessments. While it is possible to undertake only the threat or risk portion of the process, these components are complementary elements of analysis that present an integrated picture of threats, probabilities and consequences to decision-makers.

The purpose of a threat and risk assessment is to provide decision-makers with a clear picture of key undesirable events (current and potential), the probability of those events occurring, their possible repercussions, and recommendations to minimise or address specific risks and threats. TRAs are intended to facilitate decision-making regarding the setting of priorities, planning and program requirements, strategy and policy developments, and resource allocation. The clients for TRAs are generally not front-line law enforcement officers but rather middle to senior law enforcement management. As a result of findings from TRAs, management may shift resources from one criminal market to another in recognition that threat and risk levels of the latter are assessed to be more serious or increasing. For example, federal investigations into illegal gaming may be downgraded in order to increase resources targeting methamphetamine trafficking. Further, a criminal group that is determined to be an emerging threat may be prioritised over a criminal group whose threat is assessed as stable or at a lower level. For example, a threat assessment of street gangs in the US State of New Jersey resulted in the targeting of the Nine-Trey Gangsters after the assessment identified them as an emerging threat to the state (Ratcliffe and Guidetti, 2008).

Identifying and assessing the threat

TRAs begin with a threat assessment that examines the nature and magnitude of specific threats. It should also measure the probability of the threat occurring and the probability that the threat may cause harm. The determination of the nature and extent of harm from the threat falls within the risk assessment component of the TRA that will be discussed later in the chapter.

Like any intelligence product, a threat assessment should begin with a clear statement of the threat issue to be assessed and the intended scope of the analysis. Threat and risk assessments can range from high-level, broadly based assessments (for example, illicit drugs across a country) to those tightly focused on a narrow topic, such as human smuggling at one airport. The nature of the threat evaluated varies according to the needs of the agency undertaking the assessment. For example, an analyst may assess a particular criminal technique (for example, hydroponic marijuana cultivation), a series of crimes (for example, serial arsons), an individual of interest, or criminal groups involved in a specific criminal activity or region.

A market-based approach

There are numerous ways to approach an assessment of the criminal environment. Not all criminal activities are profit driven. Street gangs, for example, are involved in a variety of activities without direct financial gain, such as graffiti to promote and protect gang identity and territory. However, in order to assess the majority of criminal activities that are financially motivated, criminal intelligence has adapted economic theory to approach criminal activity from a market-based perspective. In a criminal market-based approach, theories and models of legitimate businesses and the legal market are applied to criminal markets (Smith, 1980). The criminal market can be understood as a network in which buyers and sellers interact to exchange goods and services for money or barter. Goods in the criminal markets may be:

- illegal (for example, illicit drugs);
- legal but illicitly sold (for example, smuggled, untaxed tobacco or stolen property); or
- legal in one country but not in another (for example, weapons that are prohibited in the destination country).

Within broad markets like illicit drugs, there are sub-markets that have different components, such as different source countries, manufacturing processes, consumer demographics, or specific geographic niches. As a result, heroin, cocaine and methamphetamine can be seen as sub-markets within the broad illicit drug market. While there may be an overlap between some sub-markets, a strategic value of a TRA may be to highlight not only areas of overlap but also the substantial differences between sub-markets.

A market-based approach often begins with a macro-level overview of general indicators to contextualise the particular threat issue. These indicators are often referred to as PESTEL – political, economic, sociological, technological, environmental and legal – events and trends. An assessment of PESTEL indicators can identify how and why an illicit activity is appearing; and, more importantly for decision-makers, where and when it may appear next. Indicators that determine the conditions by which the phenomenon is enabled are called *risk factors*, while those that constrain the phenomenon are *protective factors*. For example, in the case of vehicle theft, sophisticated anti-theft devices (protective factor) make some vehicles more difficult to steal. However, some criminal groups have side-stepped this constraint by legitimately leasing vehicles from dealerships, illicitly exporting them and then falsely claiming they were stolen (risk factor) (see Chapter 8 in this book for further details on PESTEL analysis).

Naylor (1997, 2002) provides further structure to Smith's market-based approach by classifying profit-driven crimes into three broad categories; enterprise (also known as market-based), predatory, and commercial. Enterprise crimes involve the production and distribution of new goods and services (for example, illicit drugs or counterfeit goods) while predatory crimes involve the involuntary distribution of already-earned wealth or property, often through deception or force (for example, extortion, theft, or human trafficking). Commercial crimes involve the production of legal goods and services using illegal methods, such as price fixing, insider trading, or bribery.

It's recognised that some crimes overlap between Naylor's categories and others are difficult to classify; however, using Naylor's categorisation within a market-based approach enables analysts to determine the relative threat from different crimes and the individuals committing those activities. Vander Beken (2004) suggests analysis of the following multiple micro-level indicators can identify the activities, transactions and roles undertaken by criminal groups within a particular criminal market:

- product (quantity/quality);
- prices (static/change);
- market dynamics (product innovation, technology impact, and level of cooperation/competition between groups);
- convergence with other markets; and
- actors (regulators, offenders, location, and market share).

From these indicators, analysis can determine the economic conditions for each illicit market and, consequently, estimate the nature, complexity and magnitude of a group's criminal operations in each illicit enterprise. An evaluation of the roles that each criminal individual or group plays within specific criminal markets (for example, supplier, transporter or financier) determines market share and supply/demand dynamics (CISC, 2007). Furthermore, the analyst can estimate which criminal individuals or groups represent key threats within any given market and their level of threat.

Another key component of the market-based approach is the examination of the nature and extent that the market in question intersects with legitimate economic sectors. Passas (2002) argues that analysis should focus on how and to what extent legal and illegal actors work together, and if their interactions take place primarily before or after crimes are committed. This information can be used to determine the benefits, risks or crime-facilitative roles of legal actors. Passas also stresses the importance of examining the nature and strength of linkages between legal and illegal actors as measured by the frequency, duration and intensity of interactions.

A final dimension of criminal market analysis is the measurement of each market's magnitude in terms of illicit activity. Magnitude can be calculated in monetary terms based on factors such as estimates of illicit profits and the numbers of consumers and suppliers. Based on a calculation of market magnitude, the analyst can determine whether a particular market is emerging, increasing, remaining stable or decreasing in scope, size and threat. Market analysis can also indicate the potential magnitude of proceeds of crime associated with a specific market which can facilitate the development of a criminal group's financial profile.

Evaluating criminal individuals and groups

In addition to an economic market-based analysis of profit-driven illicit activities, it is important to assess the actors themselves through a structured evaluation of their:

- capabilities;
- intentions;
- limitations;
- vulnerabilities; and
- opportunities.

These five components, examined in concert, indicate the particular level of threat of an individual or criminal group. *Capabilities* are the resources and knowledge available to an individual or group that allows them to engage in the activities. *Intentions* refer to the likely desire of a subject or group to engage in a specific activity and the level of confidence of success in that endeavour. For example, a group may express intent to expand into mortgage fraud but may currently lack the contacts within the financial industry to undertake this activity. While some capabilities can be readily observed, intentions can be more difficult to discern.

Limitations constrain or impede an individual or group from fulfilling its criminal intent. For example, incarceration is often determined to place some limitation, perhaps only temporarily, on a criminal group. However, some individuals are organisationally or operationally resilient to law enforcement disruption, or remain criminally active despite incarceration, so incarceration should never be assumed to be a limitation.

Vulnerabilities are conditions that weaken an individual or group, exposing it to rivals or law enforcement. For example, a criminal group may rely on one individual for a vital function, such as cross-border smuggling or the supply of fraudulent documentation. If this person is removed from the group through homicide or incarceration, the group loses access to a vital service.

Opportunities are a quantification of how a subject or criminal group is able to take advantage of circumstances for criminal benefit. One group's vulnerabilities or limitations may be an opportunity to another. For example, the incarceration of a key individual may provide an opportunity for other crime groups that are capable of exploitation or expansion. Successful criminal groups have a demonstrated ability to switch commodities, routes, or methods, in order to respond defensively to law enforcement action or proactively to exploit perceived vulnerabilities or changes in demand.

These five components can each be assigned a value. For example, in a qualitative evaluation of criminal capabilities, the knowledge and resources could be rated as ranging from *extensive* and *moderate* to *limited*. Each level would have to be clearly defined and preferably illustrated with examples to ensure consistency of application. For example, within Criminal Intelligence Service Canada (CISC), a group with *extensive* knowledge and resources is defined as one that regularly conducts multiple criminal operations that involve specialised expertise or a higher level of sophistication, particularly importing illicit commodities directly from a source location and/or exporting internationally, and manufacturing of illicit commodities at the wholesale level.

An alternative approach is to employ *resiliency theory*, a method that can be used by criminal intelligence analysis to examine how criminal markets function. In his work examining the illicit drug trade, Bouchard (2007) uses resiliency theory to measure how criminal markets are affected by or resistant to law enforcement action. Bouchard defines *resilience* as the ability of criminal market participants to preserve the existing levels of exchanges between buyers and sellers, despite external pressure (that is, law enforcement) aimed at disrupting the market.

Bouchard measures criminal market resiliency through three characteristics: vulnerability, elasticity, and adaptive capacity. *Vulnerability* is the degree to which a market can remain stable (for example, quantity/quality of illicit commodities or the number of criminal actors) in response to pressure, typically arrests and seizures. In resiliency theory, *elasticity* refers to how the level of supply of illicit commodities within the market (for example, heroin) responds to law enforcement pressure (for example, seized goods that are quickly replaced so supply is unaffected). *Adaptive capacity* is the extent to which a market can change (for example, commodity substitution or technological innovation).

Using resiliency theory, analysts can determine which criminal markets are resilient, which aren't, why these market conditions exist, what this indicates about the threat and risk levels of the criminal groups involved, and how law enforcement can exploit changes in resiliency. The determination of resiliency can also help determine which criminal markets pose the most significant threats and risks which will enable the ranking of criminal markets.

Sleipnir: A threat measurement technique

A common quantitative technique to measure the relative threat posed by organised criminal groups is the Sleipnir threat measurement technique. Sleipnir,[1] created by the Royal Canadian Mounted Police (RCMP), uses a numerical rank-ordered set of criminal attributes to assess each group's capabilities (see Figure 9.1). Values, typically colour-coded to visualise the threat, are assigned to each attribute; *high* (red), *medium* (orange), *low* (yellow), *nil* (green) or *unknown* (blue). Figure 9.1 replaces these colours with shading to aid comprehension.

Figure 9.1 Sleipnir – Threat measurement technique

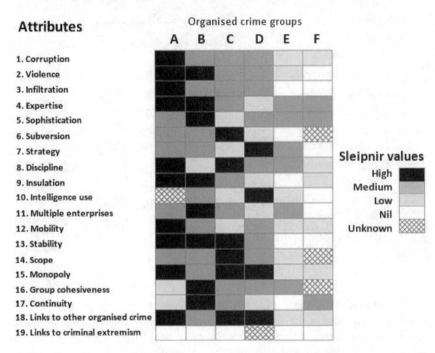

Figure adapted from Strang 2005

The 19 attributes are a set of criteria assessed by the RCMP to represent a group of key criminal capability indicators. Figure 9.2 depicts each value having a specific numerical score for each attribute. Note that the scores for *medium* and *unknown* are identical. The tally of all the attributes' values gives the aggregate Sleipnir score for each criminal group. The groups are arranged in order of threat level (by Sleipnir score) from left to right in a matrix that enables a group-by-group comparison.

---

1   Sleipnir was named after the eight-legged horse belonging to Odin in Old Norse mythology. See Strang 2005.

Figure 9.2 Sleipnir – Attribute scores and values

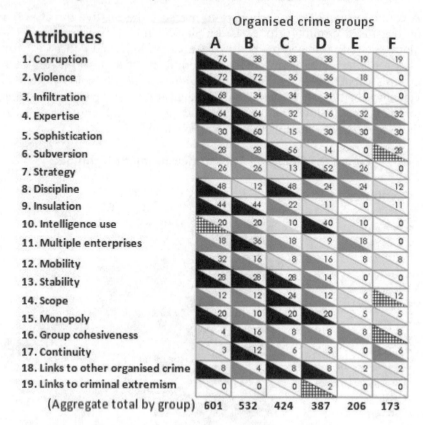

Attributes	Organised crime groups					
	A	B	C	D	E	F
1. Corruption	76	38	38	38	19	19
2. Violence	72	72	36	36	18	0
3. Infiltration	68	34	34	34	0	0
4. Expertise	64	64	32	16	32	32
5. Sophistication	30	60	15	30	30	30
6. Subversion	28	28	56	14	0	28
7. Strategy	26	26	13	52	26	0
8. Discipline	48	12	48	24	24	12
9. Insulation	44	44	22	11	0	11
10. Intelligence use	20	20	10	40	10	0
11. Multiple enterprises	18	36	18	9	18	0
12. Mobility	32	16	8	16	8	8
13. Stability	28	28	28	14	0	0
14. Scope	12	12	24	12	6	12
15. Monopoly	20	10	20	20	5	5
16. Group cohesiveness	4	16	8	8	8	8
17. Continuity	3	12	6	3	0	6
18. Links to other organised crime	8	4	8	8	2	2
19. Links to criminal extremism	0	0	0	2	0	0
(Aggregate total by group)	601	532	424	387	206	173

Figure adapted from Strang 2005

While several of Sleipnir's attributes are harms as well as capabilities, notably corruption and violence, Sleipnir is not designed to assess the harm resulting from a threat nor the probability of that threat occurring. Assessments of harm and probability must be calculated using other methods, or be included in analysis that must accompany each Sleipnir matrix.

In Canada, the CISC network of over 380 law enforcement agencies uses Sleipnir as the national technique to assess criminal groups in the annual integrated provincial and national threat assessments on organised and serious crime. In 2007, CISC evaluated over 900 criminal groups and identified to senior management the criminal groups that posed the most significant threats nationally.

Sleipnir has been modified by law enforcement agencies in the UK and Australia who have streamlined the number of attributes and integrated an assessment of harm. The Canadian criminal intelligence community is modifying Sleipnir and is liaising with agencies in the UK and Australia to adopt best practices from their adaptations of the technique.

Risk, vulnerability and harm

While a threat assessment examines the nature and magnitude of specific threats, a *risk assessment* evaluates the context within which the particular issue is located. At its most fundamental level, risk is measured in terms of the *probability* that an adverse event may occur and the *impact* of that consequence in terms of extent and severity. Both probability and impact should be evaluated in the risk assessment process. After risks are assessed, the management component of the risk cycle incorporates risk acceptance, control and monitoring. This chapter focuses here on the identification and analysis component of risk assessment. Figure 9.3 depicts a threat and risk assessment model.

Figure 9.3 Threat and risk assessment model

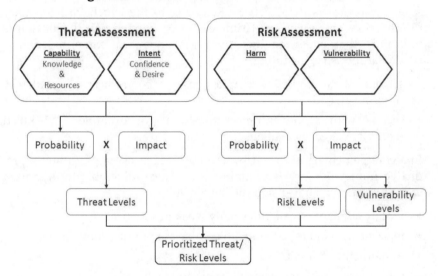

On the risk assessment side of Figure 9.3, *vulnerability* is defined (at its simplest level) as the probability of a threat occurring and the prepared-ness of the target to respond by preventing or dealing with the threat. The focus of a risk assessment is to identify and examine vulnerable areas that could be exploited by criminals. As Vander Beken (2004) notes, vulnerability depends on the intentions of criminals, the state's regula-tions, the standards of the sector itself, and the intentions of those involved in the sector. However, Vander Beken also points out that eco-nomic sectors may have attributes that are attractive to criminal groups but may not necessarily be vulnerable.

Vulnerability analysis of the legitimate market can begin with the same step as an evaluation of a criminal market – with a macro-level overview of general indicators. For example, in his development of a methodology for the assessment of vulnerability in economic sectors to organised crime, Hansens et al (2004) evaluated the sector in terms of:

- related and supporting sectors domestically and abroad (for example, production and processing);
- financial and legal actors;
- social and economic organisations;
- government; and
- crime.

Within a TRA, vulnerability analysis can then determine indicators that constrain or facilitate criminal involvement in certain economic sectors and determine why certain sectors are attractive. Indicators that are specific to individuals or groups are often defined as *agency indicators* while those that enable or promote particular conditions to occur are *structural indicators* (CISC, 2006). Referring to the Dutch Parliamentary Commission on Organised Crime in 1996, Vander Beken (2004) lists indicators that could be incentives for organised crime to enter a particular industry, including:

- sectors with limited, complicated or contradictory regulatory procedures; and
- sectors with a low-entrance threshold (for example, low-skilled workforce or easily available financing).

In a complementary study, Albanese (1987) focuses on providing a predictive framework for determining businesses vulnerable to organised crime infiltration. High-risk indicators include:

- readily available small, financially weak businesses;
- inelastic demand for product (that is, lack of product substitutes);
- easy-to-enter market;
- open market with many small firms; and
- prior history of organised crime infiltration in industry.

Albanese and Vander Beken (2004) caution against the wholesale adoption of these indicators in the absence of understanding that there may be fundamental organisational or geographic differences between industries. There are also varying standards and controls in place at different industries to identify, deter and prevent organised criminality. Analysts should use caution in developing and using indicators, remembering that an individual indicator could be indicative of a number of possible conditions. However, when multiple indicators are assessed in the context of a macro-level legitimate market overview, a clearer picture begins to emerge.

Particular economic sectors can be assessed for their relative level of vulnerability to organised crime using the opportunistic and predictive indicators described above. Vulnerability indicators can then be numerically ranked from most to least significant or relative levels can be assigned; high, medium, low, nil or unknown. After relative levels of vulnerability are established, more intensive analysis can be focused on industry sectors (or specific businesses) that have *high* or *unknown* indicators.

Harms

The negative consequence from an adverse event (often defined in risk assessment terminology as a *hazard*) is commonly described in criminal intelligence analysis as a *harm*. Most commonly Maltz (1990), and Black and Vander Beken (2000) categorise harms into broad groupings ranging from physical, economic, psychological and social to environmental.

Harms can be direct and tangible, such as fraud or theft, with effects that can be quantified in terms of monetary loss, or more difficult to quantify, such as a diminished quality of life. Some victims pay costs of crime directly; for example, replacing stolen property. Other harms affect society as a whole such as the costs of law enforcement, medical care, victim services, courts, legal aid and correctional institutions. Some individuals fear crime and seek to reduce their risk of victimisation through spending on security or insurance.

Harm analysis adds another layer of assessment for law enforcement management in their decision-making regarding the allocation of resources for further intelligence or enforcement action. This analysis enables decision-makers to prioritise specific criminal offences or groups in relation to an assessment of the harms caused. Intelligence agencies in the UK and Australia have integrated a harm component into their threat assessments that measure and rank both threats and harms from criminal groups. CISC is leading an effort on behalf of the criminal intelligence community to implement harm analysis within the CISC network's 10 integrated provincial threat assessments and national threat assessment on organised and serious crime.

Harm analysis can involve a cost-of-crime estimate by crime type that includes all costs, both tangible and intangible, associated with the crime, including; victim, enforcement, justice system and incarceration costs. The Home Office in the United Kingdom (see Duborg and Prichard, 2007) has published a number of useful assessments on the costs of crime, assessments that can help estimate the measure of social or economic harm attributable to a specific criminal market (for example, illicit drugs) or to a type of criminality (for example, organised crime). This work has also been undertaken in Australia (for example, Mayhew and Adkins, 2003).

Harms can also be determined by ranking the seriousness of crimes along with the prevalence of each of those crimes. Alternatively, each crime can be ranked according to its prison sentence along with a measure of the crime's prevalence. Distinguishing between the relative negative effects of harms contributes to determining the harm magnitude of different types of crimes within the total volume of all criminal activity. Harm analysis can distinguish between crimes that may have a high-volume / low-harm factor (for example, simple theft) versus crimes with a low-volume/high-harm factor (for example, counterfeit pharmaceuticals).

Harm analysis can focus on a specific criminal market, such as illicit drugs or vehicle theft, and assess the scope and magnitude of specific negative consequences to communities, businesses or society. For example, vehicle theft has a high economic harm, with the burden of financial costs affecting the insurance industry, but relatively little social harm. In contrast, the social harms from human trafficking are significant.

The harm from individual criminal groups can be determined based on harm scores from the group's involvement in each of its criminal markets. As shown in Figure 9.4, the aggregate harm score of each group's activities could be combined with the group's Sleipnir threat score from Figure 9.2 to determine an overall group ranking. Rankings would have to take into account the prevalence and magnitude of the group's activities within each market. As well, in order to track changes in the criminal marketplace, harm analysis must have a capability of evaluating criminal groups as posing short-, medium- and long-term harms within specific markets.

Figure 9.4 Measuring threat with harm

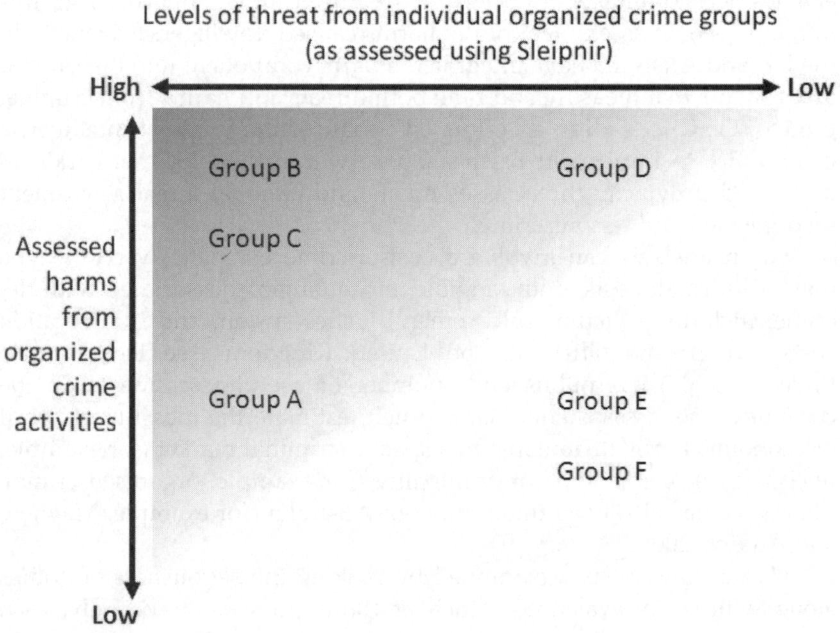

Levels of threat from individual organized crime groups
(as assessed using Sleipnir)

Estimating potential futures

Thus far, the TRA process discussed in this chapter has focused on current intelligence in the assessment of criminal threats and risks. Current intelligence represents the 'what is happening' component of the assessment and answers questions of who, what, when, where, and why. It assesses ongoing threats, events or illicit activities. While current intelligence forms the backbone of most TRAs, strategic assessments should also have a component of *estimative intelligence*.

Estimative intelligence is a forward-looking type of analysis that uses predictive judgments to project probable future developments and assess the implications. This type of intelligence lets decision-makers know 'what will happen', often within a specific time period such as 12 or 24 months. Within TRAs, estimative intelligence is commonly conveyed through forecasts. Forecasts are concise, focused analytical judgments that estimate future developments regarding a particular issue over a specific period of time. Specific techniques that can be used for forecasts at the strategic level are discussed in Chapter 10 in this book.

Intelligence involves assessing uncertainty and conveying judgments that are unambiguous to the client. When undertaking a TRA, analysts must evaluate a great deal of information, all of which can have different levels of accuracy and reliability. Expressions of probability, such as *possible* and *probable*, can result in ambiguously worded analysis if the analyst and client each have different interpretations regarding the level of probability.

In the context of a TRA, *probability* refers to the likelihood of a threat or risk occurring. As with other measurements, the description of probability should be consistent to ensure comparability. It is useful to adopt common parameters in terms of verbal or numerical expressions of probability. If expressions of probability, such as 'probable', 'highly likely', 'likely', 'improbable' and 'highly unlikely' are to be used, these terms should be defined. Where the probability is difficult or impossible to determine, the rating of 'unknown' should be given with a different colour code to facilitate the identification of intelligence gaps.

In his oft-quoted article, Kent (1964) discusses the necessity of obtaining greater precision in the use of qualitative expressions of probability and the difficulties – both cultural and bureaucratic – of aligning qualitative expressions with numerical values, either percentages or number ranges. As Kent notes, probability tables can neither have too many graduations of probability (unwieldy) nor be too narrowly rigid so that the analyst is constrained in making estimates. See Figure 9.5 for an example with five levels.

An important process to undertake throughout the TRA is the evaluation of what is known and unknown about the issue assessed. A system of criminal intelligence requirements provides an over-arching framework that coordinates the collection of information or the production of intelligence for any subject. Within this system, there is a standardised,

Figure 9.5 Probability key

Term	Colour	Key
Certain	Red	Event already occurring or its eventual occurrence is 'almost certain'. Probability at or above 85%.
High	Orange	The occurrence of the event 'probable' to 'highly likely'. Probability at or above 70% but below 85%.
Medium	Yellow	There is a 'better than even' to 'likely' chance that the event will occur. Probability above 55% but below 70%.
Low	Green	Event occurrence is possible but 'improbable'; 'little chance' to 'about even' chance of occurrence. Probability above 20% but at or below 55%.
Nil	Blue	Probability of event occurrence is negligible or 'highly unlikely'. Probability at or below 20%.

Source: CISC (2006) Strategic Early Warning for Criminal Intelligence: Theoretical Framework and Sentinel Methodology, CISC, Ottawa.

rigorous process by which all information is rated for reliability and validity. The completeness of intelligence about a particular issue is defined as a *level of knowledge,* and is evaluated as excellent, good, fair or poor according to defined parameters. What is unknown by the intelligence community about a subject is determined to be an intelligence gap. Intelligence gaps are then prioritised according to their magnitude and seriousness. The magnitude and seriousness of an intelligence gap will vary depending on its nature (for example, relating to a particular group or a broad market component, such as an illicit good's source country), and the relative importance assigned to the gap (for example, by government, public or police). Priorities are then assigned to specific collection targets. As TRAs are part of a continual cycle of analysis, the prioritisation and targeting of intelligence gaps will identify new information that may result in changes to threat and risk levels.

CISC in Canada and the Serious Organised Crime Agency in the UK both use intelligence requirements at a national level to coordinate levels of knowledge and intelligence gaps in their threat assessments. Within each agency, the national intelligence requirements are collaboratively produced between analysts and intelligence officers and are used within each agency as 'road maps' for internal planning and intelligence collection. Externally, the requirements are used to advise partner agencies of the nature and extent of intelligence gaps and of key collection priorities.

All of this is necessary because the identification of priorities from TRAs is an integral part of intelligence-led policing as it informs the decision-making process for resource allocation, strategy and policy development at all levels. The determination of priorities can also be used to develop recommendations in regards to intelligence or enforcement action. As priority-setting efforts may occur in multiple jurisdictions representing local or regional issues, there should be standards to ensure comparability between different prioritisation exercises.

After threats and risks are assessed, they're each ranked according to their relative threat levels, the seriousness of potential impact, and the probability of occurrence. If both the threat and risk scores are quantitatively scored, the level of prioritisation can be calculated by multiplying the scores from both these factors. Threat levels can also be calculated qualitatively – high, medium, low, and nil. Priorities are then ranked from most serious to the least.

A TRA may also add extra weight to a priority score in consideration of particular issues, such as whether the threat assessed is an emerging phenomenon, an increasing trend, or a designated priority for a specific jurisdiction or agency. Persistent, extensive or high-priority intelligence gaps may be considered as an extra weighting factor when evaluating a particular priority score. Priority rankings should not be considered in isolation as absolute scores but accompanied by relevant analysis in the TRA. Rankings should be re-evaluated regularly as fluctuations occur in both the criminal marketplace and within organised crime groups.

TRAs in practice

The TRA's structure, like the methods used to assess threats and risks, must be flexible enough to encompass threat and risk assessments with different purposes and clients. The individual components of a TRA can be thought of as separate modules. Each module can be as detailed or as concise as needed or excluded altogether. In order to ensure comparability between TRAs, there are key aspects to consider when determining the report's format. The following components are based on CISC's threat assessment format and are a suggested framework for thinking how TRAs can be structured:

- Executive Summary (key findings, forecasts and recommendations)
- Background (brief background of issue and aim of assessment)
- Main Body (analysis of threats, harms and vulnerabilities)
  - Determination of threat/risk levels and priorities
- Conclusions
  - Intelligence forecasts
  - Intelligence gaps and requirements
- Recommendations
- Appendices (for example, definitions of terminology, charts and Sleipnir matrices).

Operationalising a TRA

It's essential that completed threat and risk assessments do not merely sit on a shelf but meaningfully contribute to the setting of priorities, strategy, policy development and resource allocation. The principles of intelligence-led policing stress that intelligence analysis play a key role in the setting of intelligence and enforcement priorities (Ratcliffe, 2008). Where it is applicable, enforcement units need to be able to take relevant intelligence regarding the prioritisation of threats and risks within a TRA and translate it into operational action such as investigative priorities.

Threat and risk priorities identified in a TRA will rarely be simply adopted wholesale but will inevitably be considered in concert with other factors, including target viability and available resources. As a result, there is value in developing structured approaches for translating intelligence into enforcement. For enforcement units, this may involve a method for developing and ranking enforcement priorities using clearly defined criteria and definitions. Enforcement criteria must be broad enough, where necessary, to encompass variations in threat from organised crime, specific local or regional concerns, and differences in mandate between diverse agencies and regions. As priority-setting becomes increasingly common across multiple jurisdictions, there is also a need for standards so that priorities identified in one jurisdiction are comparable with those in another place.

Measuring disruption

Given the resources involved in determining which criminal groups pose the most significant threats and harms, it is fundamental to evaluate the level of disruption caused by law enforcement against a particular criminal group, especially when the operation is the result of a TRA. The RCMP's Federal and International Operations Directorate introduced a performance measurement method – the Disruption Attribute Tool (DAT) in 2005 to measure the effectiveness of law enforcement's operations against organised crime groups. After law enforcement disrupts a group through arrests or seizures, the lead investigator for each organised crime investigation rates the impact to the group's core business, personnel, and finances. The level of disruption observed in each attribute is scored as high, medium, low, nil, N/A (not applicable), or unknown based on provided definitions.[2]

Building upon information provided by the DAT, analysis of disrupted groups can provide further insight into a group's capabilities, limitations and vulnerabilities. Disruption analysis can also determine if and to what extent the targeted groups have left voids, however temporary, in specific criminal markets. This can help when attempting to forecast which groups may attempt to fill those voids. A greater understanding of the extent of a group's disruption and how disrupted attributes change over time will undoubtedly contribute to the development of enforcement strategies targeted at vulnerable components of specific groups.

---

2   Further details on the DAT, with an explanatory table, are available in Ratcliffe (2008).

Conclusion

This chapter stresses the importance of using structured analytical methods to logically assess intelligence problems in a systematic way. The underlying methodological rigour of the processes and methods outlined in this discussion of TRAs can be applied to other aspects of criminal intelligence analysis, such as intelligence collection and collation, requirements, management and sharing. Just as a common framework can be established for TRAs, common standards on intelligence processes and protocols ensure that intelligence services and products can be employed across different agencies, jurisdictions and countries.

The adoption of common frameworks for the coordination, prioritisation and application of intelligence is a key aspect of intelligence-led policing. The United Kingdom's National Intelligence Model (National Centre for Policing Excellence, 2005) and CISC's Canadian Criminal Intelligence Model (Atkins and Fahlman, 2007) focus on the effective management and integration of intelligence-led policing at all levels of law enforcement. The models, which must be flexible enough to serve the diverse needs of different law enforcement agencies, emphasise:

- the professionalisation of intelligence;
- protocols for shared intelligence across jurisdictions and between agencies;
- national standards for the delivery of intelligence products and services; and
- intelligence-led tasking through the prioritisation of intelligence work.

Within this environment, the importance of structured, multi-disciplinary approaches in intelligence products will become more pronounced and commonplace.

References

Albanese, J, 1987, 'Predicting the Incidence of Organised Crime: A Preliminary Model', in Bynum, T (ed), *Organised Crime in America: Concepts and Controversies*, Criminal Justice Press.

Atkins, I, A/Commr. 'H' Division (Nova Scotia) RCMP, and Fahlman, R, A/Director General, CISC, 2007, Presentation to the CISC National Executive Committee on the Canadian Criminal Intelligence Model, Ottawa.

Black, C, and Vander Beken, T, 2000, *Measuring Organised Crime in Belgium: A Risk-Based Methodology*, Maklu.

Bouchard, M, 2007, 'On the Resilience of Illegal Drug Markets', *Global Crime*, vol 8, no 4.

CISC, 2006, *Strategic Early Warning for Criminal Intelligence: Theoretical Framework and Sentinel Methodology*, Criminal Intelligence Service Canada (Central Bureau, Ottawa), <www.cisc.gc.ca/products_services/sentinel/document /early_warning_methodology_e.pdf>.

CISC, 2007, *Integrated Threat Assessment Methodology*, Version 1.0, Criminal Intelligence Service Canada (Central Bureau, Ottawa).

Duborg, R and Prichard, S, Home Office, 2007, *Organised Crime: Revenues, Economic and Social Costs and Criminal Assets Available for Seizure*, Home Office Online Report 14/07 (www.cscs.ucl.ac.uk/club/e-library/organised -crime/organised.pdf).

Hansens, J, Black, C, and Defruytier, M, 2004, 'Measuring the vulnerability of legal economic sectors for organised crime', Science Policy Office, <www.belspo.be/belspo/home/publ/pub_ostc/SoCoh/rSO0218_en.pdf>.

Kent, S, 1964, 'Words of Estimative Probability', *Studies in Intelligence*, vol 8, no 4, 49-65, <www.cia.gov/library/center-for-the-study-of-intelligence/kent-csi/vol8no4/html/v08i4a06p_0001.htm>.

Maltz, M, 1990, *Measuring the Effectiveness of Organised Crime Control Efforts*, OICJ Press.

Mayhew, P, and Adkins, G, 2003, 'Counting the costs of crime in Australia: An update', *Trends and Issues in Crime and Criminal Justice*, No 247, Australian Institute of Criminology.

National Centre for Policing Excellence, 2005, *Guidance on the National Intelligence Model (United Kingdom)*, Produced on behalf of the Association of Chief Police Officers, <www.acpo.police.uk/asp/policies/Data/nim2005.pdf>.

Naylor, RT, 1997, 'Mafias, Myths and Markets: On the Theory and Practice of Enterprise Crime', *Transnational Organised Crime*, vol 3, no 3, 1-45.

Naylor, RT, 2002, *A Typology of Profit-Driven Crimes*, Research and Statistics Division, Justice Canada.

Passas, N, 2002, 'Cross-Border Crime and the Interface Between Legal and Illegal Actors', in Van Duyne, PC, Von Lampe, K, and Passas, N (eds), *Upperworld and Underworld in Cross-Border Crime*, Wolf Legal Publishers.

Ratcliffe, JH, 2008, *Intelligence-Led Policing*, Willan Publishing.

Ratcliffe, JH, and Guidetti, RA, 2008, 'State police investigative structure and the adoption of intelligence-led policing', *Policing: An International Journal of Police Strategies and Management*, vol 31, no 1, 109-128.

RCMP, nd, Organised Crime Disruption Attribute Tool (DAT 2.0), Strategic Services Branch, Federal and International Operations, Royal Canadian Mounted Police.

Smith, DC, 1980, 'Paragons, Pariahs, and Pirates: A Spectrum-Based Theory of Enterprise', *Crime and Delinquency*, vol 26, no 3, 358-86.

Strang, SJ, 2005, Project SLEIPNIR: An Analytical Technique for Operational Priority Setting, Royal Canadian Mounted Police, <https://analysis.mitre.org/proceedings/Final_Papers_Files/135_Camera_Ready_Paper.pdf>.

Vander Beken, T, 2004, 'Risky Business: A Risk-Based Methodology to Measure Organised Crime', *Crime, Law and Social Change*, vol 41, no 5, 471-516.

CHAPTER 10

Futures work in strategic criminal intelligence

Neil Quarmby

Introduction[1]

Intelligence is an essential component of law enforcement capability. It exists at all levels of decision-making to support leaders and policy makers to make effective decisions. Intelligence provides the decision-maker with a timely and accurate understanding of criminal threats and the components of operational environment. No less important is the need to deprive criminals of knowledge of our law enforcement actions, dispositions, capabilities and intentions.

In the law enforcement context, it is sometimes difficult to obtain the factual information necessary for effective planning and decision-making. This is principally because much criminal activity is undertaken in such a way that it is deliberately concealed; empirical evidence is not readily available. The whole rationale for developing criminal intelligence is therefore to assist law enforcement agencies to plan, and through planning to maximise their operational and organisational effectiveness.

It is even more difficult to project what could occur. Hence, law enforcement futures work has a number of limiting factors. Not the least of these is the uncomfortable requirement for inductive analytical processes to be meshed with a policing culture that is bred on deductive reasoning processes and the evidentiary dictates of the judicial system. Law enforcement has a history of piecemeal, stove-piped or self-directed approaches to futures work. With this history in mind, there are three key assumptions especially pertinent to the successful implementation and conduct of futures work in criminal intelligence:

- there is an identifiable decision-making system to support;
- there is a will to think ahead in both the intelligence system and the decision system to be supported; and

---

1   The material in this chapter is drawn from the knowledge of the author gained from 25 years experience in intelligence practice and training. It is also drawn from various sources including a number of Australian Defence Force training courses, and law enforcement's National Strategic Intelligence Course.

- there is a will to apply the results in both the intelligence system and the decision system to be supported.

Strategic intelligence is that required by the senior executive and policy makers for the formulation of strategy, policy and long-term plans. It may have current or explanatory components by its nature, as covered in Chapter 8 in this book, but given the requirement to service forward-looking decisions, it must inherently have a 'futures' component. Given a wide range of clients can include government ministers, senior law enforcement executives and policy makers, a comprehensive service will need to include a mix of national current intelligence, forward looking assessments, open source reports and strategic warning. Here the purpose of futures work in strategic intelligence is to:

- provide a strategic context within which to understand emerging threats;
- provide a foresight capacity to allow the development of targeted strategies (provide warning of the need for new or different capabilities, policies, responses, priorities, powers and so on);
- narrow the range of uncertainty; and
- ensure that this understanding is provided in an appropriate form to the appropriate policy makers at the right time.

Importantly, strategic analytical product must always be explicitly policy relevant. It is less about descriptive intelligence and more about explanatory and estimative (predictive) intelligence. In the 'estimative' sense, this means providing a range of possibilities, with attendant assessment of likelihood, such that decisions are made with full view of the range of possibilities and the potential consequences of actions.

A significant difference between futures work conducted in law enforcement and the national security services, is that strategic criminal intelligence is often oriented towards consequence management rather than situation management. That is, national security related intelligence often focuses on event issues, whereas, strategic crime assessments are often focused on consequences of future trends, such as the mutation of criminality, the unintended consequences of social experimentation or legislative or regulatory reform.

Products for futures analysis

There are four categories of product relevant at any level:

- **Basic (background) intelligence**. (What has happened?) This type of product contains background intelligence, usually encyclopaedic in nature, that provides a broad range of baseline information and intelligence. While not futures based, such products provide a useful historical start point for analysis of futures.

- **Current intelligence**. (What is happening?) Specific assessments related to the status and significance of an ongoing operational threat, event, environmental condition or indication of illicit activity. Usually incorporates a section on the issue or indication and an assessment of implication by 'who/what/why/when/ where/how'. An assessment will normally be made on the significance of the problem over the short term.

- **Warning intelligence**. (Is a future unfolding?) Warning intelligence is that which provides warning of threats to law enforcement or national interests in time to take effective action. Warning intelligence bridges the current and estimative intelligence gap by focusing on agreed warning problems as part of a decision support mechanism that requires rapid alert and some form of policy, intelligence or operational response.

- **Estimative intelligence**. (What could occur?) Estimative intelligence is that which provides forward looking assessment and predictive judgments, and attempts to project probable future developments in the law enforcement environment and analyses their implications. Assessments normally have an explanatory section (environmental and stakeholder analysis) culminating in a discussion of key change agents or drivers. Finally the types of futures or future implications are discussed.

This chapter will focus on the processes assisting estimative and warning product development, which exist in the medium- to long-term future, as can be seen in Figure 10.1.

Figure 10.1 Different intelligence products along the time continuum

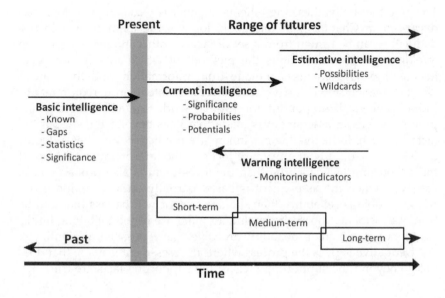

Concepts of the future and the present

At each level, customers generally have a different expectation of time frames. At the tactical level this may translate to days or minutes. As a rule of thumb, at the national strategic level (that is, beyond the specific strategic requirements of single agencies) the past is measured in years. Single agencies may view the past in a slightly shorter time frame. The 'present' is generally measured in months either side of today. The 'future' in a warning sense is generally measured out to about two years, while the 'future' relevant to decisions on broad policy and capability development is normally seen in terms of two to five years. Such temporal perspective allows the analyst to not only define the scope of the product but also decide on an analytical approach. In futures work the question of how much the past and present is allowed to colour the analysis of the future is fundamentally important to the analytical methodology used and needs to be defined early.

Foundation analytical processes

There are four types of inferences: predictions, estimates, conclusions, and hypothesis. Strategic futures work in criminal intelligence normally deals in estimative type inferences. The common ingredients in all estimative product are:

- the environment (facets may include political, social, economic, threat, and technological);
- the stakeholders who inhabit that environment;
- forces and factors of change; and
- possible change over time.

The glue that holds these ingredients together is reasoning and logic. As discussed in Chapter 8 in this book, logic is the method by which a deduction can be drawn from a set of facts or other inferences. From an intelligence perspective, it is the method by which intelligence conclusions and assessments are made from information, and the way in which an analyst will arrive at answers to intelligence requirements. Inductive logic is important for futures work. Inductive logic is the process where an assessment is made that goes beyond the supporting facts. As such, inductive logic is inherently predictive, involves a degree of risk, and should be the primary focus of the interpretation process. If the supporting facts are true then the assessment is also probably true, however, when the assessment is based partially on assumption or on facts of dubious reliability then the assessment will be less likely to be true. Assessments should be qualified by the use of the following terms, in order of decreasing probability: probable, likely, possible, and unlikely.

Deductive logic is the process where an assessment is made that does not go beyond the supporting facts. If the supporting facts are true then the conclusion must also be true. If deductive logic is used to draw a conclusion, then that conclusion is rarely predictive in nature. Deductive logic is therefore not predictive and its main use in the interpretation process is to provide conclusions for use as facts in the making of inductive assessments.

General tools

New and evolving trends in criminality flow from a combination of political, economic, technological and social factors epitomised by continuing globalisation, alertness to international terrorist and transnational threats, and myriad domestic pressures. This provides a complex qualitative problem for strategic analysts – not resolved through the application of simple scenario generation tools.

Futures tools cannot be used in isolation. They are fundamentally reliant on the structure and inferences of collation and explanation tools not covered in this chapter but covered elsewhere in this book. Futures tools often come with various names and snake-oil salesmen. Ultimately they are relatively simple to understand but it can be difficult to know when to apply them, let alone *how* to apply them. It should also be borne in mind that intelligence will not simply 'fall out' of the application of a tool or even a combination of tools. The analyst still needs to generate the ideas. If you know where you are going before you apply a tool, it will tell you what you already believe. Best practice is to not know where you are going when you start to use a tool. Finally, consider that the mind rarely works in a linear fashion, and one person's rational process may create dissonance in the thinking patterns of others. Therefore, engaging in a range of techniques that generate a creative atmosphere among the types of analytical personalities involved should be pursued where possible.

No matter what the type of product, strategic intelligence normally has the following ingredients:

- description of events or a situation with an eye to identifying essential characteristics (what, who, when, where, how);
- explanation of underlying causes (why);
- what could happen or develop (so what?); and
- implications (now what?)

Hence analysis normally follows the stages of consideration of: Environment – Stakeholders – Causalities – Futures – Implications. For an analyst dealing with an issue on a daily (current) intelligence basis, aspects of the study of the environment and stakeholders may be intuitive, but they still need to be ordered logically for the less-aware customer. It is useful to keep the same terms of reference for analysing the current situation as for the future. Reference points are generally divided conceptually into:

- **Events** – observable actions or activities that provide a conceptual framework for 'what has happened' and 'what may happen';

- **Patterns** – partially observable relationships related by time, sequence, association and/or effect. These patterns allow the analyst to link or associate events and stakeholders; and

- **Drivers** – an inferred fundamental force that creates or underpins change over time (note that drivers are also often called change agents, underpinning influences, or causal factors). These are inferred factors that assist the analyst to understand or explain why something is occurring, why it will change, and how patterns and events may emerge over time.

Significantly, the answer sought generally shapes the tools to be used and clearly if there is any degree of uncertainty as to the outcomes being sought (in an intelligence sense – the decisions to be serviced) then successful futures analysis will be unlikely. More often than not the analytical question posed is 'what's the nature and extent of problem X?' Many analysts will provide statistics – generally over a year old – and 'dress them up' as the current situation; concluding that 'observed trends are likely to continue'. This analytical cop-out not only devalues intelligence as a product, but also leads the customer into a false sense of security that what was evident a few years ago is likely to be the norm in the years to come.

So it is worth examining the question that should be asked. In the case above, the question may indeed be; 'What is the nature and extent of the problem, is it likely to get worse, and is the agency vulnerable in some way?' Hence, the warning here is before embarking on any of the following processes, be clear on the requirement and also have it clear who the 'real', 'intended', and 'intermediary' clients are; each of these may have different perspectives on the analysis produced.

Normally the futures component of the answer sought is one, or a combination of, the following:

- What potential events could occur?
- What future patterns could emerge?
- What will be the effect of future fundamental drivers?

Using events, patterns and drivers as a central framework, there are two general approaches to considering the futures part of this process. First, it is possible to examine the present in order to extrapolate change out into time. A second option is to examine possible futures and consider the range of events and factors that may connect the 'there' to 'now'. The first option can entail the use of tools that 'look from here to there'. The first set of tools that follow this section are designed to do precisely that. The second range of tools allow the analyst to 'look from there to here', as is the aim of the second set of tools in this chapter. These two different approaches to futures tools are shown diagrammatically in Figure 10.2. We begin with tools that 'look from here to there'.

Figure 10.2 Two different approaches to futures work

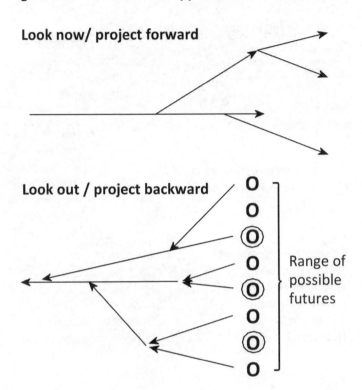

Looking from here to there

Written estimates

The most common form of futures tool used is the individually written analytical paper in which the analyst wades through a series of deductive and inductive thought processes on the environment, stakeholders, influencing or causal factors, future scenarios, and implications. This is quite a useful tool as the 'estimative' narrative may translate readily into the ultimate product released to the client. This saves formatting time. It is also useful where one individual is charged with carriage of most of the analysis. Critically, the estimative flow often provides the best framework for the inclusion of results or products from other types of analysis.

The estimative process brings explanatory and futures argument together in the one seamless process as shown in Figure 10.3. Strategic intelligence estimates normally consider the range of events, patterns and drivers associated with the topic under analysis. The aim of such work is to support deliberate decision-making and planning processes which may act on only the key judgments but must be informed by the supporting analytical process. Additionally, aspects of such analysis will be

Figure 10.3 The estimative process

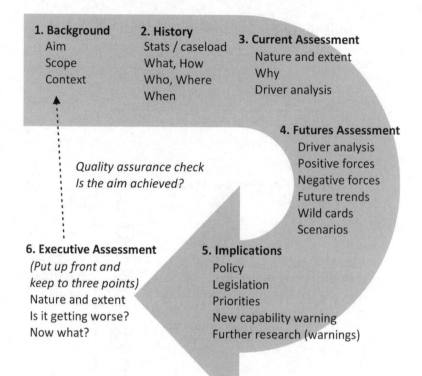

1. **Background**
   Aim
   Scope
   Context

2. **History**
   Stats / caseload
   What, How
   Who, Where
   When

3. **Current Assessment**
   Nature and extent
   Why
   Driver analysis

4. **Futures Assessment**
   Driver analysis
   Positive forces
   Negative forces
   Future trends
   Wild cards
   Scenarios

Quality assurance check
Is the aim achieved?

6. **Executive Assessment**
   (Put up front and
   keep to three points)
   Nature and extent
   Is it getting worse?
   Now what?

5. **Implications**
   Policy
   Legislation
   Priorities
   New capability warning
   Further research (warnings)

Pulling it all together using an Estimative approach

useful to a range of associated intelligence analysts and hence, if the analysis is packaged as a complete product, it usually gets broader dissemination than other more tailored products.

For example, an analyst tasked with completing a quite complex strategic assessment on the nature and extent of an issue that is not quantifiable – as often occurs in the law enforcement environment – will need to develop a number of methodologies with which to assess the extent of the problem. Methodologies should provide a minimum size and a maximum size, with several methodologies providing indicative numbers in between. With commodity imports (for example, people or drugs), the minimum may be what we seize or find while the maximum may be extrapolations of the highest estimated import rates internationally. Mid-range figures can be estimated based on extrapolating from various control groups, such as the potential consumer base or the known criminal base. The future then can be assessed based on drivers affecting these control groups as to whether they will seek to import more or consume more.

Futures wheels

The futures wheel is a consequence analysis tool mainly designed to consider the effects of an event of action, but may be used to consider a particular trend. Diagrammatically displayed, this tool provides rapid visualisation of the cause and effect relationships of consequences. The method is described here, and is shown diagrammatically in Figure 10.4.

Step 1: Scope the future event to be tested. Such events are normally expected to happen based on current or historical occurrences – such as an election, an economic downturn, an Olympic Games, a trade pact being signed and so on. The event to be examined is placed in the centre of a visual display.

Step 2: 'Big picture' or first-order results are arranged out from the event and connected by solid lines indicating direct outcomes. The first-order result is surrounded by secondary results, associations or con-sequences and connected by double lines. A good place to start is what happened last time this event occurred.

Step 3: The process is then continued by using triple lines to add third-order consequences, and may be developed to further levels of consequences and beyond. All of these stages can be seen in Figure 10.4.

Note that branches may be coded with a negative or a positive symbol based on the (positive or negative) implication for the decision-makers. Additionally, competing outcomes should be highlighted as a potential area to influence or manage consequences, and should be annotated by level of comparative likelihood.

Figure 10.4 Futures wheels model

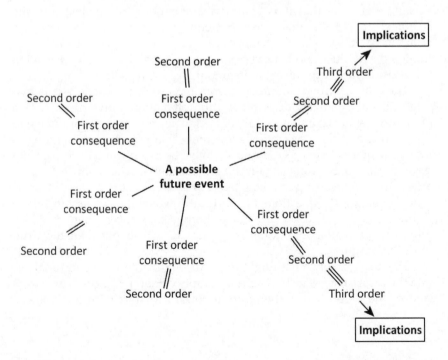

The tool is often useful in brainstorming sessions that have already successfully employed such tools as Ishikawa diagrams (see Chapter 8 in this book) to explain the current context. It is a useful divergent tool that takes the analysis away from known factors to a range of other issues that might, in themselves, warrant further analysis.

For example, as strategic criminal intelligence is frequently a study into unintended consequences, futures wheels (Figure 10.4) are often used when considering an event that could possibly impact on the shape of the environment; for example, impending legislation. Creating additional offences or legalising aspects of criminal behaviour often have unintended consequences for law enforcement and it is the strategic analyst's role to advise on how the environment may change. In such cases it is important for the analyst to think like the 'threat'. Normally criminals simply shift business in the face of legislation change, so 'how might this unfold?' Legalisation of previously illegal activity may see new entrepreneurs, new forms of business franchise emerging, or countermeasures being undertaken. Each of these stems of analysis may form part of the first-second-third order sequence in the diagram.

Trend analysis (also known as time impact analysis)

Trend analysis is one of the most common futures tools because it is one of the most common explanatory tools and is supported by a wide variety of commercial software applications. Moreover, consciously or unconsciously, all of us use qualitative trend analysis all the time in our daily lives. However, trend analysis (in a futures context) is also one of the most failure-prone tools. The common problem in extrapolating from existing trends is that it is comfortable for both the analyst and the customer to believe that existing trends will continue. Without the addition of other tools, or perspectives, such analysis will display only limited possibilities and hence be of less use in intelligence terms; leaving the decision-maker prone to 'strategic surprise' (Gray, 2005).

The other complication arising from the use of trend analysis is that often current trends are determined through a quantitative process. This often leads analysts into an intuitive backwater where they are unable to assess future conditions until they actually happen! Future trending is indeed a qualitative process and is often best performed strategically through the analysis of mega-trends, their consequences and how they affect the system being investigated. For example, this methodology is more applicable to questions of the future availability of heroin or the future social predilection for mood-altering substances, than to determine if a particular individual or group will be involved in the drug trade in the future.

The process of extending trends through a time-impact analysis into the future has, as its basis, the assumption that the future is an extension of the present. It is therefore important to start with a graphical, statistical, or some other representation of historical and current trends. The analyst then asks the following questions:

- What are the current observables and drivers of the trend?
- What forces are acting on this trend causing it to continue? Will those forces continue in the future?
- If the direction of the trend continues, what will be some positive or negative consequences?
- What is likely to alter the trajectory of the trend over time in terms of events or drivers?
- What forks in the trajectory will this produce?
- What are the positive or negative consequences of these forks?
- How much of this trend can be influenced by actions of the supported decision-maker?

A graphical example of a trend analysis is shown in Figure 10.5. The example projects three scenario futures for a hypothetical drug market, based on a price and purity index. Three outcomes are depicted from the current time into a future. The outcomes are shown by dashed lines. In the example shown in Figure 10.5, the analyst goes against the statistical trends of previous years, assessing that a particular driver will impede a recurrence of the previous, cyclical peaks and troughs.

Figure 10.5 Example trend analysis projecting futures for a drug market based on a price/purity index

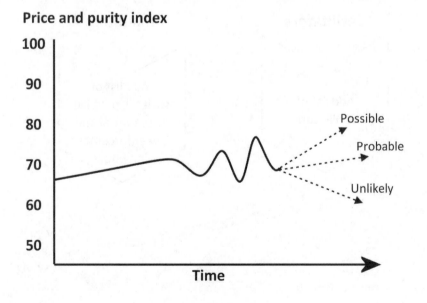

Price and purity index

Analysing drivers with 'Force field' analysis

Force field analysis is a comparative tool that assists examination of the relative weights of drivers that act for (facilitators) or against (inhibitors) change. The concept may also be used to assist weighing the pros and cons of consequences arising from decisions or future events. Hence, analysis should show where policy effort would be most rewarding.

Before conducting force field analysis, the key drivers should have already been identified by another analytical process. An explanation of the relative strengths of drivers on the current situation can be displayed as follows:

- list all forces for change in one column, and all forces against change in another column;
- assign a score to each force, from 1 (weak) to 5 (strong);
- the table may be converted readily into a diagram showing the forces for and against change. Show the size of each force as a number next to it or by different sized arrows pushing at a centre line forming a pendulum effect. Or if turned on its side a see-saw display can be created, which is often more effective as it shows the relative strengths of each driver (see Figure 10.6).

A similar process can be followed for future force field analysis. Here a projected future point in time can be taken and the diagram overlayed

Figure 10.6 Lists of facilitators and inhibitors can be added to the arrows, which are scaled to indicate relative weights

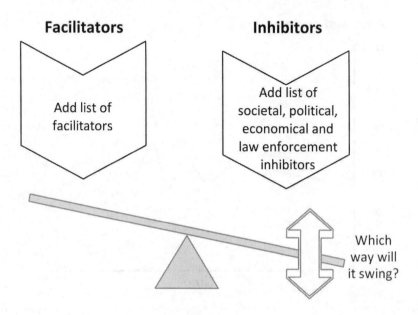

Figure 10.7 Hypothetical force field analysis.

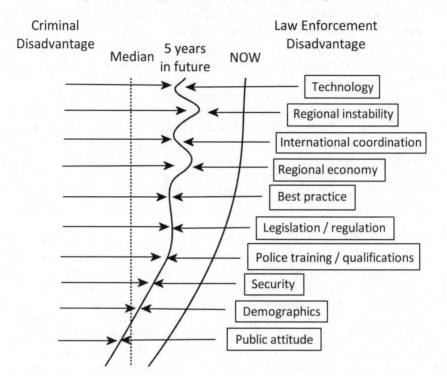

against the current situation to show which inhibitors or facilitators will be more important in future (see Figure 10.7). In the diagram, hypothetical force field analysis considers different drivers affecting an issue over the next five years. Over a five-year period it can be seen that the general trend is still towards a law enforcement disadvantage, though less so than at the present (NOW).

A derivation is to arrange facilitators and inhibitors in conjunction with trend analysis to show on a time line when inhibitors or facilitators are likely to weaken or strengthen (this is discussed later in this chapter, see Figure 10.8).

The key to force field analysis is to assess which inhibitors or facilitators are vulnerable to external policy pressure and where effort is likely to be best expended. Many analysts find continuing with a tabular approach to driver analysis of most use; as shown in the blank table here. Additional columns can be added for the types of perspectives that the analyst wishes to consider.

	Positive impacts	Negative impacts	Future Issues	Implications
Driver 1				
Driver 2				
Driver 3				

Threat assessments

Much of criminal intelligence processes have a genesis in security intelligence processes. Hence (as stated in Chapter 9 in this book) there are a range of threat assessment and risk assessment tools that assist an articulation of threat levels and potential priorities of response. Many techniques that are based on an attribute weighting system – that cumulatively provides a threat assessment – are relatively difficult to apply in a futures context. Often analysts who use and design such models have a focus on present issues. Hence it is very rare for emerging threats to rate well against known threats simply due to attribute weighting (see Chapter 15 in this book for a more detailed discussion of this point). Ultimately such methodologies are an attempt to quantify what may be ultimately unquantifiable and thereby add some level of comfort to assessments. In other words they are a tool that attempts to make a science of an art.

However, there is a use for such techniques in a futures sense if the analyst is comfortable with using descriptive or quantitative techniques in an inductive manner. 'Harm' (or 'consequence') ratings can be allocated by an analyst to an issue according to its potential economic, social, or political impacts. Hence, assessing *harm* often provides the simplest strategic mechanism for advising an 'order of merit' of issues of criminal significance warranting action over time. See the various methodologies and discussion of threat, risk and harm in Chapter 9 in this book.

Capability and *intent* are two further perspectives on threat that can be analysed in a futures context, where *capability* relates to the means and knowledge to facilitate a crime, and *intent* relates to the willingness to conduct the crime. Capability attributes can be given a relative weighting according to the potential or willingness to develop levels of capability related to the crime type under analysis. Clearly here though, a level of subjectivity needs to be imposed by the analyst by considering emerging ways to conduct criminality in the face of likely environmental change. This may lead to a spectrum of capability considered.

An area of difficulty remains when attempting to quantify future intent. This is often speculative in explaining current threats, let alone considering future criminal issues. A useful approach here may be to retain intent as a constant from current assessments, allowing a controlled variation of capability to assist in assessing the impacts of targeting capability over time.

Competing hypothesis

Competing hypothesis is an analytical technique used to objectively create a range of possible answers to a question. It is covered in detail in Chapter 8 in this book.

This technique uses a multi-step technique to explore a range of hypotheses in order to evaluate them and identify the most plausible of the options. As such it is a useful technique to establish a current perspective on an issue and especially as a framework to collect against components of the problem. However, it can also serve as a futures tool, in that subsequent analysis of unfolding events or patterns (through the examination of indicators or evidence) will be conducted against these hypotheses.

Combining techniques

Like any use of tools, the best analysis is achieved from a combination of approaches. A particularly useful combination is to take time lines or pattern lines forward and add the balance of competing drivers in a weighted fashion over time as shown in Figure 10.8. This not only provides an interpretation of how trends may branch or emerge over time, but also which key drivers are required to create that divergence. Of note is that many of the best models or techniques that build analysis from 'here to there' are an extension of explanatory techniques noted in the Chapter 8 in this book.

Figure 10.8 Combination scenario generation model

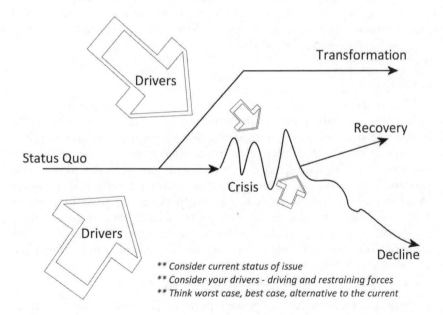

** Consider current status of issue
** Consider your drivers - driving and restraining forces
** Think worst case, best case, alternative to the current

Looking from there to here

Delphi technique

The Delphi method was discussed in Chapter 8 in this book, and it can also be used in futures work. The main result sought in futures analysis is to gain a consensus forecast. However, alternative views that arise during such processes remain important as potential hypotheses that must still be collected against over time. Hence, such techniques are useful supporting processes to development of competing hypotheses and scenario generation.

The ability to select the right panel of 'experts' is crucial as is an ability to convey to them the key question being asked. Many experts in a field in criminal intelligence are more comfortable dealing in the 'here and now' and are reticent to assess the future without evidence. Moreover, many personality types within law enforcement are similar or are based in set cultural perspectives on criminality. Hence, establishing a panel of experts for futures work will normally require drawing from a broader field of interests and then attempting to apply a level of objectivity in viewing the results.

Given the analytical complications inherent in the tool, many futurists see Delphi Technique as a last resort. In many ways it can be a mechanism by which analysts abrogate their analytical responsibility. However it also remains a useful technique to gather expectations and judgments on which to make further interpretations, or to see whether or not you have missed a critical point.

Analogies

Analogies involve analysis of a certain issue by comparing it to a different issue with similar characteristics – one that may be expected to develop in similar ways. Events in the past may appear to have parallels to current events. It is therefore a possibility that a past or current situation may also be repeated in a different context in the future. This process uses an inductive form of argument that asserts that if two or more entities are similar in one or more respects, then a probability exists that they will be similar in other respects. In analysis of futures this is important where a great deal of work on the future of the analogous issue has occurred and some relevance of this analysis can be translated to a similar issue being considered.

Key steps to the development of an analogy are:

- **Step 1**: examine the component parts of the issue under analysis. Especially consider the way it manifests and the environment it manifests in;

- **Step 2**: search for a known situation which exhibits the same characteristics. Often the best place to start is in the same environmental context;

- **Step 3**: draw on futures work or develop futures models for the analogous issue;
- **Step 4**: overlay the outcomes of this analysis on the issue under consideration;
- **Step 5**: examine relevant similarities and differences; and
- **Step 6**: extrapolate those properties worth pursuing in a futures context.

A basic example is to analyse the future of one particular illicit commodity through developing an understanding of how other commodities are likely to be exploited by criminal enterprise. Another common analogy in law enforcement is that criminal enterprise tends to conform to many of the developments of corporate enterprise – especially given current levels of globalisation. Here proposed future developments in the corporate sector can be used as analogies for how criminal organisations may develop. An example here could be an analyst viewing the blossoming use of franchising arrangements in the corporate world in the 1980s-1990s projecting such models onto the criminal sector for the 1990s-2000s. Such analysis may be pertinent to organisational structure, methods of operation and technology take up.

Analogies are only as sound as the cause and effects links drawn and parallel relationships established. Cross cultural and social imperatives must be clearly argued. Pitfalls in the correlations may exist. For example, in the hypothetical criminal–corporate correlation noted above, potential problems may include non-conformity motivation, the extent and dynamics of the black market and so on. However, analogies may still be useful even if only subsets of the contexts are able to be correlated.

Scenario methods

Scenarios are the most commonly used *look out/project backward* tool and can be defined as self-consistent pictures of the future or an aspect of the future. The best scenarios are carefully created to be internally coherent and useful. They are mainly to illustrate continuities from, and contrasts to, the present in order to reveal choices, consequences, and so on. They are normally an exploratory tool in which the scenarios themselves should never be expected to come to pass in their entirety, especially if they support decisions which will over time shift the nature of the scenarios generated. Here the aim is not to foresee the future, but to show how different interpretations of drivers can lead to different possible futures. Secondly, scenarios are used to make better decisions in the present about issues that have long-term consequences for the future.

The best scenarios need to be plausible, creative, internally consistent, and relevant. They should contain reference to those events, patterns and drivers encompassed by the scenario. They are produced as a narrative, and are normally reduced to a small number (3-4) to assist perspective.

A variety of different scenarios are usually prepared in order to emphasise the possibility of different alternative futures. By setting up several scenarios, a 'possibility space' is created. It is somewhere within this 'possibility space' that the future is likely to unfold. Here typical plots include winners and losers, crises and response, good and bad news.

Considering the stakeholders of the analysis, the current strategic setting and the main protagonists, the steps in developing scenarios are usually:

- **Step 1**: Identify which drivers will be important over time, as discussed previously. Assess the importance and the uncertainty of the drivers. Other tools can assist this process such as either a force field analysis process (where positives and negatives can be arranged in a table as in Figure 10.9) or a morphological construct (taking the best and worst combinations of factors from a morphological table – see Chapter 8 in this book).

- **Step 2:** Two possible scenario generation paths normally follow. If the problem can be reduced to two central drivers, they can be placed on the 'x' and 'y' axes of a graph, and using 'significant impact' to 'little impact' at either ends of both axis, four scenario quadrants are formed. This is shown in Figure 10.10, where one axis discusses the utilisation of best practice by criminal groups, and the other axis examines the use of communication and information systems. This graph is of course an example, and different axis titles may be chosen. The graph has four quadrants, and a short script should be inserted in each box to discuss the nature of the environment that the competing drivers create. Alternatively, where the situation is not reducible to the influence of two forces, the positive and negative consequences of all drivers can be logged.

Figure 10.9 An example force field table that assists derivation of positive and negative influences

Stakeholders Trends Uncertainties	Positive (from criminal perspective)	Negative (from criminal perspective)
Legislation	Gaps in international regulation	Increased punishment
Law enforcement	Periodic success but insufficient to be an effective deterrence	Detection and reaction capability increases
Technology	Law enforcement lack of funds to enforce and detect illegality	Inability to exploit due to lack of expertise

**Figure 10.10 Potential impacts of technology and
business practices on money launderers**

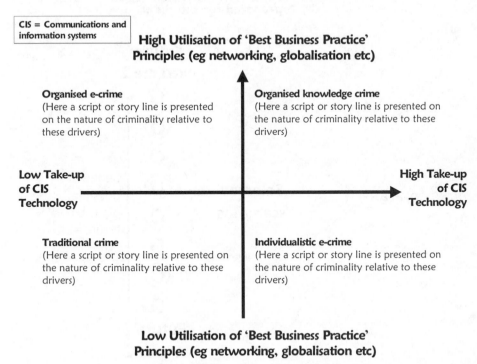

CIS = Communications and
information systems

**High Utilisation of 'Best Business Practice'
Principles (eg networking, globalisation etc)**

Organised e-crime
(Here a script or story line is presented
on the nature of criminality relative to
these drivers)

Organised knowledge crime
(Here a script or story line is presented on
the nature of criminality relative to these
drivers)

**Low Take-up
of CIS
Technology**

**High Take-up
of CIS
Technology**

Traditional crime
(Here a script or story line is presented on
the nature of criminality relative to these
drivers)

Individualistic e-crime
(Here a script or story line is presented on
the nature of criminality relative to these
drivers)

**Low Utilisation of 'Best Business Practice'
Principles (eg networking, globalisation etc)**

Two parameter scenarios can be formed by using all the negative consequences and another with all the positive consequences articulated as a future picture. Between these two extremes a larger number of possibilities can be derived based on variances in the accepted consequences (Figure 10.11, next page).

- **Step 3**: A narrative is then developed to show how each end state picture could emerge from the present.
- **Step 4**: Reconsider the range of scenarios using wild card or Devil's Advocate techniques.
- **Step 5**: From this narrative, determine the key indicators that would show whether or not each of the potential futures were unfolding.

Wildcards and Devil's Advocate

Analysis should always be followed by a process of reconsidering some of the fundamental assumptions that underpin the futures concepts developed. In nearly all circumstances, futures work has some degree of current continuity of either an analytical perspective or of a cultural, social, political or economic norm.

Figure 10.11 A range of scenarios are mapped from best to worst, and individual scripts for selected intervening possibilities are prepared for the client

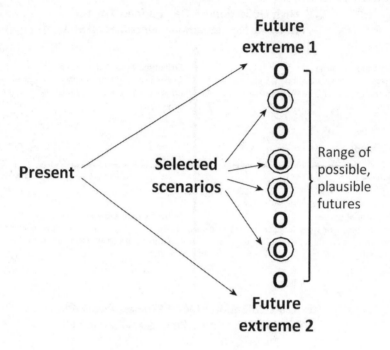

Reflection on the veracity of futures work normally involves questioning these perspectives and 'givens'.

One approach to questioning assumptions is to develop wildcards. The process here is to consider the key judgments formulated from the analysis and brainstorm those key events or patterns that, if occurred, would fundamentally alter the judgment or require a review of the analysis.

Another approach is to establish an adversarial brainstorming session in which key players adopt a sceptical Devil's Advocate approach to the analysis or a different point of view. Often this approach can be formalised as a 'game'.

Such alternatives do not, of themselves, fundamentally undermine the analysis provided but can actually improve the effectiveness of the advice provided by caveating the 'so-whats' and highlighting some of the key underlying premises.

Indications and warnings system

The aim of a strategic indications and warnings system (IWS) is to provide timely warnings to decision- and policy makers of potential or likely threats and issues that may adversely impact on the jurisdiction's specific environment. IWS can be used to orient collection and warning on specified issues to service potential policy decisions, by using a process-based analytical method to consider the impact of observed threats, events and trends on the criminal justice environment. The system works on the basis of information supplied by sources and agencies, often already collected for other operational and strategic purposes, and the analysis and synthesis of this information. When firm indications of strategic change emerge, a warning product results (an Alert).

The risks associated with this process are threefold. First, there is often a level of analytical difficulty in defining the types of problems that will require strategic response. Secondly, there is the possibility of friction from agencies having to consider potentially confronting possibilities outside their stated view of the direction in which they seek to progress. Finally, there is an issue of corporate courage in acknowledging that the IWS, while providing a comprehensive framework, is not infallible. An IWS must have:

- a client base for warning products;
- client-defined threats (where possible);
- a stated indications and warnings problem or problems related to the threat;
- an intelligence requirements or collection management system on which to levy collection requirements;
- an ongoing monitoring and environmental scanning resource associated with the problem;
- a collation system to record change in indicators (indications); and
- a reporting mechanism.

IWS practice normally conforms to the following processes in order to be effective. It may seek to develop a warning problem. This is normally encapsulated in a threat statement that focuses the issue for decision-makers (such as 'the threat to law enforcement interests from X, includes …). An IWS may also aim to develop data so as to create a baseline level of activity or pattern from which possible change could be interpreted. It may also seek to refine futures concepts to 'most dangerous'. By discussing with key clients the scenarios in a future context, developed from estimative work, it may be possible to align criminal futures against projected policy and strategy. Most importantly, an IWS should aim to develop indicators for each scenario. Here the analyst works back from each possible projection and seeks to interpret the future paths that may develop that lead to the 'futures of concern'. Along these paths there will be indicators (events, activities or trends) which will provide an indication that this future may be unfolding. Special note should be given to identifying critical (unique) indicators that are specific to single scenarios or future developments. Finally, the indicators are then cross-matched against existing collection processes and flagged as critical warning issues. Ongoing monitoring and reporting then occurs.

Conclusion

If a strategic intelligence system does not include a futures function, then it inherently does not fulfil a strategic intelligence function. As an extension of a strategic decision-making system that involves policy, capability, strategy and operational development, strategic intelligence must include analysis of significance and consequence over time. This then establishes the context in which decisions are made.

Such futures work does not have to be necessarily lengthy, involved or grounded in the unknown. It should, however, seek to challenge and provide the broadest context for decisions and be supported by a robust collection system. The analysis required to support such intelligence processes can be assisted by a range of futures tools usually aligned to either look out from where we are or look back from where we may end up.

Reference

Gray, C, 2005, 'Transformation and Strategic Surprise', Strategic Studies Institute of the US Army War College, <www.strategicstudiesinstitute.army.mil/pdffiles/PUB602.pdf>, accessed June 2008.

CHAPTER 11

Influencing decision-makers with intelligence and analytical products

R Mark Evans

Introduction

The value of intelligence staff, and in particular analysts (a role pres-cribed by most law enforcement agencies), is heavily influenced by the quality of their outputs and products. Commanders (who have a particular set of requirements) and front-line officers (who have a very different set of needs) expect intelligence products to provide insights, direction, guidance and (often) 'the answer' (even if no question has been set). Typically analysts need to balance competing demands and work to multiple timescales because some products must be generated very quickly, while other tasks will demand hours, weeks or months of work. It is often necessary to produce material for each client group which is focused on their particular and specific needs. Immediate, tactical advice will often be the core function of an intelligence unit and this work is usually essential to support effective day-to-day policing activity. But ultimately, products must be designed to inform, assist and influence decision-making if they are to make a positive, sustained and long-term contribution to crime control strategies. Achieving this is not straight-forward and requires the effective alignment of multiple factors – some of which fall outside the direct influence of even the most senior intel-ligence personnel.

This chapter explores the critical importance of intelligence and analytical products in influencing decision-making in a policing environ-ment and highlights those key issues faced by analysts in the effort to make a sustained contribution to crime control strategies.

Intelligence and analytical products: How do they fit together?

The recent literature of operationally focused police intelligence describes what, to a non-expert, must seem like a bewildering array of different products or outputs. For example a 2004 US report noted that; 'as a general rule, only about three products may be needed' (Carter, 2004: 81) and goes on to describe reports that aid investigation and apprehension of offenders, reports that provide threat advisories (to harden targets) and strategic analysis reports to aid in planning and resource allocation. By contrast, the New Jersey State Police (NJSP) Practical Guide to Intelligence-Led Policing (NJSP, 2006) describes producing 'finished intelligence products within ... four categories'; current intelligence (addressing day-to-day events); estimative intelligence (deals with what might be or what might happen); warning intelligence (sounds an alarm); and, research intelligence (in-depth studies). The types of finished analytical products described by the NJSP include briefings, spot reports (time critical intelligence), quarterly trends reports, threat assessments and after action reports.

There are multiple variants of this list in agencies across the law enforcement spectrum. Indeed, it is arguable that the lack of consistency in outputs (products) is a key weakness in the ability of law enforcement agencies to talk a commonly understood language in ways that allow intelligence to be stored, analysed, understood and used effectively.

In the United Kingdom (UK) the introduction of the National Intelligence Model (NIM) proposed for the first time that all police forces in England and Wales would adopt a standard set of intelligence and analytical products (the model was later adopted in Scotland and Northern Ireland and increasingly by other UK law enforcement agencies). The model is backed by practice advice and minimum standards. Guidance on the UK NIM states that 'the use of defined analytical techniques and products created using recognised analytical tools and methods is fundamental to the development of intelligence products. The specifics of the situation will determine the number and combination of analytical techniques and products that should be drawn on to inform intelligence product requirements' (NCPE, 2005: 61).

The NIM defines nine analytical options; crime pattern analysis, demographic social trends analysis, network analysis, market and criminal business profiles, risk analysis, target profile analysis, operational intelligence assessment and results analysis. There is debate within the UK analytical community as to whether these are actually *techniques* or *products*. Arguably some have a lengthy and well understood history as techniques – crime pattern analysis falls into this category, while others – such as risk analysis – are better understood as products. Equally, as extensive as the list is, it does not cover everything. For example, there are specific techniques and products used in support of serious and major crime investigations that fall outside the core set. Nevertheless there is an expectation that these analytical options will contribute to the production of the four intelligence products that are described in the NIM:

- *Strategic Assessments* – designed to provide an overview of current and long-term issues affecting the police force and, crucially, to inform the setting of strategies to deal with the highest priority issues;

- *Tactical Assessments* – identifies shorter-term issues that require attention;
- *(Target) Subject Profiles* – designed to provide greater understanding of a person(s) of interest;[1] and
- *Problem Profiles* – aimed at providing greater understanding of policing problems such as crime series or hot locations.

It should be noted that NIM can, if not thoughtfully implemented, lead analysts (and intelligence units) to become remote from the core business of operational policing. There are particular challenges where the relationship between decision-makers and analysts is weak or immature, because it will usually stifle any notion of NIM as a forward-looking, innovative framework that can add real value. It is also clear that there are dangers associated with adopting any approach that does not reflect local circumstances. NIM products work best with clear ownership, when they are crafted by intelligence staff given the freedom and autonomy to focus on real problems, and where they provide the basis for action.

For example, in the Police Service of Northern Ireland (PSNI), the NIM provides a robust corporate framework; however the frequency, type and range of products varies to reflect the differences in policing areas. Within this framework police analysts combine frequent and rigorous intelligence analysis. This work is often focused on traditional investigation (case) support aimed at uncovering networks, associations and links, but is combined with broader crime analysis that seeks to provide a holistic view of the criminal environment. Importantly, PSNI analysts perform crime and intelligence analysis, and this is why staff are deliberately not labelled 'intelligence' analysts; they are employed in flexible ways that maximise the value of the NIM framework.

Furthermore, the NIM provides direction to intelligence collection activity. PSNI analysts work closely with intelligence managers to target and develop the right collection opportunities – a critical factor in the value of subsequent intelligence analysis and products. Finally, PSNI does not employ performance analysts. This means that NIM type products do not directly compete with statistical analysis for time and attention.

There are many models across Europe, North America, Australia and beyond. For example in 2005 European Interior Ministers agreed on a European Criminal Intelligence Model (ECIM). But since its UK introduction NIM-type products have become widely known and used in other parts of the world, though usually with some refinement to reflect the circumstances of local policing.

Figure 11.1 illustrates the way in which the New Zealand (NZ) Police is seeking to build a flexible but consistent national portfolio of intelligence, analytical and knowledge products to meet the needs and expectations of local Area, District and Service Centre Commanders.

---

1   In many jurisdictions, the term *subject profile* has replaced the original NIM term *target profile*.

Figure 11.1 NZ Police Intelligence Product Framework

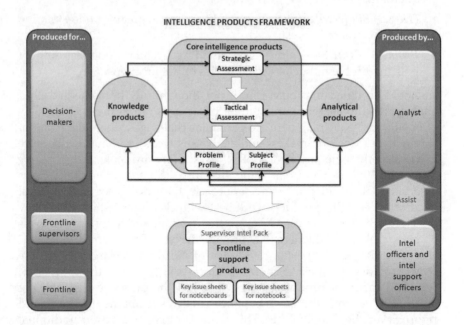

The Intelligence Product Framework (Figure 11.1) demonstrates the interaction and mutual support provided between the four distinct product groupings (*Core*, *Knowledge*, *Analytical* and *Frontline Support*). The left hand side of the framework highlights who the target client groups are for each of the product groupings while on the right hand side are an indication of which intelligence staff function, own or contribute to the production of these products.

The NZ Police framework is designed to support staff at all levels – from front-line officers to middle and senior management – through a combination of:

- *core intelligence products*, regular, action orientated outputs generated within Area, District, Regional and National Intelligence Units;

- *analytical products*, which provide insight into specific problems – for example a homicide Detective needs statement and telephone toll analysis to support a suspect interview – and which may inform intelligence products or be used directly in support of decision-making;

- *knowledge products*, which may include reports that 'scan' an issue and provide background, context and understanding to a law enforcement issue or problem but aren't usually designed for immediate action; and

- *front-line support products*, which are designed specifically to assist supervisors (for example with shift briefings) and to meet the immediate needs of community policing, patrol, investigation or other areas (for example a reliable piece of intelligence about a person or crime may need to be dealt with quickly by a local operational team). These front line support products can have a short shelf life and often be presented in non-written forms, for example police notebook sticker entries or verbal briefings. Such products reflect the traditional notions of crime intelligence analysis as case support and briefing tools.

To be fully effective (and recognising both resource constraints and the fact that some entities can often be 'one person' operations) intelligence units need to be able to generate a wide range of outputs. Often, however, short-term immediate issues are the only focus. This may be because; intelligence units lack an effective analytical component; because they do not have access to the right (quality) information; are staffed by personnel, including sworn officers, who have little or no understanding of longer-term problem-solving and crime control strategies; or because there is no management demand or expectation for a more considered approach. Often all of these factors are at play. The role of intelligence analysis should not be underestimated as a tool to support critical operational priorities. Often it is the insight provided by high quality, painstaking intelligence analysis that can break open a case that traditional investigation techniques have failed to uncover. Such short-term focused units may actually be well regarded in policing circles and will often be very busy; however, their role will always be marginal.

The preparation of strategic products is particularly important if decision-making within individual command units is to avoid a recurring emphasis on short term, response and/or incident focused policing. Strategic assessments (produced every 6 or 12 months) linked to tactical assessments (produced every two to four weeks) and subject and problem profiles, and more specialist analytical products (produced on demand), provide a robust intelligence reporting framework that enables command unit decision-makers to align available resources against actual priorities.

While no single model may be regarded as providing definitive guidance it may be important for agencies to at least agree on some common outputs (products) – particularly in circumstances where cooperation between them is necessary.

The components of good products

In the UK the NIM is accompanied by extensive guidance and national templates that set out in considerable detail what each product should contain, what it should look like and how it should be used. It is a highly prescriptive framework that, on the face of it, offers little room for local interpretation. In practice, the NIM framework, however implemented, remains incomplete and still requires analysts to apply their thinking in creative and critical ways and to reflect the culture, context and expectations of their organisational environment. These all have a very significant impact on 'what good analysis looks like' and there are a number of axioms that all analysts need to be aware of in the development of high-quality products.

The better you understand your subject the more likely you can produce material with insight (Pease, 2006). This may seem obvious but too often analysts work with single data sets, fail to read widely around their subject and miss the latest research or thinking. There are different ways to think about problems and there are many fields outside law enforcement – medicine, geography, science, mathematics, philosophy, business – that all have ideas, concepts and methodologies that can assist effective crime and intelligence analysis. By limiting solutions to traditional fields it may be possible to make a short-term or marginal difference – but real progress is likely to require new (or at least innovative) thinking. The best analysts have a broad view of the world around them and can effectively apply the learning from other disciplines.

Products will be better informed by involving others. A community or neighbourhood profile for example will always benefit from input of those working closest to the problems on the ground. Consultation and taking advice is essential – a computer system and its captured data only contains some of the information necessary for effective analysis.

Poorly written products will often confuse facts and opinions. At best this can lead to criticism – at worst it can lead to flawed decision-making and action. The separation of facts, evidence, opinions, judgments, hypotheses, conclusions and recommendations is a critical element of the analytical tradecraft and fundamental to the generation of effective product.

Good analysis needs to add real value. The biggest criticism of many intelligence products by operational staff is that they simply provide 'news and weather' – information already known about events that have occurred and with no sense of how they relate to the future. Analysts should avoid the temptation to simply reorganise or represent information that is already widely available.

Timeliness is always a factor. There will always be intelligence gaps (unknowns) and it is usually the case that conclusions and recommendations need to be made on incomplete data. But this needs to be set against the fact that timeliness in the dissemination of law enforcement intelligence product is almost always critical – and this will often mean exercising judgment about when to publish or report. Though negotiation around deadlines can help, it takes insight and bold analytical decision-making to know when to call it a day.

Executive summaries are key to focusing attention. Analysts will often know that a subject is complex and that reaching a clear and firm view can be difficult, but for decision-making simple is often best. For analysts this is a particular challenge and writing accurately and in a style that allows non-experts to understand the argument and action the product is a skill that needs significant practice. Lengthy products, for example, may never be read in full by busy decision-makers. Using an executive summary, stressing key findings and highlighting action points may all be essential to focus attention on the right issues.

Good products get to the point. There is a temptation for analysts (particularly those new to the field) to want to 'show all their workings'. Sometimes this may be necessary or needed, but in general such detail is best avoided in the main body of a report. The 'noise' it creates can often detract from the main message. Detailed workings need to be available to defend any challenge, but it shouldn't be necessary for them to be fully reported, particularly in a situation where analysts and decision-makers have confidence in their respective roles.

Experience for police officers is mainly about evidence. In writing for a policing audience it is important to remember that the search for facts is often paramount. Poorly drafted prose that meanders across a chosen subject, or reports written in the style of a work of fiction may come to be regarded as a good read but are unlikely to positively influence serious decision-making over an extended period of time.

Good law enforcement analysis should be bold (but not foolhardy) and seek out the truth. Good analysts bring a professional, objective approach to law enforcement. If analysts don't make decision-makers uncomfortable at least some of the time then it's likely that they are not doing their job properly.

Products must comply with policy, procedure and legislation. This is particularly the case where sensitive intelligence is concerned. This means recognising the need-to-know principle (balanced against the principles of the obligation-to-share), adherence to any restrictive disclosure obligations – for example law enforcement partners will often place limits on what can be done with their intelligence products – and most products should carry the appropriate *security classification*. It is important that intelligence officers and analysts understand these issues because slack application of the rules will undermine trust and confidence and may threaten sensitive sources or operations. Equally, over-classified material, which is too tightly controlled, can seriously hamper the effective use and application of products for decision-making. The observation 'If I can't use it don't tell me about it' is still a familiar (and wholly flawed) comment heard in many police investigation units.

The issue of recommendations

There is much debate about whether analysts should make recommendations. Some operational staff believe that analysis should only provide the facts; that decision-makers are responsible for reaching a view on what should be done and do not need guidance. Some also suggest that if analysts make recommendations, this somehow gives them alone a stake in 'solving the problem' and reduces the obligations on other staff to contribute. Finally, some argue that analysts – particularly non-sworn individuals that have never been involved in operational policing – lack the necessary currency and knowledge to know what the right options are.

While superficially attractive, in general such thinking mainly reflects weak analytical product, a relatively unsophisticated decision-making model and a lack of understanding about the purpose and value of recommendations. Well informed, carefully considered recommendations represent options and possible actions that can be taken, but they are *not the same* as decisions taken by those with the authority to commit resources, a point echoed by Cope (2004).

In making recommendations, analysts should bear in mind the following considerations.

There are many types of recommendation. The UK NIM for example, highlights *intelligence, prevention (intervention)* and *enforcement priorities;* while routine activity theory may suggest a focus on the *victim, offender* and *location;* and other models of policing may emphasis the value of a PIER approach (*prevention, intelligence, enforcement* and *reassurance*). PIER has been adopted in some UK police agencies as a way of adding public reassurance to the core NIM principles of intelligence, prevention (intervention), and enforcement. The organisational style and context, together with the expectations of the audience will often dictate which recommendation type is most likely to achieve impact.

In law enforcement the best recommendations will be SMART (*specific, measurable, achievable, realistic* and *time-bound*) and should be seen as practical by those for whom they are written. For example, a decision-maker faced with significant short-term pressure to reduce budgets is unlikely to welcome a proposal that demands immediate and significant investment in police overtime or the recruitment of new staff to solve a crime problem.

It is important to distinguish between *short-, medium-* and *long-term* recommendations and between *tactics* (designed to suppress a problem) and *treatment* (which may be aimed at solving problems over the longer term). All may be valid but the expected outcomes, resources required and time taken will be very different in each case.

The best recommendations will usually be written in ways that include an *element of choice* in how they are applied. Prescriptive, closed-off options should generally be avoided because intelligence staff may not be fully aware of all the constraints placed on the decision-maker.

It is easy for intelligence products to make a strong case but to lack credibility when it comes to proposing solutions. It must always be the case that 'recommendations should follow from the analysis or be credited to research' (Pease, 2006).

Finally, credible recommendations can only ever be made by those with insight and understanding. They should always be written after careful consideration and, wherever possible, in consultation with subject matter or other experts. Often, front-line staff, practitioners, academics, researchers and others will have tried many options and have spent a good deal of time thinking about what works. This experience can often be invaluable in generating ideas and highlighting obvious pitfalls. The most effective products will reflect – and build on – the learning that comes from such contacts. While there is room for debate about how recommendations might be drafted, presented and ultimately used, there can be no doubt that in a mature environment they ought to be a useful aid to (but not a substitute for) decision-making.

Decision-makers:
What do analysts need to know?

While the skills, training and knowledge of analysts is clearly crucial, in law enforcement the expectations and maturity of decision-makers are just as important in determining what sort of analysis can be done, how ambitious it seeks to be and the overall impact that this will have on crime control strategies.

In law enforcement decision-makers will generally be individuals that control access to resources *and* have the ability to make reasonable choices about how those resources are actually used.

What constitutes 'choice' can often be a complex matter in itself. For example, all police departments are required to respond to emergency calls, and while call management initiatives can provide some assistance, there are few real opportunities to allocate these resources on an entirely free choice basis. But beyond emergency response, much law enforcement work does involve making decisions about how best to use people, information and other assets. Across police organisations such decisions are made all the time and at every management level. It is also the case that many police organisations lack effective and robust decision-making structures that enable intelligence products to be turned into operational outcomes.

In the UK the NIM Tasking and Coordination Group (T&CG) process provides one such framework and, properly applied, is critical in the effective use of intelligence. Unfortunately in too many places such structures do not exist at all or are weak in application, and even where the T&CG works well, there are still many decisions taken outside the formal processes. This requires analysts and intelligence staff to understand the world of decision-makers in ways that enable products and other outputs to meet different and particular needs. For workers in the intelligence field, there are some key tenets that are useful to know, as the next section explains.

Linking products and decision-making

Intelligence officers and analysts must know who the key decision-makers are and what 'pushes their buttons'. Usually this is clear but often key individuals are not on the organisational hierarchy chart. For example long-standing and experienced detectives will often have significant influence over how investigation units work, even if they have no formal management responsibility. Equally, a crime reduction strategy may require the involvement of partner agencies whose direct interests may be quite different to the police. Identifying and understanding how key individuals operate, what their interests are and how they see the world will often be important in influencing how intelligence outputs are received and subsequently used.

Decision-makers are rarely intelligence professionals. This usually means that they need clear, straightforward advice written in a language free of jargon and complexity. To be useful intelligence products need to be understood and this generally means they need to be written for non-experts.

Pick the right presentation style and format. For many analysts lengthy written reports or detailed briefings, backed by extensive data, may appear to be the only way to 'get the message across'. These are often necessary and important, but in reality, there are many other, and often better, ways in which to communicate material. According to the management guru Henry Mintzberg, 'It is more important for the manager to get ... information quickly and efficiently than to get it formally' (Mintzberg, 1973). In this respect, options for analysts include:

- **Visualisation**. Many individuals prefer to receive information through visualisation tools, such as mind mapping, link charting and 'painting pictures'. While there are multiple software programs that will provide high quality charts, spreadsheets or maps, it is important for decision-makers to understand that while they support and facilitate effective presentation *they do not represent the actual analysis*. Deciding what to map, how to manipulate data in a spreadsheet or represent information on a time line is analytical – the visualisation product itself is not a substitute or proxy for the thinking (analytical) element of the intelligence process.

- **One-to-one informal briefings**. These allow for two-way questions and answers, can often supplement written reports, and are an effective way to quickly get the main points of a message across. For information to flow effectively, analysts must be embedded around and have access to decision-makers at every level.

- **Text and electronic messages**. Email has become the major tool for communicating within law enforcement agencies but in some places the sheer volume of information that requires attention can be overwhelming. This means analysts need to find ways to differentiate their product.

- **Corridor sessions**. Often the opportunity to influence arises at odd and unexpected times. Meetings in the tea/meal room, in the lunch queue or riding the lift (elevator) together can be key moments in winning time and attention. A brief exchange of views and ideas can lead to more substantial analysis. The ability to network effectively – both formally and informally – is a critical skill.

- **Visibility**. Getting out from behind the computer terminal and being seen around (for example, turning up to listen to the Police Commissioner's speech to a local business group) and offering general views and ideas about policing will create an expectation that the analyst already has something to offer. Sharing good news, making a point of explaining the impact of a piece of work, contributing to newsletters and so on, all create visibility, making it more likely that when the intelligence product arrives on the decision-maker's desk it is seen as coming from a person who already has valuable ideas to offer.

- **Understand the power of different formats**. In policing many analysts have no idea what happens to their products and therefore little or no idea about the impact they have made. Knowing what style and format works is clearly important. The overall message is summed up by Gardner (2004: 101); 'Individuals learn most effectively when they can receive the same message in a number of different ways, each re-presentation stimulating different intelligence'.

Understand that decision-makers are faced with multiple, competing demands. Intelligence may be important in making choices, but other factors will also weigh heavily. A long-running media campaign against a particular crime problem or a sensational headline will often set the agenda. Though such issues may appear to be a distraction they cannot be ignored. Intelligence has an important role to play in helping decision-makers to deal more effectively with these problems.

Know what's important. Generating intelligence products and firing them out in the hope that 'something' will stick is a recipe for frustration and failure. Commanders with few staff, policing a limited geographical area need products with a distinct, detailed and well-informed local flavour. Regional commanders may expect to see what the common issues are – and where opportunities exist for attacking shared problems – while Chiefs of Police will normally require a broader, more strategic viewpoint that perhaps addresses a problem from a whole-of-organisation, or even whole-of-government approach. It is very unlikely that a single report will adequately address each need or interest and analysts need to determine what's important at each level.

Seek clarity on what decision-makers expect. Decision-making priorities are often ill-defined and subject to change. New requirements can emerge very quickly and what was a major issue last week can be off the agenda today. For analysts this means staying in touch with the latest thinking so that outputs can be directed at the right issues. Agreeing on terms of reference with clear objectives – and keeping these updated – will help, but effective, frequent communication is vital. Crucially, analysts must know *who* they are writing for and *why* the product is needed. In most agencies decision-making will go on regardless of whether or not the intelligence picture has been painted, and adding real value is about the ability to deliver the right product, in the right format at just the right time.

Focus on people and context. 'If you are interesting people will want to be with you. People will seek your company. People will enjoy talking to you ...' (De Bono, 2004). The best analysts have presence, engage in effective verbal and non-verbal behaviour, and have the ability to read a situation and tailor their contribution accordingly. While these may be qualities that appear intangible they can be practised and when used successfully will contribute to the impact made.

Key decision-makers may be outside the immediate policing environment. The drive towards multi-agency partnership working and the blurring of lines of responsibility that accompany the move towards a more holistic all-of-government approach to tackling crime, leads to a more complex and flexible decision-making environment. This has clear implications for police intelligence which needs to respond effectively to such new demands.

Be aware of the constraints on decision-making. All law enforcement decision-makers operate in a world of finite budgets, limited resources and time constraints. Most are burdened with the expectations of more senior managers, organisational performance regimes, and unmet public expectations. Equally, the introduction of electronic forms of communication has significantly increased the amount of information circulating to managers. All of this is competition for analysts. Intelligence outputs that fail the test of real-world understanding are likely to be of limited value, and analytical units that establish a reputation for being disconnected from the day-to-day realities of policing will generally find it difficult to have any meaningful input in decision-making.

Intelligence-led policing concepts have brought the link with decision-making into much sharper focus in recent years and have significantly raised decision-maker expectation levels. There is now a sense that intelligence outputs ought or should be able to provide 'the answer'. While such notions are not new in some other intelligence fields – such as national security (see for example Lowenthal 2008) – it does not reflect the way that most law enforcement agencies have traditionally worked. Equally, law enforcement intelligence needs to be alive to dangers posed by raising unrealistic expectations or failing to explain what is (and what is not) possible. Those police decision-makers who complain that intelligence is too often wrong, fails to 'predict' the future or does not tell them exactly which is the best option, will always be disappointed. Nevertheless, by putting intelligence at the heart of a policing style such as intelligence-led policing (Ratcliffe, 2008) the link to decision-making becomes absolutely critical.

The matrix in Table 11.1 illustrates how the combination of different types of intelligence analysis and the sophistication (or maturity) of decision-making structures has a significant impact on crime control strategies.

Table 11.1 Combining products and decision-making

Time focus?	Current State (Informing Products)		Future State (Directing/Action Products)		
Type?	Knowledge and Front-Line Support Products (FSP)		Intelligence and Analytical Products		
Analytical Range?	Description of Facts	Facts & Interpretation	Opinions/ Judgments	Recommendations/ Conclusions	Forecasts
Typical content of intelligence product?	Will often be drawn directly from files, IT systems etc.	Will often draw together qualitative and quantitative data and may offer some guidance.	Will often draw together a range of data and offer relevant views/ advice and direction.	Will often reflect good practice and/or what works. Can draw on research material. Quality outputs will be heavily influenced by the skills, knowledge and experience of the analyst.	Will often seek to project forward previous trends or patterns. Seeks to highlight key future risks.
Sophistication of decision-making structures required to use product ?	Very Low	Low	Low-High	High	Very High
Designed for immediate action?	No [FSP – Yes]	Probably No [FSP – Yes]	Probably Yes	Yes	Yes
Likely impact of product combined with sophistication of decision-making structures on crime control strategies?	Will provide reassurance and evidence that the problem has been identified. Can be used to explain performance, allocate investigative resources and justify decisions that have already been taken.	Will provide useful knowledge and can offer some new ideas. Can be used to direct short-term resources in a business-as-usual environment.	Will offer guidance on current risk areas and issues. Can be useful in planning new strategies and will often influence the commitment of resources in the short-to medium-term. Can be used to inform reduction and intervention strategies.	Will provide clear advice on key issues/problems and proposals/ options on how best to address them. Will drive new strategies, provides basis for long-term planning and can be useful in engaging non-police agencies and partners. Can often be used to help identify cures/ solutions to problems through Problem-Oriented Policing (POP) and Intelligence-Led Policing (ILP).	Will provide focus on future issues that will probably need attention. Can drive very significant changes in strategy but can also be seen as crystal ball gazing and too ambitious if not properly managed.

Knowledge, intelligence, analytical products and decision-making matrix

At the first level of development intelligence products will often be *backward-looking* and seek to describe the facts. Facts may be lifted from database systems and reorganised in a more useful or convenient form (for example tabular data may be represented in the form of bar or pie charts). The product may add to overall knowledge and may influence a decision-maker's thinking but without any expectation that it will necessarily result in immediate or short-term action or that resources will need to be allocated. Often the product can be seen as an end in itself because it provides comfort or reassurance around a particular issue. As such, products contain limited analysis and they can often be prepared by researchers, intelligence support officers or (for example) work experience intelligence students. The decision-making structures required to exploit this type of product do not need to be well developed.

At the next level of sophistication intelligence analysis will provide some interpretation of the available information. Together with factual descriptive products, these knowledge-type products can be used to raise awareness around a particular problem; for example high risk criminals and crime. Such products may also represent an extensive examination (scan) of a problem and can often be the necessary first stage in the creation of a more action-orientated product. In general such products will be based on known and/or existing data and will look back at crime, issues or problems that have already occurred and highlight short-term risk areas. Most decision-makers are comfortable with these tactical types of product as they can often be useful in justifying or explaining the allocation of resources.

Action-oriented intelligence and analytical products anticipate opinions, judgments, recommendations, conclusions and (in some cases) forecasts. Such products will always be *forward-looking* and will seek to provide decision-makers with options and advice. By offering opinions and judgments intelligence analysis provides guidance and direction which can be useful in planning immediate action (for detectives for example) and/or short- to medium-term strategies (for crime prevention officers). By offering recommendations and conclusions there is an expectation that the analyst will have identified critical opportunities based on good practice, research material and/or a clear and a detailed understanding of the key issues. Forecasts will often seek to identify active criminals, project trends or patterns so as to add significant value to action plans and strategy development. All these forward-looking approaches are useful in providing multiple options on how best to address a problem or issue, for undertaking long-term planning and for developing intervention strategies. See Chapter 10 in this book for methodologies applicable to futures work.

The decision-making structures required to maximise these directing/ action orientated products will have to be more sophisticated than those required to deal with informing products. In practice this means:

- Decision-makers must have the training, education and knowledge necessary to read and then translate an intelligence product into some kind of operational outcome. This is not straightforward and is made more difficult by the fact that in most places it isn't a skill routinely taught to police officers.

- There must be a well understood decision-making framework capable of receiving intelligence products. This may be through a Tasking & Coordination Group, an Operational Action Meeting or some similar arrangement.

- Management structures must have the ability to choose how to allocate discretionary resources and objectives must be clear. This latter point is critical but often missed in planning a course of action. Without it subsequent results analysis is impossible to carry out. Some link to the organisational business planning process is normally an essential component for success.

- There must be clear and unambiguous accountability when decisions are taken, who owns them, what is expected and how success is to be measured.

- Rigorous follow-up is necessary to check what has been done, what has changed and to confirm whether objectives have been met or expected outcomes achieved.

- Some type of evaluation, learning, assessment or review must take place as a matter of routine so that 'what works' can be repeated. Sometimes, this is difficult with small data sets or individual case studies. The solution is often to link results to a wider body of research which can provide context and understanding.

- Evidence-based knowledge transfer takes place both internally and externally so that good practice becomes embedded widely.

The most sophisticated decision-making structures include all the above elements. In practice, very few police organisations *routinely* appear to make decisions in this sort of rigorous way. More likely, some elements are applied as and when necessary, and often in response to questions around value for money or efficiency. Some units within the organisation may even be recognised as having good processes while others in the same organisation may appear to have few or no systems (what is per-haps more surprising is that many police organisations allow such arrangements to coexist without much pressure for change). Often a formal decision-making process is used for special operations and events, or after a crisis, but not for day-to-day business. The process also appears to be highly dependent on local personalities who know and understand what to do.

The most sophisticated decision-making structures revolve around robust, routinely applied processes and activities. Where these are combined with excellent intelligence products there is an expectation that the combination will have a positive impact on crime control strategies.

Intelligence and analytical products: The key to making an impact with decision-makers

Although the future may look very different in terms of technology (more data available for analysis, better and quicker ways to deliver product, automated decision-support systems and multiple channels of communication), the critical elements required to make an impact are likely to remain unchanged. What underpins everything is the fundamental need for analysts to build good relationships. These are needed, first, to capture data. Without good links to those with information – community officers, investigators, partners, and others – no product can be well informed. Computer systems just don't have all the answers. Secondly, effective relationships are needed to make good recommendations. Failure to exploit the knowledge of those who have probably tried many solutions before and failure to learn lessons will ultimately undermine the credibility of the intelligence and analytical product. Finally, an ability to market the intelligence product requires a skilled approach to relationship building. In police organisations where performance information is often (and mistakenly) a proxy for intelligence and almost everyone has the ability to generate statistical reports automatically, this puts even greater pressure on analysts to add real value. A clear understanding of the necessary separation between performance analysis and crime intelligence work is particularly important in this regard (though recognising that decision-makers often, and rightly, need to consider both).

Ultimately, it is clear that the key to making an impact through intelligence and analytical products in a law enforcement environment depends on three essential elements. First, *the integration of effective thinking* (that is, good analysis) is essential. This requires that products are well informed, clearly written, based on good evidence and drafted with a clear understanding of purpose. Secondly, products must be *tailored to the needs and interests of decision-makers* (analysts have to understand their audience). Analysts must seek out those individuals who have the authority to make decisions, must understand their world and must be willing to move rapidly to address changing requirements. Finally, intelligence analysis and decision-making must be conducted within *a management framework that has the ability, maturity and authority to turn intelligence into action* (that is, sophisticated decision-making structures). It is this last area that is most challenging because it will normally be owned by non-intelligence staff who may have little or no interest in the complexities of the other two critical elements. Without this understanding, however, intelligence and analytical products will always struggle to make a sustained contribution to crime control strategies.

References

Carter, DL, 2004, 'Law Enforcement Intelligence: A guide for State, Local, and Tribal Enforcement Agencies', Office of Community Oriented Policing Services (Washington DC).

Cope, N, 2004, 'Intelligence led policing or policing led intelligence?: Integrating volume crime analysis into policing', *British Journal of Criminology*, vol 44, no 2, 188-203.

De Bono, E, 2004, *How to Have a Beautiful Mind*, McQuaig Group Inc.

Gardner, H, 2004, *Changing Minds: The Art and Science of Changing our Own and Other People's Minds*, Harvard Business School Press.

Lowenthal, M, 2008, 'The Real Intelligence Failure? Spineless Spies', *Washington Post*, 25 May 2008.

Mintzberg, H, 1973, *The Nature of Managerial Work*, Harper and Row.

NCPE, 2005, 'Guidance on the National Intelligence Model', National Centre for Policing Excellence (UK) on behalf of ACPO.

NJSP, 2006, 'Practical Guide to Intelligence-Led Policing', New Jersey State Police.

Pease, K, 2006, 'Tools for Tomorrow: Predictive Analysis and Self Selection Policing' and 'Polishing your Tools: A Review of Products', presentations to the Police Service of Northern Ireland, Police Analyst Conference, Belfast, 17 November 2006.

Ratcliffe, JH, 2008, *Intelligence-Led Policing*, Willan Publishing.

CHAPTER 12

Project management

Patrick F Walsh

This chapter provides the reader with an overview of basic project management theory and how it can be applied to strategic intelligence projects. After a brief discussion of project management theory, the chapter will discuss some of its key elements using a case study. The case study is an ongoing project (Project Nimbus) within the Victoria Police, Australia. The case study highlights some of the lessons about how project management principles can be applied to improve the management of complex intelligence projects that impact upon an entire agency. The chapter concludes with a simple checklist for those thinking about using project management theory in their intelligence practice.

Project management and intelligence

While most readers would agree that intelligence projects need to be planned and managed it can be less clear to those working in the industry as to which projects might benefit from the application of formal project management methodology. Most intelligence practitioners are familiar with planning projects of varying size, from strategic assessments to implementing new intelligence structures or processes. Planning for such projects requires going through similar steps each time: specifying outcomes, scheduling (start and end dates) and considering resourcing issues. So the question is, what can project management add to what many analysts do already?

In the first instance, project management theory offers intelligence practitioners a framework that they can draw from to ensure that their project remains within the overall strategic interests of the organisation. It also provides a number of strategies to match skills to work, track progress, and monitor costs and scope once the project is underway.

The critical importance of project management theory to the business world is well known. Changes in the nature of globalised business over the last two decades have resulted in many companies developing a more strategic approach to meeting client needs in order to remain competitive. In public sector management there is evidence that organisational approaches to providing public goods and services have also resulted in a new way of doing business. Government programs are increasingly under pressure by budgetary constraints and greater calls for accountability in the expenditure of public funds.

For example, in Australia, since the 1980s a new public management culture has arisen in many public agencies resulting in their funding becoming increasingly tied to delivery of specific products and services whose outputs are seen as relevant, measurable and cost-effective (Mitchell and Casey, 2007: 75). Hence many government agencies are now engaged in similar formal project management processes as their private counterparts to track limited resources and measure the impact of their important initiatives.

The impact of the new transnational security agenda, particularly post-11 September 2001 (9/11), has also changed the way intelligence agencies do business. A more fluid threat environment has driven profound change within many of our intelligence agencies and new organisational responses require the application of effective project management principles if agencies are to adapt and remain relevant. Further, since 9/11 and the invasion of Iraq in 2003, a series of reviews have also occurred into the capabilities of intelligence agencies in the United States (US), Australia and the United Kingdom (UK). These very public processes have thrust the business of intelligence (somewhat uncomfortably for its practitioners) into the public and political domain. There is now greater interest in what intelligence does and whether it is worth the investment. In this environment of greater openness and scepticism, community confidence in these agencies will be partly measured by the ability of intelligence managers to adeptly manage their projects – particularly those where a public reform process has called for greater evidence of cost-effectiveness, transparency or operational success.

Historical perspectives

The field of project management theory has become a growth industry since its formal recognition as a management concept in the 1950s and 1960s. However many researchers argue that most large scale projects in history, such as the pyramids, Great Wall of China, the armies of the Roman Empire and more recently the building of the Panama Canal, are evidence that project management has been with us for a lot longer. There are also a number of historical examples of project management in an intelligence context. Lientz (1998) suggested that the detailed project planning by the KGB in the 1960s to install 100 nuclear missiles and over 40,000 scientists into Cuba could well be a good example of project management in intelligence; however, others would argue the initial delay in US intelligence agencies detecting Soviet missiles in Cuba was a good example of intelligence failure!

Either way, the roots of what we now call modern project management only emerged with operations research associated with complex aerospace projects such as the Polaris and Apollo programs. NASA and the US Defence Department developed methods and specialised tools to manage expensive and high profile projects, including articulating standards that they expected their contractors to follow.

These project management methods and tools were then picked up by the private sector, especially in the construction and engineering industries in the 1960s and 1970s. From the 1970s there was also a growing volume of publications on project management theories, methods and standards. By the late 1980s, project management theory had become a mainstream academic research area.

The growth in project management theory building and its application by the private sector has increased steadily. However, project management researcher Larry Richman, states that the trend through the 1990s also saw an increased uptake of project management practices by industries in the non-profit sector. He argues that this sector like their business colleagues came to realise that the size and complexity of many of their activities were in his words, 'unmanageable without adopting formal project management processes and tools' (Richman, 2002: 4).

Project management defined

There are thousands of books on the subject each with their own definition of project management. Very simply project management can be defined as a systematic process of guiding a project from its beginning through its performance to its end using a range of specialised tools. However, many researchers provide a more specific functional definition of project management. For example, Richman (2002) defines it as 'a set of principles, methods, and techniques that people use for effective planning, scheduling, resourcing, decision-making, controlling and replanning'. Other authors define it contextually, whereby an organisation may choose to apply project management methodology (Cleland and Ireland, 2002). A contextual approach goes some way towards defining the distinctiveness of project management theory as opposed to any other planning process. After all, there must be a threshold reached by organisations where they assess on balance that the context of the project lends itself more to the use of formal project management theoretical tools over less structured approaches.

In summary, it is difficult to provide a precise holistic definition of project management as a range of methodologies and tools fit loosely underneath an overarching discipline. Project management can partly be understood by examining its methodologies and associated tools. However, gaining insight into the fundamentals of the project management lifecycle is the best way to define and understand project management theory.

There are differences between theorists both in the number of phases and their naming conventions that make up the project management lifecycle. Yet despite these differences, the theoretical underpinnings of each functional phase remain similar. For the purposes of providing a brief overview of project management theory, I have modified Cleland and Ireland's five phases approach: *conceive, define, start, perform, close.*

Conceive phase

Clearly the project management lifecycle must start with the birth or conception of the project idea. The central question in this phase is what are the business reasons for the project? At its broadest level the **conceive phase** is about defining the problem or opportunity and understanding your client's motives in tasking you to manage it. In the law enforcement intelligence context, there are numerous issues and initiatives that may provide the spark for new projects, large and small. For example, changes in the operating environment such as the increased criminal exploitation of an emerging technology, a new directive from govern-ment, or the desire to integrate intelligence more closely within corporate decision-making processes are all possibilities. This phase and the next (define phase) are similar functionally but a distinction can be made between the two. Activities undertaken in the conceive phase are at the wider strategic level.

The questions that need to be addressed under the define phase are still strategic but the conceive phase focuses on operationalising the client's broad requirements. At the conceive phase the project manager wants to understand the strategic fit of the project; that is, how it fits into the wider business objectives of the organisation. By the time managers get to defining the project, they hopefully know what the client wants resolved and how it fits into the broader strategic requirements of the organisation.

Define phase

With a broad conceptual understanding in place, the **define phase** is next. It uses processes, methodologies and tools to operationalise specific project objectives in terms of time, cost, and scope. It is clear that it may take some time to define the project properly. So getting a clear definition from the client or assisting them in defining the problem remains a key activity of the first two phases of the project management cycle. Time spent doing this in the planning stage is much less than what it may cost to fix the problems after the project is completed. Jonathan Nicholl explores task definition techniques in some depth in Chapter 5 in this book.

In the define phase the principle project management tool used to describe what the project will accomplish and the steps required for its implementation is the project plan. Project managers may give their plans different names across different agencies operating in different contexts. There are also, in project management theory, many approaches to draft-ing a project plan. Again, like most other phases in project management, the general approach taken by the project manager is influenced by the complexity of the project. Clearly someone managing the drafting of a strategic assessment does not require the same level of detail in their plan as a manager developing a project plan for the implementation of a new intelligence function within a law enforcement agency.

Nevertheless regardless of the size, complexity or scope of the project, a plan is an essential building block for a systematic approach to determining purpose, objectives, constraints and assumptions for any project. It articulates and expands on what has been agreed upon as a result of the ongoing dialogue between client and project manager. It is also a vehicle for the manager to identify secondary clients who may be looking for results from the project and want to buy-in at an early stage.

The project plan should also be viewed as a dynamic document to be updated and refined as required, as long as any fundamental changes in the plan are managed through a formally agreed change process. As Richman (2002) suggests, any good system must be flexible enough to operate in the real world, but still rigorous enough to provide sufficient control.

Depending on the size, complexity or scope of the project, the plan may include some or all of the following features:

- purpose of project (including business need the project addresses);
- scope statement;
- scheduling details (time and cost);
- cost-benefit analysis; and
- description of the final product or service the project will create.

The project plan may also include relevant legal attachments including a statement of the authority of the project management to apply resources to project activities, schedules and budgets.

Again, with consideration of our two examples of the strategic assessment and the implementation of a new intelligence function within an agency in mind, the presentation of all activities contained in the project plan is a product of the size, complexity and scope of the project. In the case of developing a plan for the strategic assessment it is likely that an intelligence project manager requires one that breaks down each scheduled activity to only a few relevant tasks. However this lack of detail would not suit his counterpart who needs to build a new intelligence capability.

For example, in our case study, Victoria Police used project plan features detailed in the project management software *Microsoft Project* to track the complexity of many tasks over a lengthy period. The phases included were similar to those articulated here, but project planning also included regular status reporting which recorded regular project information under headings such as; 'planned schedule', 'status narrative', 'milestones', 'major deliverables', 'issues' and 'dependencies' (dependencies refers to how this project related to other projects being implemented).

The most common tool used in project management to show greater project planning detail is the *work breakdown structure*. A work breakdown structure provides a more organised and hierarchical representation of all work to be performed in the project, broken out in sufficient detail to support planning, assignment of roles and responsibilities, and ongoing monitoring and control. The work breakdown structure could be broken down to individual work assignments then divided again to tasks and even sub-tasks. It can then be represented using a range of project management derived scheduling tools. These tools can also be employed by the project manager to illustrate the sequence in which activities will be performed, and track the time and costs associated with their start and completion. Many of these tools are maintained throughout the lifespan of the project as monitoring and control mechanisms to assist in the completion of the project on time.

The scheduling tools in project management range from those most commonly used such as basic organisation (or bubble) charts and network diagrams to more elaborate representations such as Gantt or PERT (Program Evaluation and Review Technique) charts. Gantt charts are bar charts with time graduations along the horizontal axis, and activities along separate lines down the vertical axis, making it easy to see the relation between activities and time (see Figure 12.1). PERT charts track activities and time spans for their completion. PERT charts are a network analysis technique originally developed by project management theorists to estimate project duration for complex longer-term planning such as defence projects with a high degree of uncertainty in individual activity duration estimates (Kerzner, 2001; Cleland and Ireland, 2002). However, the author has not seen them used in law enforcement intelligence projects, whereas Gantt charts are becoming more commonplace.

In recent years, Gantt charts and other project scheduling and cost monitoring activities have now become easier with the development of a range of project management software such as Microsoft Project 2004, @task, Faces and Project Desk. Again much depends on the complexity of the project. Microsoft Project may be more applicable for complex lengthy projects such as the development of a new intelligence capability for an agency. Smaller projects that are shorter in duration, such as intelligence support to a multi-agency investigation or the drafting of a strategic assessment, could be managed using simpler IT tools such as Excel or the various functions of Microsoft Outlook.

In addition to considering resource and budgetary requirements the other critical tool frequently used in the project planning phase is the development of a risk management plan. Risk management planning has been standard practice in private enterprise project planning for decades and more recently has become increasingly part of strategic project planning in the public sector. Natasha Tusikov and Robert Fahlman discuss threat and risk management in detail in Chapter 9 in this book. In

Figure 12.1. Victoria Police Project Nimbus Gantt chart

On the left side of the screen tasks are assigned durations, start and end dates, and on the right managers can monitor progress both as bars and in a percentage indication

#	Duration	Task Name	Start	Finish	%
68	242 days	⊟ Pilot Region 1 & Region 4 Div 2 & 5	Thu 3/17/05	Fri 2/17/06	69%
69	80 hrs	Appointment of SPOC	Thu 3/17/05	Wed 3/30/05	
70	42 days	⊟ Pre-Pilot Evaluation	Thu 3/17/05	Fri 5/13/05	
71	160 hrs	Information Collection Plan	Thu 3/17/05	Wed 4/13/05	
72	160 hrs	Role of the Community Cultural Division Personnel	Thu 3/24/05	Wed 4/20/05	
73	25 days	⊟ Divisional Information to gather from SPOC	Thu 3/31/05	Wed 5/4/05	64%
74	200 hrs	Compstat Data	Thu 3/31/05	Wed 5/4/05	50%
75	200 hrs	Staffing profile	Thu 3/31/05	Wed 5/4/05	80%
76	200 hrs	Sample T&CG Minutes	Thu 3/31/05	Wed 5/4/05	100%
77	200 hrs	Products used at T&CG	Thu 3/31/05	Wed 5/4/05	80%
78	200 hrs	Demographic	Thu 3/31/05	Wed 5/4/05	50%
79	200 hrs	Meeting Schedule and Composition	Thu 3/31/05	Wed 5/4/05	50%
80	200 hrs	ID existing regional initiatives	Thu 3/31/05	Wed 5/4/05	0%
81	200 hrs	Impact of Clarendon & LEDR	Thu 3/31/05	Wed 5/4/05	100%
82	35 days	⊟ Info to Gather from Intelligence Personnel	Mon 3/28/05	Fri 5/13/05	76%
83	200 hrs	Intel Staffing Resources & Issues	Mon 3/28/05	Fri 4/29/05	100%
84	280 hrs	Workload Analysis for intel	Mon 3/28/05	Fri 5/13/05	20%
85	280 hrs	Intel Extraneous duties	Mon 3/28/05	Fri 5/13/05	50%
86	280 hrs	IT available	Mon 3/28/05	Fri 5/13/05	70%
87	280 hrs	Identify Skill gaps of intel personnel	Mon 3/28/05	Fri 5/13/05	20%
88	280 hrs	Line management of intel areas	Mon 3/28/05	Fri 5/13/05	100%
89	280 hrs	Current Intelligence Issues of Concern	Mon 3/28/05	Fri 5/13/05	100%
90	120 hrs	Gap Analysis	Mon 5/9/05	Fri 5/27/05	100%
91	200 hrs	Establish Baseline Measurement	Mon 5/9/05	Fri 6/10/05	
92	360 hrs	Strategic Assessment of Pilot Areas	Mon 3/28/05	Fri 5/27/05	
93	200 hrs	Implementation Plan	Mon 5/9/05	Fri 6/10/05	

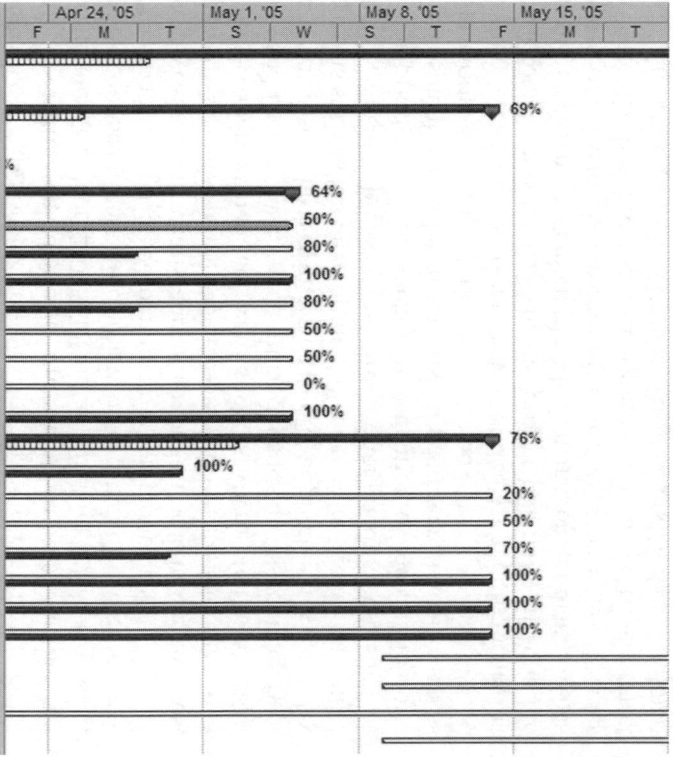

our case study from Victoria Police, the identification, prioritisation and control of risks were very important processes built into the implementation of Project Nimbus.

Start phase

The **start phase** marks the point where all the tasks conceived and designed in the last two phases are actioned according to sequences articulated in the project plan. For some readers, a description of the 'start phase' may seem a bit obvious and unnecessary; given most projects have a start, middle and an end. However, in the lexicon of project management, the start phase is not the actual beginning of the project. As noted earlier, the project 'starts' at the *conceive* phase. In reality, the start phase marks the beginning of the perform phase and the end of all the initial planning and scheduling of the two earlier phases. This phase could also be thought of as the 'review phase' as the project manager should also be checking once more; the scope, sequence of tasks, and other activities such as any contractual and budgetary arrangements prior to the execution of the perform phase.

Perform phase

The fourth phase (**perform phase**) is a logical progression from the define phase. The focus of the perform phase is to action all the activities articulated in the project plan. This phase is also known as the control phase as it relates more to controlling how project objectives are achieved than about merely performing them. Key concepts critical in this phase are time, cost, scope and quality control. All four are interdependent and the project manager must have a hand on the lever of each if the project's intended outcome is to be realised. The links between time and cost control are perhaps the most obvious. As noted earlier, project management theorists have developed a range of scheduling tools to monitor the effects of time and costs of activities throughout the project lifecycle.

These tools are in a sense time control reports that allow project managers to compare actual schedule performance to the baseline recorded in the work breakdown structure. This comparison can determine variances, evaluate possible alternatives for slippage or completion ahead of schedule, and take appropriate actions. For example, in large complex engineering or defence projects with multiple stakeholders and external contractors, project managers need to track carefully the actual start and end time of each activity, assess the impact of any variances and determine what courses of action may be required to bring an activity back on schedule. Again, as discussed earlier, scheduling tools developed in the planning phase such as Gantt charts in combination with the use of project management software become critical in this phase – particularly tools that assist in controlling time schedules.

Time and cost are frequently linked, particularly in large resource intensive projects that require more complex management. As with time monitoring, effective cost controlling relies on the project management team preparing sufficient cost details in the planning phase. The cost control process of the project broadly follows similar procedures to time monitoring. Cost performance data should be collected and actual expenditure compared to the baseline cost plans. Analysis of variances and their impact on project outcomes needs to occur early in order to identify possible alternatives to control any significant potential cost changes. Some of the same tools used to monitor time (such as PERT charts) can also be used in cost control.

In contrast to their private sector counterparts, law enforcement agencies have not historically engaged in formalised cost control mechanisms in managing projects. However, as noted earlier, a growing culture of measurement and the desire for evidence-based evaluations of the impact of publicly funded projects has resulted in greater consideration of tracking costs against effectiveness. More recently, in the UK and to some extent among Australian law enforcement agencies, the implementation of intelligence-led policing models has also influenced the development of evidence-based mechanisms that seek to track performance and cost. In Australian law enforcement agencies these mechanisms have included COMPSTAT processes. For example, in June 2006 Victoria Police implemented its first COMPSTAT process on all its intelligence projects. It was called 'Maximising the Value of Intelligence' and focused on three themes of intelligence (collection, use and gaps). It was designed to evaluate negative and positive factors that impact on intelligence across the agency. The Australian Federal Police carried out a similar process, called the 'Business Activity Analysis', on its strategic intelligence function (Walsh, 2007a).

In addition to time and cost control, there is also a nexus between scope and quality control concepts in project management. The project manager in the perform phase needs to avoid what some theorists refer to as 'scope creep' (Cleland and Ireland, 2002). Scope creep occurs when project performance starts to deviate from planned objectives. Scope creep remains a constant possibility in strategic intelligence projects due to the usually lengthy time frames and number of stakeholders involved. Again in the world of project management there are a number of tools and processes that can be employed to evaluate actual performance to planned objectives, and identify possible alternatives to get things back on course if required (see Cleland and Ireland, 2002, for a discussion of scope creep and the problems of getting back on track).

Close phase

The **close phase** marks the end of the project lifecycle but the beginning of its two final and critical processes: project evaluation and termination. Evaluation is a continual process throughout the project lifecycle. Project plans (work breakdown structures), network diagrams and scheduling tools discussed earlier provide road maps to help team members measure whether they are on course and evaluate their overall effectiveness. These tools should therefore be seen as part of an overall evaluation process. Depending on the project there may be legal requirements for periodic review, inspections and/or evaluations on a number of aspects including; safety standards, security issues, licensing requirements, and other contractual requirements. Feedback from periodic evaluation also has another important function in motivating team members towards achieving project milestones.

In addition to the ongoing evaluation process, a final project audit or post-project evaluation may also be carried out to verify everything was completed as agreed to by the client, customer and project team. This auditing of projects is becoming more frequent in the law enforcement intelligence context. For example, the activities described in our case study will be subject to audit as part of a wider review of the implementation of the Victoria Police Intelligence Model. Part of this evaluation process could include an assessment of lessons learnt, what was done well and what could be improved. The post-project evaluation process may also include a benchmarking process to measure the quality of the product and how it compares with competitors or industry average. However, reflecting back on evaluating intelligence projects we can see that some qualitative measurement remains difficult. Nevertheless, further consideration needs to be given by practitioners and researchers on how we can develop evidence-based evaluation tools that can measure not only the impact of projects but also the intelligence products and processes that make up these projects. In Australia, some progress is being made particularly with a greater willingness by agencies in allowing independent researchers to evaluate such projects (Walsh, 2007b).

Project termination logically flows from the evaluation process if the objectives have been met. However, project termination can also occur anywhere in the ongoing evaluation process if some project constraints have been violated (scheduling, scope or costs) or if management consider that the project no longer strategically fits into the organisation's purposes. In either scenario, team and project leaders need to consider human resource issues that come with the termination of a project.

Leadership and organisation

Merely tracking project scope will not necessarily ensure a quality product. Quality control in the perform phase is also a function of a number of other concepts that loosely fall under two major themes – leadership and organisational design. Both of these themes have a profound effect on project quality.

All the monitoring tools available in project management will amount to nothing unless there is effective project leadership. As highlighted earlier, good project leaders are those who, from the onset, understand the objectives of the project and who they are managing the project for. On the latter issue the project manager needs to identify and manage effectively the involvement of an entire project audience throughout the lifecycle. In project management parlance the audience will be a diverse array of people in addition to the client or customer whose feedback is important, and who must be kept appraised of the project's status.

For example, secondary stakeholders who are not regularly engaged in the day to day running of the project may still be able to exert influence over the project and their needs need to be managed as much as customers or 'project champions'. A project champion is usually someone in a senior position who has influence within the organisation and can rally support for the project. The best outcome is achieved when the project champion is *not* also the project manager. Successful project leadership involves understanding the 'what's in it for me' factor for each stakeholder and employing effective communication strategies to engage each member of the project audience.

The other critical side to successful project leadership is being an effective leader to the people on the project team. The leader brings their own approach to project team management based on their experience, skills and unique personality. It is clear that a certain level of drive, passion, perhaps even a certain obsessive quality (or what Paul Gaddis referred to in his classic 1959 article on the project manager as 'reasonable projectitis'), is needed by the leader to generate the momentum in the team for success.

Many project management theorists have made a sub-discipline out of studying the effects of different leadership styles on project outcomes (Lewis, 2003). While there undoubtedly are certain elements of leadership style which will encourage teams to high performance, taxonomic rigidity in their application should be avoided. In the end, an effective leader needs to adopt a flexible style that is determined by the task at hand rather than a pre-ordained style.

Quality project leadership also hinges on the project manager's ability to understand the interaction of a number of organisational and behavioural variables which can impact on the project's success. The behavioural variables relate to things like creating a participative and professional working environment, encouraging peak performance, promoting effective team communication and minimising dysfunctional conflict. For the intelligence officer responsible for managing a project these skills are critical particularly in the policing context where organisational cultural understanding is sometimes not optimal across intelligence, investigative and other functions.

There are also a number of organisational variables of a structural nature which the project leader needs to be aware of and manage effectively if project teams are to deliver on activities as planned. Unfortunately some of these variables may not be ideal for harnessing efficiently all the resources required to do the job. The project leader needs to position themselves to maximise the positive and minimise the negative structural constraints on project performance.

In project management theory, there are the two extremes in organisational structure. At one end, organisations are structured for projects purely along functional lines; at the other management is based around a pure project perspective. The structure adopted may be dependent on a number of factors external to the project's lifecycle including, product type, skill base, organisational size and cultural predisposition. These factors may reflect more closely managements' broader interests but they can all have a significant impact on the project leader's ability to command and control teams to perform project related tasks.

The ideal organisation structure for the project manager to operate in is a combination of both organisational structures. A hybrid of both or a matrix structure should give the project leader the authority to deploy the right skills and resources at the appropriate time in the project plan. The matrix design has a number of advantages. First, it allows the project leader to have the sole authority to oversee the project and utilise resources as required. Second, it also allows the unique skills of team members to be employed under their functional line of management for other non-project work. Under this structure, project management involvement from functional areas ensures expert advice is taken into consideration by the project leader on not only what has to be done but how the task should be done (Kimmons and Loweree, 1989).

These concepts will now be demonstrated with a concrete example using a case study from Victoria Police in Australia.

Case study: Victoria Police Project Nimbus

Project conception (conceive phase)

The Victoria Police Project Nimbus[1] is a complex set of programs aimed at implementing the agency's new intelligence model, the Victoria Police Intelligence Model (VPIM). Due to space limitations, we will be restricting our discussion to the delivery of one of its key programs, the pilot implementation of a strategic intelligence capability for Victoria Police. However, the reader should keep in mind that the focus of Project Nimbus is wider than the implementation of just the new strategic intelligence capabilities described here. Other initiatives including new governance structures and information management systems are also linked to the project's objectives. Nimbus was itself the result of an

---

1   The author wishes to thank Victoria Police for granting permission to use Project Nimbus as the case study for the chapter. I would also like to thank Inspector Gillian Wilson for her assistance with the case study.

earlier project, when in September 2002; an Intelligence Review Project recommended to the executive that the agency's intelligence function needed to be more proactive so that it could meet new and evolving business requirements. The report suggested that there was also room for improvement in intelligence service delivery at the operational and tactical level in conventional policing areas such as volume crime issues (Walsh, 2005).

In addition to the 2002 review, other important corporate drivers such as the introduction of Local Priority Policing – a new initiative to focus on the unique service needs of particular communities, and the Chief Commissioner's *Five Year Strategic Plan (2003-2008) The Way Ahead* (Victoria Police, 2003) were important catalysts driving organisation reform of intelligence and the creation of Project Nimbus.

The Strategic Plan emphasises four key value areas. The first of these is *intelligent policing* which is to be achieved, among other things, by the 'introduction of integrated information systems and enhancing early intervention and proactive capacity' (Victoria Police, 2003: 5). Hence the business case for Chief Commissioner Christine Nixon's establishment of Project Nimbus was to implement a new intelligence model, one that could help the agency better identify emerging problems and one that could better support proactive decision-making.

In February 2005, a separate command for Project Nimbus was established within Victoria Police and a team of five people were given responsibility to manage all aspects of this project, including the pilot implementation aspects of a strategic intelligence capability, the focus of discussion here.

Project definition (define phase)

As noted in the conceive phase, a key expected and defined outcome of this project by the executive was the full implementation of a new intelligence system in order to progress the initiatives in the agency's Strategic Plan *The Way Ahead*. The implementation of the strategic intelligence aspects of Project Nimbus was seen by the executive as particularly important to the successful implementation of all other aspects of the VPIM. The strategic aspects of Project Nimbus included two broad objectives. First, an ability to produce district, regional and, State-wide strategic assessments. Second, to build a strategic tasking and coordination function at all levels of the agency to integrate the outcomes of these assessments into pro-active decision-making, particularly in setting policing, intelligence and enforcement priorities for Victoria Police.

Establishing the strategic intelligence capability objectives of Project Nimbus relied on the development of a project plan which could identify a number of key priority tasks falling out of the above two critical objectives. The project plan for the strategic intelligence aspect of Project Nimbus was drafted in early 2005, and the Nimbus team used mind-mapping software to identify and map all relevant tasks for the pilot project plan. The many tasks to building a strategic intelligence capability could be summarised briefly as:

- the development of strategic tasking and coordination groups at all levels across the agency (local, regional and State-wide);
- the development of a strategic intelligence education program to train analysts in developing assessments; and
- the development of processes and procedures to integrate strategic assessment outcomes into organisational planning.

In this early phase of project definition, the Project Nimbus team opted for a pilot implementation of the above strategic intelligence tasks involving two regions of Victoria Police rather than an organisation-wide launch. The rationale for this approach was simple. Much of what was to be achieved related to socialising staff into a new way of 'doing intelligence' according to the VPIM standards. This socialisation process involved implementing several initiatives that would shift mind-sets and encourage intelligence staff and managers to use intelligence proactively rather than reactively. For instance, there were shifts to be made in getting middle-level managers to start linking strategic intelligence products into setting their prevention, intelligence and enforcement strategies. In addition to a number of challenging organisational cultural issues, the pilot project also needed to develop strategic intelligence expertise where it hadn't previously existed. All of these issues were challenging enough for the pilot regions so the project team felt it was important to get them right in these regions first before attempting to launch such profound change agency-wide.

A snapshot of the kind of detail provided in the project plan for the pilot implementation can be seen in Figure 12.1. Here the Gantt chart screen shows the level of tasking detail for some of the education aspects of the pilot project. The education tasks involved a number of internal and external stakeholders and their roles will be discussed in the perform phase. Project planning was also managed through other formal mechanisms such as the use of project status reports which allowed Nimbus staff to track progress through providing short updates in narrative form in addition to using visual aids available in Gantt charts. These reports allowed the Commander of Project Nimbus to track the detail of planned schedules, tasks and view milestones not normally represented by Gantt charts. Finally, determining budgetary allocation for all aspects of the Nimbus 'roll-out' was key to activities in this planning phase.

Project commencement (start phase)

Project Nimbus commenced with a final review of planned milestones, budget and stakeholder analysis, both internal and external. This was to ensure deliverables were in the correct order of priority prior to their implementation.

Project performance (perform phase)

The pilot implementation of the new VPIM including its strategic intelligence capability took place in two regions (regions 1 and part of region 4) from July 2005 to February 2006. The key objective of the trial period can best be understood by an entry made in the project *status report* which in summary suggested the pilot aimed to set the minimum standards for intelligence practice (Victoria Police, 2008). In practice, setting minimum standards meant that the pilot will assess the role intelligence practitioners were performing and focus their efforts onto developing intelligence products (including strategic) that were prescribed to the standard set in the new VPIM requirements. Other important objectives of the pilot were to link better intelligence products into improved tasking and coordination of intelligence processes, and to evaluate pre- and post-pilot improvements in these areas.

The implementation of various tasks in the pilot was managed by the Project Nimbus staff but progress was also facilitated by 'project champions' elsewhere in the organisation. For example, at the highest level project implementation was supported by a corporate steering committee and on the ground Project Nimbus staff introduced specific points of contact in each area of the pilot to garner support for organisational change.

While the pilot on the whole progressed well – particularly at the tactical intelligence level – much of what was being implemented at the strategic level was still new and the Nimbus team identified early that existing project communication and consultative mechanisms needed to be enhanced to encourage greater understanding and 'buy-in' from Victoria Police members. An improved communication strategy was identified and greater focus was placed on getting out to staff via a range of media, project achievements and information demonstrating a clear direction for future steps. Part of this communication strategy included workshops to engage middle management and even a DVD was released by the team to educate staff on the VPIM, including its strategic intelligence objectives.

Project completion (close phase)

The pilot implementation of the VPIM and its strategic intelligence capability was completed by February 2006. As expected, the ongoing monitoring and evaluation process throughout the project lifecycle had already highlighted what tasks had been achieved as well as those that had not or required modification. This regular review process throughout each stage of Project Nimbus has been a key strength of the project. However, after the conclusion of the pilot the Nimbus team commissioned a formal evaluation that identified strengths and weaknesses in the pilot. The view was that 'lessons learnt' were important to incorporate prior to the agency-wide launch of the project. An evaluation report was submitted to the executive in June 2006 indicating that the objectives of the pilot phase of Project Nimbus had been delivered largely as planned, but it also identified areas for improvement.

In particular, the quality of the strategic assessments produced and the strategic training of staff were areas tagged for improvement. As a result of the pilot evaluation process, Victoria Police contracted Charles Sturt University in Australia to deliver fully accredited strategic intelligence training to all of its analysts across the agency in preparation for the State-wide implementation of Project Nimbus in late 2006. The engagement of an external education provider added another layer of complexity to managing a new strategic intelligence capability under the auspices of Project Nimbus. Under the education priorities identified in Project Nimbus, close to 100 analysts have now been given training in strategic intelligence.

While the pilot phase of Project Nimbus was completed in 2006, this project continues to monitor progress in the area of strategic intelligence assessments and education. As noted earlier, the objectives of Project Nimbus were never just about building a strategic intelligence capability within Victoria Police. Nimbus is also about the effective use of intelligence more broadly across the agency. Many of its other critical objectives, including; building better accountability for the use of the VPIM, improved professional development of intelligence practitioners and achievement of key objectives in its strategic plan, are still in progress. However, much of its activities are now more focused on auditing and compliance in the areas just discussed.

Conclusion

In law enforcement and in the national security environment, a project management approach places at an intelligence agency's disposal, a useful set of tools that aid development of a range of intelligence projects. However, the use of project management theory in an intelligence setting will always require a flexible application of these perspectives. The project lifecycle and its plan will need to be tailored to the unique needs of the intelligence user or client rather than merely adopting a generic business or commercial approach. For example, intelligence project managers who frequently rely on in-house resources may not need to factor in extensive cash flow analysis or budgetary planning and there may be less emphasis on legal, procurement, inspection or other technical activities seen in the private sector.

In addition while some of the scheduling and risk management tools discussed above can be used to better manage intelligence projects, project management is more than developing and maintaining Gantt charts. Over-planning or the obsessive and inappropriate application of elaborate scheduling tools can just as easily lead to project failure. Effective project management in the intelligence setting is just as much a product of strong leadership with a clear sense of what you want to achieve.

For most, project management theory does not ignite flames of intellectual passion. However, the Nimbus case study underscores that some projects intelligence practitioners are confronted with will be complex. In these cases, success will also depend on applying sound project management principles, but the 'excitement' will come from knowing that through these principles we can change profoundly the strategic directions of the organisations we work in for the benefit of our communities.

Tips for better intelligence project management

- Be clear on why you are managing the project and who it is for.
- Keep stakeholders informed throughout the project lifecycle.
- Identify or cultivate project champions and supporters.
- Spend most of your time getting the conceive and define phases right.
- Don't be afraid to change the project's scope during planning.
- Use a simple project lifecycle template as the basis for your plan.
- Break your plan down into tasks and sub-tasks as required.
- Consider whether your project requires a cost-benefit or risk management plan.
- Determine control mechanisms for team performance, scheduling activities and costs.
- Consider using graphical representations and commercial software to assist in controlling project variables (though keep in mind these are merely tools and you will need to manage the project!).
- Assess communication strategies.
- Engage team members to either be committed to or own project outcomes.
- Implement periodic project evaluations and audits to monitor progress.
- Project management is estimative, not factual, and so it alone cannot guarantee project success.

References

Cleland, DI, and Ireland, LR, 2002, *Project Management: Strategic Design and Implementation*, McGraw Hill.

Gaddis, PO, 1959, 'The Project Manager', in 'Managing Projects and Programs', *Harvard Business Review*, 1989.

Kerzner, H, 2001, *Project Management: A Systems Approach to Planning, Scheduling and Controlling*, John Wiley & Sons.

Kimmons, R, and Loweree, J, 1989, *Project Management: A Reference for Professionals*, Dekker.

Lewis, JP, 2003, *Project Leadership*, McGraw Hill.

Lientz, BP, 1998, *Project Management in the Twenty-First Century*, Academic Press.

Mitchell, M, and Casey, J, 2007, *Police Leadership and Management*, Federation Press.

Richman, L, 2002, *Project Management Step by Step*, American Management Association.

Victoria Police, 2003, *The Way Ahead: Strategic Plan* (2003-2008), Victoria Police.

Victoria Police, 2008 (January), *Project Status Report*, Victoria Police.

Walsh, P, 2005, 'Intelligence-led policing: evolving Australian perspectives', paper presented at the International Forum on Intelligence-Led Policing, Hangzhou, China, June 2005.

Walsh, P, 2007a, Managing Intelligence: Innovation and Implications for Management', in Mitchell, M and Casey, J (eds), *Police Leadership and Management*, Federation Press.

Walsh, P, 2007b, 'Knowledge from evaluating intelligence', The Journal of the Australian Institute of Professional Intelligence Officers, Vol. 15, no 3, pp 31-48.

CHAPTER 13

Collaborative intelligence production

Ray Guidetti

Introduction

Interpreting the range of threats facing society often requires capabilities beyond those demonstrated by any single law enforcement organisation. A more holistic view of the criminal environment requires an integration and application of analytical capabilities best represented by an inter-agency collaborative intelligence effort. Unfortunately, the meritorious nature of policing invariably fuels a culture of pluralism among organisations, creating a significant challenge for intelligence managers to achieve unity of effort among analysts. Despite competing interests, diverse cultures, and dissimilar priorities intelligence managers can defeat this autonomy and in doing so cultivate, sustain, and reinforce interagency collaboration. The end result is a more inclusive and complete intelligence product.

This chapter proposes that by focusing on six key activities intelligence managers can establish and preserve an integrated intelligence enterprise capable of generating strategic intelligence products, the six activities being:

- clarify mission, roles, and responsibilities;
- communicate priorities through a defined governance process;
- create a culture of collaboration;
- construct a platform for knowledge sharing;
- coordinate collection, analytical, and production capabilities; and
- create performance assessments that focus on jointness.

Why interagency teams?

Interagency collaboration among law enforcement intelligence partners is a thorny venture rife with challenges. Parochialism, unwillingness to share information, and difficult egos all combine to confound intelligence managers who dare engage this noble cause. Moreover, the adherence to the traditional mindset that perpetuates the notion of information as a source of power that ought not to be shared further adds to the complexity of achieving collaboration. With so many hurdles for intelligence managers to tackle in building interagency teams, why bother? The answer lies in two main reasons. First, today's law enforcement threat environment can often require capabilities and access beyond those of any single organisation. Second, interagency teams offer increased opportunities for knowledge exchange and growth because of their ability to draw on others' experiences and expertise.

The 9/11 Commission Report (2004) documented that stovepipes present within the United States (US) Intelligence Community hampered information sharing and critical analysis required to provide intelligence and warning related to the September 11, 2001 attacks on US soil. Al Qaeda's ability to carry out its asymmetric strategy took advantage of these silos, silos that were considered, pre-9/11, intrinsic to US intelligence agencies. Bogdanos noted that 'it was apparent that this new threat required [from the intelligence community] a breadth of vision, speed of action, and management of resources that could be accomplished only through synchronising all the elements of national power to achieve integrated operations' (Bogdanos, 2005: 10). While national intelligence agencies are slowly coming to understand that asymmetric threats of terrorism, radicalisation, and crime are best addressed through integrated operations, domestic police intelligence arrangements may still be struggling with implementing this concept.

The situation is not improved by the daily pressures of the immediate situation that often prevent agencies finding the breathing space to develop interagency relationships. At any given time, domestic law enforcement agencies the world over face a range of threats presented by terrorists, violent criminals, Internet predators, burglars, and even weather. These threats often run concurrent creating an interesting quandary for intelligence managers charged with interpreting their local environments. As one senior police officer wistfully described the situation; 'the constant need to exercise for the possibility of multi-event crises is often preempted by their occurrence' (Fuentes, 2008).

Strategically assessing a jurisdiction's threat or producing comprehensive assessments, which take into account varied perspectives, may require skills, knowledge, and talents outside of those a single police organisation can usually resource. For example, access to data sets needed to craft intelligence products is often specific to an analyst's assignment. In the US, each of the primary federal law enforcement investigative agencies (Federal Bureau of Investigation, Coast Guard, Drug Enforcement Administration, Alcohol Tobacco Firearms and Explosives, and Immigration and Customs Enforcement Administration) maintain their own databases containing information specific to the crimes they are charged with investigating. These independent databases present challenges for analysts whose work requires access to diverse data sets. The necessity for interagency analytical teams becomes apparent at this point. Careful development of relationships can broaden the range of data sets intelligence producers can draw on when interpreting a dynamic and diverse criminal environment, but these relationships have to be nurtured and encouraged.

Positive byproducts of successful interagency intelligence teams are the increased opportunities for knowledge exchange and development that have a lasting synergistic effect on enhancing analytical support to a broad range of clients and partners. In other words, as a result of agencies pooling their analytical resources the results become exponential. There are more tools in the analyst's arsenal (data, information, and knowledge) to draw from, while the stakeholder and constituent base amplify. This is significant for intelligence entities that are usually understaffed to support often wide-ranging missions. Analysts with diverse backgrounds bring with them different tools that can be shared and developed in the right professional environment.

The ever-present challenges the criminal environment presents clearly necessitates the need for integrated intelligence production teams; however, developing and sustaining such teams requires effort, care and attention. What follows are six key areas that serve as recommendations for intelligence managers seeking to build this capacity.

Clarify mission, roles, and responsibilities

Unity of effort begins with unity of purpose. For interagency teams this purpose must be clearly expressed within a mission statement. It allows for divergent team members from different agencies to anchor their efforts to a common purpose while working on disparate projects. An integrated intelligence entity will continuously manage several ongoing projects; some run concomitantly, while others run to longer or shorter time frames. This mix of various deadlines and overlapping projects often results in an increased operational tempo within an intelligence entity and is enough to unhinge joint efforts where analysts work on their individual projects. The mission statement, by aligning analytical efforts to a common purpose, distinguishes the collective operational aims from other analytical ventures. This is especially important when partners who make up the interagency team come from neighbouring analytical entities. Without a clear understanding of participants' roles and responsibilities confusion or dissonance will likely result as the home base analytical unit will begin to exert increased influence over intelligence projects they may see as their own.

While the mission statement identifies the scope of operations and provides a sense of direction to the interagency team, a vision statement answers questions related to expectations, aspirations, and performance. Vision statements unite team members towards a common purpose and promote the goal of mission accomplishment instead of autonomous ownership of a particular project or initiative.

Once the mission is established, intelligence managers can then identify the essentials needed to carry out its operation. Sometimes referred to as a Mission Essential Task List (METL), mission requirements identify those tasks critical for mission accomplishment. Constructing a METL is a potent planning process that can offer intelligence managers a strategic way of thinking about long-term initiatives and associated capabilities. Similar to a mission statement, the METL provides analysts with a strategic document to guide their efforts while working on intelligence products. It is important to note that essentials listed in a METL can be broken out further into individual objectives that personnel need to carry out in order to satisfy the essential.

Regardless if an intelligence unit is an autonomous entity or an interagency team, intelligence production is dependent upon a defined management structure which guides analysis and production, or as Quarmby (this volume) puts it, an identifiable decision-making system. In the zeal to hire analysts to produce intelligence products, law enforcement organisations are often mistaken in their belief that analysts alone will create a robust intelligence production capacity. Like any other industrious enterprise, intelligence production requires management. Interagency teams require greater management attention in order to keep them operating at an optimum level.

The Memorandum of Understanding (MOU) has become the standard tool for organisations to communicate and recognise collaborative partnerships. MOUs identify the formal relationships and established guidelines needed for collaborating agencies to achieve their common goals. MOUs also outline the level of support and commitment that participating agencies will provide to an interagency initiative. The MOU facilitates the building of stronger working relationships between interagency partners because it formalises the relationship.

While unity of effort may begin with unity of purpose, it can only be attained when individual analysts understand what is expected of them from their managers. Reliance on mission and vision statements, Joint METLs, and MOUs alone are not enough. Intelligence managers must drill expectations down to the individual level in an effort towards gaining greater understanding of mission, roles, and responsibilities. When an analyst recognises what exactly is expected, it is far easier for a manager to gain commitment and ownership. This in turn creates tremendous benefits towards the success of the interagency team.

Communicate priorities through a defined governance process

In general, law enforcement organizations, which tend to support performance cultures, indirectly reward information hoarding over information sharing thereby making the presence of a collaborative environment a difficult if not rare occurrence. Given that multiple stakeholders have committed their resources to the interagency analytical operation, intelligence managers should expect that these entities seek to exercise some level of influence over the mission, roles, and responsibilities. By introducing and applying a defined governance process, consisting of oversight procedures that maximise value creation, ensure accountability, and provide a level of transparency, stakeholders can effectively delineate policies and procedures for collaborative analytical operations to follow. Prescribing protocols from this macro perspective can increase the relationship among stakeholders around a defined analytical mission while at the same time allowing these key figures the opportunity to have some sway over day-to-day expectations of analytical practices.

Key stakeholders can offer a strategic decision-making framework in which daily analytical operations can align. When governance committees establish standing information needs, analysts can:

- request, collect and exchange information against them;
- prioritise their importance; and
- produce finished intelligence products in line with them.

These information needs represent intelligence gaps that a governance committee can institute after coming to consensus over their strategic importance for the analytical enterprise to address.

Performance measurement regarding analytical enterprises is all about customer satisfaction. Yet, the nature of most interagency analytical enterprises lends themselves towards servicing diverse constituent groups. This can be challenging and problematic when attempting to evaluate customer approval ratings of an analytical unit. Governance committees, because of their own diverse make up, can provide an alternative, yet fastidious, evaluative body over intelligence products and services. As stakeholders in the enterprise, their willingness to assess customer satisfaction can be exacting, while at the same time encouraging for individual analysts.

Governance bodies are a powerful and practical way for collaborative analytical enterprises to see the world through their constituents' eyes. In essence, these bodies can synthesise diverse views into a single message that translates into command guidance over operations. Their leadership contributes positively towards aligning the interagency intelligence unit around a unified, collaborative and value-added purpose that is right for consumers.

Create a culture of collaboration

In general, government organisations continue to reward information hoarding over information sharing, making the presence of a collaborative culture a rare occurrence. Since the success of interagency teams rely heavily on collaboration, intelligence managers ought to be mindful of the dangers of autonomous behaviour to the team while introducing actions to facilitate collaboration. One technique to foster collaboration is to focus team efforts on a common goal. This technique works to align efforts while serving to motivate participating members. For instance, analysts from different backgrounds and skill levels who come together to work on a joint project will each bring with them their own perceptions and ideas of how a project should progress and what the project's end state will resemble. Left unchecked these independent measures will often result in discord when a project comes due and analysts disagree on the finished product – their tensions heightened because of the time spent on the project. Trying to reconcile differences late in the project's life will frequently result in shattered relationships again owing to the time spent by analysts 'travelling down the wrong path' and being directed to make corrections.

Joint projects which start off focused on a common goal have a greater probability of achieving collaboration. Reaching consensus for a common goal at the beginning of a project's life may in fact be convoluted because of independent perspectives; however, egos seem to be less fragile during brainstorming phases as opposed to when it is time to review final content. Time spent on developing a common goal, aims, and objectives not only forces the collaboration process itself, but is well worth the price in time. This is why Chapter 5 in this book emphasises not only the definition of the task, but also the format of the final product. Put another way, to help lessen the effects of a final reviewer's red pen, 'the more time spent sweating at the beginning of the project, the less time spent bleeding at the end'.

Although it should be obvious that establishing trust among team members is central to creating a culture of collaboration, intelligence managers must work diligently to cultivate and nurture this phenomenon. Since personal interactions in casual settings are beneficial towards developing trusted relationships, there is a lot to be said for intelligence managers encouraging team members to share their coffee breaks, eat lunch together, and participate in outside activities that encourage team-building. These dealings provide team members with a look at the 'human side' of their peers and assist with balancing inter-agency rivalries. Of course, intelligence managers can never control malcontents who may use this time to poison relationships or to undermine the interagency mission, but experience suggests that the overall net gain is worth the investment.

Another useful technique for facilitating collaboration is for intelligence managers to host brief morning meetings to kick off the day with their teams. The meetings are often referred to as huddles or scrums to connote the sports analogy of short team meetings to discuss operational objectives. These short meetings usually conducted with task force participants standing up and providing a synopsis of their projects encourage open communication among interagency participants. Even with large groups, these meetings can be shepherded along to last usually no more than 15 minutes. Huddle participants summarise three core areas:

1) what they have found of value they think others should know;
2) what they are working on and the stage they find themselves; and
3) what they need from someone else.

These face-to-face meetings not only initiate team activities, but promote transparency among interagency teammates. Everyone has the opportunity to know what their peers are working on, and what they can do to lend a hand.

Intelligence managers can ensure that workflows are done in concert by directing tasking and coordination processes to support collaborative efforts. A daily tasking and coordination meeting ensures that front line supervisors who may manage dissimilar programs synchronise work processes that may include attention from their personnel. For instance, a supervisor who oversees a violent crime analysis program may need to lend analytical support to assist with carrying out a strategic project related to critical infrastructure. Since analysts who comprise these dissimilar programs come with different skill sets and perspectives it is critical that supervisors coordinate collaboration. At the management level, this technique creates harmony among supervisory personnel and stimulates collaboration, but it does require greater managerial supervision and oversight.

Training is also a valuable technique for boosting and sustaining a culture of collaboration. Training programs in this venue should address workflow processes and the functionality of tools designed to create collaboration. For instance, analysts assigned to an interagency intelligence entity should receive training on brainstorming, strategic planning, and managing diverse projects. In addition, they should receive training on the virtual tools they will use to assist them with collaboration. The next section will discuss some of these tools. Training itself is a great force multiplier towards establishing collaboration among interagency participants. Analysts who attend training sessions together draw upon one another when they deploy the skill sets learned in training.

A final technique to assist with building collaboration within an interagency team is to develop a reward system that recognises collaboration over individual performance. An organisation's culture is dependent upon the reward system it employs, hence the cliché, 'what gets measured, gets done'. Traditionally, the law enforcement discipline maintains a meritorious reward system, which focuses on an individual's ability to perform. While this system may motivate individuals in the workplace it undercuts collaboration efforts and develops information silos among participants. Reward systems that focus analysts' attention towards information sharing, teamwork, and synchronisation can nourish the development of a collaborative culture. This type of change to reward systems away from individual investigative effort is crucial to the development of intelligence-led policing (Ratcliffe, 2008) but undoubtedly presents the one of the most significant challenges to more collaborative strategic thinking.

Construct a platform for knowledge sharing

The intrinsic value that interagency analytical teams afford to greater opportunities for knowledge exchange and development was discussed earlier in the chapter. While this is true, these activities cannot mature unless intelligence managers construct platforms for which analysts can share knowledge. Although conventional methods to exchange knowledge will continue, today's advances in technology allow analysts to convey knowledge to one another both asynchronously and synchronously. In an interagency environment this type of platform not only tears down information silos but can strengthen the collective wisdom of the intelligence entity.

In a conventional manner, analysts can share knowledge through their finished intelligence products, published works, musings, participation in working groups, and of course email exchanges. While this type of communication may satisfy existing needs of analytical entities it certainly does not take advantage of groupware tools that facilitate real time collaboration while sharing knowledge. Although groupware tools include email handling and sharing access to databases and electronic calendars, the groupware tools most effective for interagency analytical intelligence production are those that allow for collective writing and for sharing expertise.

Virtual discussion forums are great ways for analysts to collectively discuss a variety of topics or issues while at the same time construct and convey new knowledge among team members. Forums are essentially bulletin boards; however, resourceful analysts can find multiple uses for them. For instance, analysts can use a virtual forum to post and discuss reading material with the group. This becomes a real bonus when analysts begin to engage a topic resulting in a knowledge exchange. In addition, analysts can use forums to discuss and evaluate writing projects. Although the activity is asynchronous it still provides analysts a valuable environment for posting drafts for review by their peers regardless of where they sit in an interagency analytical entity.

A chat room can be used for real-time discussions among analysts. The chief difference between a discussion and a chat is that the latter has the ability to discuss issues in real-time. These synchronous discussions are a valuable way to gain an understanding about an event or topic being discussed. For instance, analysts can discuss the progress on their projects in real-time among multiple team members. Each would have the ability to participate in the discussion. As an aside from the strategic imperative, for more tactical events chats can be used to keep everyone apprised of a situation. This can be valuable when a crisis event unfolds and analysts are responsible for generating a timely situation report for clients. As analysts receive information they can report it through a chat while those responsible for crafting the situational report can formulate it collectively.

Web logs, commonly called Blogs, enable analysts or groups of analysts to exchange personal thoughts, experiences, and links to other websites for their interagency teammates to review. Essentially, blogs are a running log of events and can be a valuable asset to the collective knowledge base of an intelligence entity. When analysts working on a project choose to post their progress so others can become immediately familiar with the processes and steps required for project completion, the sharing of expertise or knowledge becomes almost instantaneous. Deborah Osborne's Analysts' Corner blog is an example of a publicly accessible blog (<www.analystscorner.blogspot.com>).

A Wiki is similar to a blog, except all analysts can add, modify, edit, and comment on the posted content. This tool enables documents to be authored cooperatively, which is a tremendous tool for interagency analytical teams. An analyst alone can use a Wiki to brainstorm with his peers on a particular subject. Additionally, analysts can use Wikis to peer review or edit documents with others. Intelligence managers can also use Wikis to produce joint intelligence products by directing analysts to participate in Wikis.

Constructing a platform for knowledge sharing can greatly assist establishing and preserving an integrated intelligence enterprise. However, some analysts may perceive this platform as just a new work paradigm and find it difficult to adopt. The point being made is that new fangled virtual tools – although useful to the resourceful analyst – may present challenges to those less inclined to participate in technological advances. Regardless, intelligence managers should explore all available virtual tools that enable the sharing of knowledge and expertise across all interagency participants. At the same time, they should mentor inter-agency personnel in the value of exchanging knowledge for the collective benefit of the intelligence entity. The result can pay dividends in the knowledge growth of all participants.

Coordinate collection, analytical, and production capabilities

The advantage of an interagency intelligence workforce over a single agency entity is the ability for intelligence managers to draw upon a varied breadth of analytical knowledge and experience when producing strategic intelligence products. Yet, for managers to reap these benefits they must act as a relationship manager to overcome the challenges inherent in coordinating the collection, analytical, and production capa-bilities of these assorted assets. One solution for achieving success in this area is for managers to focus on the processes and workflows related to producing intelligence products. By establishing practices that communicate and require group efforts, managers can supervise the relationships in a way that yields joint ventures.

Whether the strategic intelligence product follows requirements driven by the producer (analyst-driven, event-driven, or scheduled) or finds its origin with the client, it should begin with a task definition stage or (as it is termed in the New Jersey State Police) Request for Information (RFI). The RFI's purpose is to gather the necessary information needed to support intelligence production. Chapter 5 in this book addresses the value of task definition in depth. From the interagency standpoint, the RFI can be viewed through a collaborative lens, where the task definition stage is an initial opportunity for a dialog between partner agencies. Supervisors representing interagency partners at this early stage have the opportunity to weigh in on the decision to commission a project or pass. Together, the intelligence production manager and operations officer, based on the input from these supervisors, can come to an agreement on commencing a project by evaluating personnel resources and production requirements against other standing priorities.

Commencing the production process requires drafting an intelligence product proposal. By sharing the expertise represented at the tasking and coordination meeting, intelligence managers can ensure better coordination among interagency collection, analysis, and production efforts. Once the team collaborates on a research question and identifies the project's aims and objectives they can begin to assign personnel resources to the effort. At this time, the intelligence production manager– leveraging the interagency relationships – can marshal the placement of joint resources to the project. Once the proposal is completed and the priority and time to completion are noted, assigned analysts can engage their assignments.

The tasking and coordination group is also responsible for ensuring that intelligence projects not only stay on schedule and meet their strategic objectives, but maintain their collaborative focus. The group achieves this through regular updates and periodic briefings surrounding the progress of each project. If personnel are not sharing information or collaborating with one another, mid-course corrections cannot be made in a timely manner. This process compels supervisors to act as relationship managers to make certain that personnel representing disparate agencies are collaborating towards the common goal represented within their projects.

Once the team of analysts produces their final draft, they are ready to submit their work through a formal report staffing process. The process requires that specialists review the report's content, grammar, permissibility, and formatting. These specialists are made up of personnel who again represent the interagency partners. This process achieves a few critical things. First, it acts as a quality control measure. Second, it ensures that interagency collaboration is responsible for the final review of an intelligence product. Lastly, it provides a sense of ownership to all involved in the production of the strategic intelligence project. These benefits collectively work to increase the multi-agency adoption of the product and help to synchronize efforts with regard to future products. In other words, by working to increase agency buy-in from the various agencies, this reduces the chance that an outside agency will reject the findings from the product and commission its own analysts to redo the analysis and repeat the work to their own liking.

Coordinating collection, analytical, and production capabilities within an interagency intelligence team can be a challenge requiring constant 'care and feeding'. However, by applying the above processes and workflows intelligence managers can ease this effort and ensure collaboration. The processes identified start with the needs of a customer and end with a finished product.

Create performance assessments that focus on jointness

Creating and completing performance assessments that reinforce colla-borative behaviour is a key component towards structuring a unified interagency intelligence entity. Reward systems must serve to underpin and promote information and knowledge sharing among participants. Since values and rewards are central to an organisation's culture and performance intelligence, managers must implement evaluation and performance metrics that acknowledge teamwork and collaboration. Existing programs that emphasise individual performance can under-mine jointness within an interagency intelligence agency.

Responses to the *Goldwater-Nichols Reorganization Act* of 1986 (US) are extreme examples of how reward systems and performance metrics serve to foster and support joint efforts. The Act shifted US operational authority from the individual US military branches to the Joint Chiefs (Johnson and Wirtz, 2004). As a result of *Goldwater-Nichols* there have been substantial inroads towards the way interagency collaborative intelligence efforts are carried out. *Goldwater-Nichols* prevented service parochialism from being a roadblock to collaboration (Hopkins, 2004). Service members cannot advance into high command positions unless they spend time within and endure the challenges inherent in a joint command. Essentially, *Goldwater-Nichols* is an enabler for indoctrinating an interagency collaborative culture.

Yet, law enforcement on the other hand continues its tradition of parochialism and is crying out for a *Goldwater-Nichols* type Act to cut down on the stovepipes that still exist among intelligence. It is therefore critical that intelligence managers instead become the stewards for shepherding jointness among interagency participants by recognising team enterprises over individual specialties. Designing metrics that focus on collaborative ventures, information sharing, and fusion among interagency participants can strengthen the overall interagency operation. For example, individual analysts should be able to demonstrate their ability to devise, perform, and complete strategic intelligence projects *while a part of a team*. For those who fail in this domain, intelligence managers should provide training to increase effectiveness. The lack of a US equivalent to Australia's National Strategic Intelligence Course (Walsh and Ratcliffe, 2005) is a significant roadblock to encouraging greater analytical ability and cooperation in the area of strategic criminal intelligence collaboration.

When existing organisational reward structures that centre on individual performance or a specialised expertise become the standard for evaluation, joint initiatives usually break down because it is then difficult to sustain. This can easily become the case when intelligence managers retrofit new joint initiatives into old performance systems. The recommendation is to establish performance metrics assessments that are unique to the interagency operation they must assess. Failure to do so will make it extremely difficult for analysts to rationalise their contribution towards a joint venture.

When assessing personnel within an interagency intelligence organisation it is important for intelligence managers to understand their lines of authority over individual personnel. There will be some workers who the intelligence manager will only exercise operational control over. Those personnel will receive their administrative control authority from their home agencies. Although some may view performance assessments as an administrative function, it is vital towards carrying out a successful interagency operation that intelligence managers provide feedback to these assessments. It not only affords personnel the opportunity to recognise their strengths and weaknesses within the interagency environment, but it gives the home agency the same opportunity as well.

Conclusion

This chapter has examined the fundamentals of establishing and preserving an integrated intelligence enterprise. By clarifying mission, roles, and responsibilities; communicating priorities through a defined governance process; creating a culture of collaboration; constructing a platform for knowledge sharing; coordinating collection, analytical, and production capabilities; and creating performance assessments that focus on jointness, intelligence managers and analysts can implement sound interagency practices that are capable of producing joint strategic intelligence products.

Quality interagency intelligence efforts come from processes and workflows that facilitate and demand collaboration, information sharing, and teamwork. Intelligence managers and analysts who understand these fundamental principles can put them into action and reap the value of increased knowledge exchange and greater numbers of data and information sets to draw from when producing strategic intelligence products.

Interagency intelligence organisations are all about collaboration and information sharing. While the function of intelligence management is at the centre of these processes, it is the perception and backgrounds of people that will certainly influence the success of the mission. Since the law enforcement discipline has had a long history of not sharing information, major efforts need to be applied to stimulate and sustain collaborative relationships among interagency analysts and intelligence officers.

In recent years, the law enforcement community has made significant strides towards increased interagency collaboration when crafting strategic intelligence products. However, we should realistically acknowledge that the criminal intelligence community is still in dire need of significant political, cultural, policy, and procedural changes needed to formalise interagency collaboration when generating intelligence in the strategic domain. Until then, it will be the intelligence managers and analysts who will be the primary enablers for building interagency collaboration into the intelligence process.

References

9/11 Commission, 2004, 'The 9/11 Commission Report', The National Commission on Terrorist Attacks Upon the United States (Washington DC).

Bogdanos, MF, 2005, 'Joint Interagency Cooperation: The First Step', *Joint Force Quarterly*, no 7, 10.

Fuentes, J, Colonel, New Jersey State Police, 2008, Personal communication, 20 January 2008.

Hopkins, MS, 2004, 'U.S. Army Transforming For New Military Demands', *Military Review*, May–June 2004, p 61, <http://usacac.army.mil/cac/milreview/download/English/MayJun04/bob.pdf>.

Johnson, L, and Wirtz, J, 2004, *Strategic Intelligence: Windows into a Secret World: An Anthology*, Roxbury Publishing Company, p 16.

Ratcliffe, JH, 2008, *Intelligence-Led Policing*, Willan Publishing.

Walsh, P, and Ratcliffe, JH, 2005, 'Strategic criminal intelligence education: A collaborative approach', *Journal of the International Association of Law Enforcement Intelligence Analysts*, vol 16, no 2, 152-166.

CHAPTER 14

A practitioner's perspective of UK strategic intelligence

Steve Christopher and Nina Cope[*]

Introduction

The British police service (like many overseas) retains a multifunctional role (Bowling and Foster, 2002: 987) whose demands outstrip the capacity to deal with them effectively (Morgan and Newburn, 1997: 151). The past decade has witnessed the emergence of intelligence into the mainstream of United Kingdom (UK) public policing to facilitate prioritisation of resources to problems (Maguire and John, 1995; Maguire, 2000; Heaton, 2000; Manning, 2001; Ratcliffe, 2008). Paralleling trends in contemporary society that can be characterised as an increase in a range of data where control and communication of information are critical elements in defining social organisation (Castells, 2000; Poster, 1991; Lash, 2002), processing information is an 'essential and central feature of policing' (Manning, 1992: 352). Indeed the police can be viewed as 'knowledge workers' who manage and apply information to manage risk (Ericson and Haggerty, 1997: 19-30).

The development of different styles of policing interventions, including intelligence-led policing and problem-solving have at their foundation, the application of analysed information to better inform interventions. Attempts to offer a standardised framework for policing have led to increased codification of how policing is delivered and an acknowledgement of strategic intelligence as a key component of both the planning and delivery of policing services.

This chapter examines the emergence of strategic intelligence in policing from a practitioner's perspective. It briefly outlines the definition of strategic intelligence and explores its genesis as a key component of the National Intelligence Model (NIM). The chapter goes on to discuss the potential of strategic intelligence in its application and considers some of the barriers to this potential being realised.

---

[*] Nina Cope would like to thank Adrian James for a helpful discussion that informed the revision of this chapter.

Strategic intelligence and the National Intelligence Model

While the concept of strategic intelligence has a tradition in the military and national security arenas, its advent in modern law enforcement is a contemporary phenomenon. A modern view of strategic intelligence, emanating from the Yale historian Sherman Kent, is knowledge and, more importantly, foreknowledge of the world for the information of policy makers (Kent, 1949). In policing, this forward-looking view is delivered by gathering and cross-referencing a range of information from a variety of sources both open and restricted, taking account of social, economic, political and other trends. Strategic intelligence for policing, aims to understand and propose solutions to issues, essentially developing the service from being demand-driven to more pre-emptive in how it plans and allocates resources. The potential significance of strategic intelligence for prioritising policing in a modern society dominated by the evaluation and management of risk cannot be understated. For McDowell (1998), strategic intelligence in law enforcement 'focuses upon comprehensively describing and assessing a phenomenon to allow the formulation of organisational policies and plans to combat criminal activity'. Conceptually, strategic intelligence differs from other forms of intelligence work in that it deals with topics as opposed to individuals and is more aligned to social science research (Dintino and Martens, 1983).

There are differing views as to the *raison d'etre* for strategic intelligence. Hall (1998) and Wardlaw (1998) contend that strategy is a high-level, agenda setting concept restricted to the executive command which coordinates a concerted top-down approach to tackling serious problems in the long term. However, McDowell (1998) adopts a far more prosaic interpretation, in that strategy is simply the development and realisation of a structured plan to deliver an aim and is equally applicable for local management. His view is that strategic intelligence and analysis allows the nature and constructs of a subject to be understood and is a tool that informs relatively long-term management and decision-making leading to a course of tactical or operational activity. As such, there must be connectivity and reciprocal interplay between the strategic and more tactical processes. The relationship is symbiotic where 'tactical and strategic intelligence analyses are frequently interdependent and interlinked' with strategic analysis providing the framework for tactical requirements while tactical work simultaneously informs and justifies strategic assessments (Innes and Fielding, 2002: 6). As McDowell (1998: 7) describes when explaining the relevance of strategic intelligence for operational officers; 'Strategic intelligence and analysis practice focuses on being able to creatively think one's way through issues at a macro level, yet constantly retain pragmatic linkages to the inevitable tactical and operational impact and outcomes'.

The ascendancy of intelligence-led policing in the UK was ultimately formalised by the design and introduction of the National Intelligence Model (NIM), which proposed a structure and process to enable the systematic integration of strategic intelligence analysis into policing. Supported by the Association of Chief Police Officers (ACPO), Her Majesty's Inspectorate of Constabulary (HMIC) and the Home Office, the NIM was mandated by government as a core business-operating model for police forces in 2005. While catering for tactical aspects of crime reduction, the NIM was intended as a business management model, explicitly informed by intelligence, to set the strategic policing agenda at a local, regional or national level. In essence, the model unequivocally legitimised the concept of strategic intelligence, its requirement, analysis and application (NCIS, 2000).

However, the implementation of the NIM met a number of challenges. The service lacked an 'intelligence culture' (Friedman et al, 1997) as intelligence had not been particularly influential in the police force, especially in a strategic context (Maguire and John, 1995; Hook, 1998; Barton and Evans, 1999; Innes and Fielding, 2002). The standardisation that the NIM sought to achieve, along with the collaboration and sharing of information, were not realised, as forces interpreted the concepts of the model with reference to their existing processes, information technology systems and cultures (Maguire and John, 1995; John and Maguire, 2003). Arguably, it was this accommodation of the NIM that contributed to the lack of synergy between key areas, including strategic intelligence and business planning.

While this chapter will not discuss construction of the NIM (a topic covered in Chapter 4 in this book) or the theory of strategic intelligence, any evaluation of strategic intelligence must be contextualised against the persisting themes that characterise the development of intelligence-led policing. The chapter will address the context of public sector reform that increased the demand for a more strategic approach, and consider the application of strategic intelligence at a local and force level in British policing.

Demand for strategy: Emergence to centrality

The late 1980s heralded a concerted drive from central government in the UK to introduce efficiency measures and heightened financial accountability into the public sector in pursuit of value for money (Walsh, 1995). The police were not exempt from this 'managerialism' and 'new public management' (Home Office, 1984; Home Office, 1993; Clarke and Newman, 1997; McLaughlin and Murji, 2001). Conducted by the Audit Commission, the report titled 'Tackling Crime Effectively' concluded that the police were locked into a vicious circle where the volume of crime was threatening to become overwhelming and advocated the adoption of an intelligence-led approach with an emphasis on targeting the criminal in contrast to the crime. The essential ingredient of the report though was the evocation that the intelligence function should be interwoven throughout *every* aspect of police work (HMIC 1997: 5).

The aspiration represented a paradigm shift from reactive to proactive law enforcement that was conveniently attractive and therefore acceptable to government and the police. The nexus of effective use of resources, efficiency, reduced crime rates and maintaining a status as 'crime fighters' provided an appealing resolution for both parties (Gill, 2000: 79-80).

Prior to the publication of 'Tackling Crime Effectively', the trend towards intelligence-based targeting had already been identified (Dorn et al, 1991) and was an established practice of many force and regional intelligence bureaux. The underpinning rationale to the widespread extension of 'targeting' was based on Home Office research that indicated a small percentage of criminals were responsible for a disproportionate amount of crime and that focusing upon those individuals would lead to greater effectiveness and efficiency in crime control (Maguire, 2000; Heaton, 2000). The notion has a certain simplicity of logic and attraction, notwithstanding a significant degree of symbolic labelling and self-fulfilling prophecy, which belies the complexity of conducting targeted operations against 'known' offenders. As experienced intelligence practitioners will confirm, legitimately accessing often impenetrable, diverse and deviant subcultures is a difficult task.

Nevertheless, after over 150 years in the murky backwaters of policing, the Audit Commission unambiguously thrust intelligence into the spotlight. Until this watershed, intelligence had been marginal and any development was restricted to its own community. Consequently, the police were in no position to deliver upon the transition to a generic intelligence-led policing model, a point made by the Audit Commission. Acknowledging that intelligence suffered from low status and under-resourcing, it nevertheless enthusiastically encouraged forces to embark upon a 'quantum leap' to proactivity. However, it is posited that it was deficiencies in the process of change management, combined with the pre-existing state of 'intelligence maturity', which consequently resulted in diversity of implementation of intelligence processes across the country. As argued by Maguire and John (1995), 'only through a fully integrated, strategically informed approach are forces likely to reach a situation in which proactive work makes more than a marginal contribution to crime control'. The holistic reform required to deliver the full potential of intelligence-led policing did not routinely occur in UK police forces, and there was little acknowledgement of the paradigmatic shift contained in 'Tackling Crime Effectively', and subsequently the NIM. Even in the Police Service of Northern Ireland, one of the more proactive forces, the process took five years (see Ratcliffe, 2008: 103).

In the context of intelligence-led policing, where the ethos is on targeting the criminal, it would be remiss when discussing doctrine not to consider the means of gathering intelligence. The organisation of criminality, and the degree of its cohesiveness, is a vast academic debate that remains ambivalent and unresolved (Dorn et al, 1991; Hobbs, 1994, 1997; Stelfox, 1998; Levi, 1998). Suffice to say that targeted policing ultimately depends upon the capability to infiltrate 'difficult to access' criminal milieux in order to gather information.

The capacity to penetrate inimical environments and subcultures is afforded by covert policing, and the Audit Commission accordingly commended to forces the utilisation of informants and surveillance to facilitate and underpin intelligence-led policing. Yet, this recommendation was not only an operational imperative. It was also ostensibly grounded in 'value for money', thereby reinforcing the synthesis of efficiency and 'crimebusting' that has tenuously emerged in relation to proactive work. However, despite practitioner experience that human sources can serve as an invaluable gateway into criminality, research has shown that the cost-benefit gains claimed for informant management have been exaggerated (Morgan and Newburn, 1997; Dunnighan and Norris, 1999; Innes, 2000) and surveillance is an expensive commodity (Ratcliffe, 2008). Furthermore, from an 'intelligence maturity' perspective, individual forces are at varying states of covert policing development, capability and capacity. More importantly, though, there have been serious ethical dilemmas surrounding all aspects of covert policing (Colvin and Noorlander, 1998; Maguire, 1998; Sheptycki, 2000), especially concerning the use of informants (Dunnighan and Norris, 1996a, 1996b; Norris and Dunnighan, 2000). Internal regulation, compliance with legislation and the establishment of the Office of Surveillance Commissioners has seen a framework introduced and management tightened to address these concerns, because the reality is that there may be no alternative to these techniques in certain cases if the requirement for meaningful intelligence is to be satisfied.

A process for strategic intelligence

The shift to a more proactive approach in UK policing increased the requirement for strategic intelligence in three ways. First, at the most macro level there was a clear recognition that the delivery of policing services could be planned, despite being principally demand based. Effective business planning needed to be supported by information that explained both existing and potential threats that needed to be catered for. The NIM, by espousing a business process that accommodated strategic intelligence created the second impetus. In its simplest terms, the 'strategic' elements of the model were exemplified by the strategic assessment, which fed into a strategic coordinating and tasking meeting where priorities were agreed and were captured in a control strategy that would then set the framework for tactical interventions. While accepting there were limitations to this process (they are discussed later in this chapter), it did serve to introduce the vocabulary of strategic information and decision-making into police forces, reinforcing that intelligence is an iterative business process for policing (Philips et al 1997). Lastly, to support this emerging demand for strategy, an infrastructure developed. Within this infrastructure, the importance of other types of information (including social and evaluative data), and the requirement for different skills to support gathering, assessing and interpreting information in a strategic policing context, meant strategic analysts or social researchers became more common in most forces.

The potential of strategic intelligence was to provide a different kind of input into policing that would develop a broader and longer-term perspective. Developing alongside an agenda that stressed the importance of developing partnerships to tackle the underlying causes of crime and disorder provided strategic intelligence and analysis with even more legitimacy. Furthermore, for police forces to effectively respond to an increasingly centralist target-driven agenda, they needed to confidently know and understand their problems to allow them to generate an effective conversation about the kind of support and resources required from government.

Despite the logic, the impact of strategic intelligence has been variable. The next section focuses on some of the primary challenges involved in embedding the strategic principles into police work.

The challenge of embedding intelligence in police practice

Some of the challenges in embedding strategic intelligence stemmed from broader issues associated with ensuring the necessary change required to support the intelligence-led policing and the NIM – effective leadership, culture, and ensuring the right infrastructure is in place. There is little doubt that in most forces an 'intelligence lacuna' existed, and in a few, still does.

A crucial element for effective change management is executive leadership to champion transition (Schein, 1996; Chan, 1997). As Maguire and John (1995: 54) observed, 'major organisational reforms can be successfully implemented only if there is wholehearted commitment to them from the most senior officers in the force'. As with any policing innovation, certain chief officers invested unconditionally in the NIM while others were less convinced of the concept. This reluctance should be understood in the context of competing strategic priorities and in some cases an inadvertent failure to appreciate the fundamental significance of 'Tackling Crime Effectively' and the shift it required throughout policing structures, not just in particular areas, to ensure success.

Change management also relies on the ability to successfully win the hearts and minds of the workforce, particularly problematic with a police culture where 'its more negative elements act as inhibitors for change' (Bowling and Foster, 2002: 1011-1014). This manifests itself in several ways. Cultural conservatism and cynicism fuels an institutionalised inertia that is remarkably intolerant to reform (Reiner, 2000: 90-93) wherein rank and file officers have a capacity to undermine innovative strategic change by continuing to work, almost impervious at the coal-face, in a traditional, culturally defined, 'comfort zone' (Holdaway, 1983, 1989; Manning, 1997; Chan, 1997). Arguably the cultural elements were more acute in relation to the NIM, as an enduring characteristic of police culture is the retention and cherishing of information by officers who exhibit an unwillingness to share knowledge, thereby suppressing its free flow upon which intelligence-led policing depends (Manning, 1992: 369-372; Manning and Hawkins, 1989: 145; Cope 2004). There is also a tradition for police work to be extremely local in its focus and this geographical myopia militates against the exchange of information within and between police forces and law enforcement agencies. Finally, intelligence work is largely bureaucratic, painstaking, mundane and slow-paced, thereby presenting a negative image to those officers thirsting for action (Reiner, 2000: 89). Consequently, intelligence has not been perceived as an attractive career option among officers.

Change management is dependent upon the existence of an infra-structure to deliver the necessary reform. This infrastructure needs to include those factors that will act as a foundation to support the change itself, as well as its implementation. To effectively drive forward intelligence-led policing requires a workforce with a familiarity and expertise in a professional doctrine, an analytical capability and adequate mechanisms for effective data management, retrieval and presentation. Even though the police are primarily 'knowledge workers', their ability to effectively structure and optimise the use of raw data is questionable (Tremblay and Rochon, 1991: 269-283) and strategic knowledge manage-ment requires holistic coordination. The codification of the Management of Police Information in 2005 has aimed to standardise this process for UK forces. While this is important there is still some way to go to enable integration. As Gaspar (2001) highlighted; 'the history of the use of infor-mation technology for intelligence applications is one of fragmentisation. Individual forces have developed their needs at different speeds with varying views on the type of data required by various groups of officers'.

At present, the information and communication technology available across the country remains diverse, incompatible and not sufficiently sophisticated to cater for an intelligence driven model. The availability of compatible, expandable and user-friendly information and communica-tion technology is a non-negotiable essential to underpin the develop-ment of intelligence driven policing.

In relation to implementation, effective channels of communication for promulgating understanding and expectations to staff to gain their commitment and compliance are essential. Experience shows, unfor-tunately, that the service has frequently lacked adequate mechanisms with which to impart information, has failed to provide clarity and precision of detail and has diluted critical messages by inundating staff with less important material. With the NIM, a dedicated implementation team (which developed into a resource to enhance policing doctrine) aimed to address this issue by providing advice, coherence and intervention to forces. Given the limited development of the model in its early stages, the lack of formal guidance, and the scale of the challenge the team faced in persuading forces to fundamentally reshape their commands around a relatively unproven concept, it is not surprising that the result was a predictable differentiation in interpretation, implementation and outcomes (Maguire and John, 2003; Cope, 2008). The variation in progress and lack of standardisation across the country led to a thematic inspection by HMIC, 'Policing with Intelligence' (HMIC, 1997). While observing a general trend towards intelligence-led policing and highlighting *ad hoc* examples of good practice, the report reaffirmed that key aspects of the change management process had to be resolved if intelligence was to assume a central role in directing policing.

Finally, it is important that any change management process has mechanisms in place to evaluate and measure the impact of the recommended reforms. However, 'Tackling Crime Effectively' did not document the mechanisms for monitoring and evaluating the impact of the transition to intelligence-led policing so as to demonstrate the benefits of the paradigm shift. Shortcomings in these critical elements of change management are reflected in the early conclusions of Maguire and John (1995: 54-55) on the transition to intelligence-led policing and have been significantly impactive on effectively realising the model over time (HMIC, 1997; Ratcliffe, 2000; Maguire, 2000; Heaton, 2000; Maguire and John, 2003). The variability to which these vital change management challenges have been addressed characterises the extent to which the model has been adopted and it is hardly surprising that there has been a diversity of development across the country.

What does this mean for strategic intelligence?

The previous section articulated the challenges associated with shifting policing away from responding to demand to use information proactively to inform tactical interventions. These numerous and imposing challenges indicate the inhospitable context strategic in which intelligence has found itself. However, while accepting that some conditions required for intelligence and change management to flourish were absent or hostile, strategic intelligence can also restrict itself. A key issue is the label 'strategic intelligence' that complicates matters at the point of gathering information. Categorising information in this way does not necessarily serve to organise data, but potentially silos information for its perceived and anticipated outcome. Labels such as strategic, tactical, community, or covert intelligence imply that these are fundamentally different kinds of information, which will produce different products. The reality is that there will be duplication between each category, and each area will enhance and develop another. Intelligence is a highly reusable resource, which is better labelled when it is applied to the area where the intention is to add value or inform a particular decision, rather than when it is gathered.

The difficulties of defining strategic intelligence, the development of strategic products, and the methodology to support this, offers a further challenge for the practitioner. In relation to the NIM, guidance for the analysis process became overly prescriptive and too focused on the inputs to the process, rather than facilitating the creative process of interpreting information. Indeed a major dilemma surrounding strategic intelligence is the process and the extent to which it should be top-down, bottom-up or an integration of both. The methodology for compiling the UK Threat Assessment (SOCA, 2006) is very much top-down with police forces satisfying a strategic intelligence requirement, precluding the identification of topics in the reverse direction. It is the process of developing the appropriate interpretation of these high level issues and the extent to which they impact, influence or should be prioritised at the local level, which remains difficult. The same problems exist when considering the extent to which local priorities can be aggregated to inform or construct a national agenda, and is best exemplified by the development of the UK National Strategic Assessment. While the NIM aimed to allow policing organisations at each level to strategically deter-mine their priorities having regard to other strategic assessments, developing the necessary flow of information has proved difficult to achieve (Maguire and John, 2003).

Analysis is the function that interprets, facilitates understanding and attributes significance to the vast volume of data available. As Gill (2000: 211) alludes, analysis is the 'brain' of the intelligence process yet for such an intrinsic element, its organisational development was very much in its infancy when 'Tackling Crime Effectively' was published, and continues to face challenges both in relation to its definition and integration into routine policing (Cope, 2004, 2008). A specific challenge for strategic analysis is how it delivers an effective interpretative commentary on the information its assesses. That is, does it offer more than a descriptive review and summary of a range of sources? While this may provide some intrinsic value, the true potential of strategic intelligence comes when an effective analytical process is aligned to planning, thereby encouraging an organisation to prepare to respond. It is this tripartite *information – analysis – planning* relationship that is challenging both to develop and embed. The advent of the NIM as a business process mecha-nism has raised the debate without necessarily offering the solution. Initially, chief officers failed to appreciate the centrality of the NIM, and especially strategic assessments, to their annual business planning pro-cess, perceiving it as a stand-alone entity that was either in conflict or involved a duplication of effort. Arguably this was exacerbated by the relatively underdeveloped concept of strategy contained within the NIM, which had its foundations firmly routed in tactical crime reduction activity, rather than business operating or planning processes.

The analytical capability in police forces was ill-equipped to cater for the strategic intelligence and assessment requirement demanded by the NIM, irrespective that HMIC (1997: 5) had previously advocated the benefits of strategic analysis. Informed commentators, such as Wardlaw (1998) and Hall (1998), contend that strategic intelligence is a specialist analytical doctrine that must be serviced by a dedicated provision but few forces were in a position to deliver this. The issues associated with integrating crime analysis have been discussed elsewhere and there is not the space to rehearse them in this chapter (see Cope 2004, 2005; Ratcliffe, 2008). To progress, police forces will need to build into their analytical structure a strategic analytical capacity and ensure it has the necessary skills, training development and position to realise its potential, thereby ensuring the quality of the products does not serve to undermine support for the process.

The identification of a strategic threat requires the formulation of strategic countermeasures, defined in the NIM as the control strategy and broadly categorised as intelligence, enforcement and prevention. It is here the connectivity between the strategic and the tactical activity is most evident. Unfortunately, research unsurprisingly found similar disappointing issues of relevance and strategic insight for control strategies (Maguire and John, 2003: 12). To ensure any plan is successful relies on significant interagency support and cooperation, not only in building solutions, but also in developing an understanding of the problems. The problem with many control strategies lies in a limited understanding of the criminal environment.

While the discussion presents a potentially gloomy picture for strategic intelligence, it is not intended to do so. Recognising the contribution a broader and longer view can have to a specific area can bring dividends when dealing with challenging issues (such as emerging crime trends [see Cope 2005]), managing a response to opportunities (such as urban renewal), or anticipating changes (such as population shifts or migration). Police forces certainly recognise the need and have an appetite for developing strategic information, and efforts at developing strategic intelligence have demonstrated the extent to which it needs to be a collaboration of police and partners to ensure it is effective.

Conclusion

Although the last decade has witnessed the engineering of intelligence-led policing into a position as a pivotal paradigm of law enforcement in the UK, its development remains in its infancy. The lack of an 'intelligence culture' at the outset, shortcomings in change management and a deeply entrenched occupational culture hardly makes this surprising. The aggregated impact of these factors was grossly underestimated and the paradigm shift to an intelligence-driven model needs a reality check. The NIM experienced a problematic introduction, but arguably still offers the service a well-grounded structure for the intelligence process and the development of doctrine that will lead to both professionalisation of intelligence practice and, as argued by Flood and Gaspar in this book, to a professionalisation of policing management.

The widespread practice of strategic intelligence is inextricably linked with the paradigm of intelligence-led policing and any consideration of its value and relevance must be evaluated against that broader backdrop. Strategic intelligence in tandem with the business planning process of the NIM has the capability of setting the policing agenda. To deliver this aspiration, police forces have to invest in developing strategic information and expertise within their structure supported by an infrastructure that permits the free flow of data both internally and externally with partner agencies. Effective open source data sharing, especially with other public authorities, is key to meaningful strategic assessment and if conducted competently and coherently could dictate the future role of policing.

While strategic intelligence is arguably still in its infancy in terms of impact, in terms of recognition of its potential it is more firmly established. It has both utility and relevance for all strata of policing and law enforcement. Ensuring the right infrastructure is in place to make the theory a reality remains the challenge for police forces, as they continue to confront a range of complex problems and are required to manage a plethora of competing priorities.

References

Audit Commission, 1994, *Helping with Enquiries: Tackling Crime Effectively 1*, HMSO.

Barton, A, and Evans, R, 1999, *Proactive Policing on Merseyside*, Police Research Group Crime Detection and Prevention Series Paper 105, Home Office.

Bowling, B, and Foster, J, 2002, 'Policing and the Police', in Maguire, M, Morgan, R, and Reiner, R (eds), *The Oxford Handbook of Criminology*, 3rd edn, Oxford University Press.

Castells, M, 2000, *End of Millennium (The Information Age)*, Blackwell.

Chan, J, 1997, *Changing Police Culture: Policing in a Multicultural Society*, Cambridge University Press.

Clark, J, and Newman, J, 1997, *The Managerial State*, Sage.

Colvin, M, and Noorlander, P, 1998, *Under Surveillance: Covert Policing and Human Rights*, Justice.

Cope, N, 2004, 'Intelligence Led Policing or Policing Led Intelligence: Integrating Volume Crime Analysis into Policing', *British Journal of Criminology*, vol 44, 188-203.

Cope, N, 2005, 'The range of issues in crime analysis', in Alison, L (ed), *The Forensic Psychologist's Casebook*, Willan Publishing.

Cope, N, 2008, 'Crime Analysis for Policing', in Newburn, T (ed), *Handbook of Policing*, 2nd edn, Willan Publishing.

Dintino, JJ, and Martens, FT, 1983, *Police Intelligence Systems in Crime Control*, Charles C Thomas.

Dorn, N, Murji, K, and South, N, 1991, *Traffickers: Drug Markets and Law Enforcement*, Routledge.

Dunnighan, C, and Norris, C, 1996a, 'A Risky Business: The Recruitment and Running of Informers by English Police Officers', *Police Studies*, vol 19, no 2.

Dunnighan, C, and Norris, C, 1996b, 'The Nark's Game', *New Law Journal*, vol 146, 401-403.

Dunnighan, C, and Norris, C, 1999, 'The Detective, The Snout and the Audit Commission', *The Howard Journal of Criminal Justice*, vol 38, no 1, 67-86.

Ericson, RV, and Haggerty, KD, 1997, *Policing the Risk Society*, Clarendon Press.

Friedman, G, Friedman, M, Chapman, C, and Baker, JS, 1997, *The Intelligence Edge*, Random House.

Gaspar, R, 2001, *High Level Business Case for Intelligence and Information Sharing*, Unpublished, National Criminal Intelligence Service.

Gill, P, 2000, *Rounding up the usual suspects? Developments in contemporary law enforcement intelligence*, Ashgate.

Hall, R, 1998, *Presentation to NCIS Analyst Conference*, Unpublished, National Criminal Intelligence Service.

Heaton, R, 2000, 'The Prospects for Intelligence-Led Policing: Some Historical and Quantitative Considerations', *Policing and Society*, vol 9, no 4, 337-56.

HMIC, 1997, *Policing with Intelligence – A Thematic Inspection on Good Practice*, Her Majesty's Inspectorate of Constabulary, Home Office.

Hobbs, D, 1994, 'Professional and Organised Crime', in Maguire, M, Morgan, R, and Reiner, R (eds), *The Oxford Handbook of Criminology*, 1st edn, Clarendon Press.

Hobbs, D, 1997, 'Criminal Collaboration: Youth Gangs, Subcultures, Professional Criminals and Organised Crime', in Maguire, M, Morgan, R, and Reiner, R (eds), *The Oxford Handbook of Criminology*, 2nd edn, Oxford University Press.

Holdaway, S, 1983, *Inside the British Police*, Blackwell.

Holdaway, S, 1989, 'Discovering structure: Studies of the British Police Occupational Culture', in Weatheritt, M (ed), *Police Research: Some Future Prospects*, Avebury.

Home Office, 1984, *HO Circular 114/84*, Home Office.

Home Office, 1993, *Police Reform: A Police Service for the Twenty First Century (Sheehy Report)*, HMSO.

Hook, P, 1998, 'Gang Wars: The new National Crime Squad response to organised transnational crime gangs', *Police Review*, vol 106, no 5460, 14-15.

Innes, M, 2000, 'Professionalising the Role of the Police Informant: The British Experience', *Policing and Society*, vol 9, no 4, 357-384.

Innes, M, and Fielding, N, 2002, 'Intelligence Work: Police Practice in the Information Age', paper presented to British Society of Criminology meeting.

John, T, and Maguire, M, 2003, 'Rolling Out the National Intelligence Model: Key Challenges', in Bullock, K, and Tilley, N (eds), *Problem Oriented Policing*, Willan Publishing.

Kent, S, 1949, *Strategic Intelligence for American World Policy*, Princeton University Press.

Lash, S, 2002, *Critique of Information*, Sage.

Levi, M, 1998, 'Perspectives on "Organised Crime": An Overview', *The Howard Journal of Criminal Justice,* vol 37, no 4, 335-345.

Maguire, M, 1998, 'Restraining Big Brother? The Regulation of Surveillance in England and Wales', in Norris, C, Armstrong, G, and Moran, J (eds), *Surveillance, Closed Circuit Television and Social Control,* Ashgate.

Maguire, M, 2000, 'Policing by Risks and Targets: Some Dimensions and Implications of Intelligence-Led Social Control', *Policing and Society,* vol 9, no 4, 315-337.

Maguire, M, and John, T, 1995, *Intelligence, Surveillance and Informants: Integrated Approaches,* Police Research Group Crime Detection and Prevention Series Paper 64, Home Office.

Maguire, M, and John, T, 2003, *Round Targeted Policing Initiative: Rollout of National Intelligence Model,* Home Office.

Manning, PK, 1992, 'Information Technologies and the Police', in Tonry, M, and Morris, N (eds), *Modern Policing,* University of Chicago Press.

Manning, PK, 1997, *Police Work,* 2nd edn, Waveland Press.

Manning, PK, 2001, 'Technology's Ways: Information Technology, Crime Analysis and the Rationalizing of Policing', *Criminal Justice,* vol 1, 83-104.

Manning, PK, and Hawkins, K, 1989, 'Police Decision Making', in Weatheritt, M (ed), *Police Research,* Avebury.

McDowell, D, 1998, *Strategic intelligence: A handbook for practitioners, managers and users,* Istana Enterprises.

McLaughlin, E, and Murji, K, 2001, 'Lost Connections and New Directions: Neo-Liberalism, New Public Managerialism and the "Modernisation" of the British Police', in Stenson, K, and Sullivan, R (eds), *Crime, Risk and Justice: The Politics of Crime Control in Liberal Democracies,* Willan Publishing.

Morgan, R, and Newburn, T, 1997, *The Future of Policing,* Oxford University Press.

NCIS, 2000, *The National Intelligence Model,* National Criminal Intelligence Service.

Norris, C, and Dunnighan, C, 2000, 'Subterranean Blues: Conflict as an Unintended Consequence of the Police Use of Informers', *Policing and Society,* vol 9, no 4, 385-412.

Philips, D, Caless, B, and Bryant, R, 1997, 'Intelligence and its Application to Contemporary Policing', *Policing,* vol 1, 438-446.

Poster, M, 1991, *The Mode of Information,* Polity.

Ratcliffe, JH, 2000, 'Intelligence-Led Policing and the Problems of Turning Rhetoric into Practice', *Policing and Society,* vol 12, no 1, 53-66.

Ratcliffe, JH, 2008, *Intelligence-Led Policing,* Willan Publishing.

Reiner, R, 2000, *The Politics of the Police,* Oxford University Press.

Schein, E, 1996, *Organisational Culture and Leadership,* Jossey Bass.

Sheptycki, J, 2000, 'Policing and Human Rights: An Introduction', *Policing and Society,* vol 10, no 1, 1-10.

SOCA, 2006, *The UK Threat Assessment of Serious Organised Crime 2006/07,* Serious Organised Crime Agency.

Stelfox, P, 1998, Policing Lower Levels of Organised Crime in England and Wales, *The Howard Journal of Criminal Justice,* vol 37, no 4, 393-406.

Tremblay, P, and Rochon, C, 1991, 'Police Organisations and Their Use of Knowledge: A Grounded Research Agenda', *Policing and Society,* vol 1, 269-283.

Walsh, K, 1995, *Public Services and Market Mechanisms: Competition, Contracting and the New Public Management,* Macmillan.

Wardlaw, G, 1998, *Presentation to NCIS Analyst Conference,* Unpublished, National Criminal Intelligence Service.

CHAPTER 15

Setting the strategic agenda

Jerry Ratcliffe and James Sheptycki

The first chapter of this volume produced an ideal-type model of intelligence-led policing (the three-i model in Figure 1.2). In simple terms, this model shows that the impact of policy decisions regarding interventions against organised and serious crime depends crucially on the ability of the criminal intelligence system to accurately interpret the criminal environment, and that any such interpretation can be conveyed to decision-makers in a useable way.

Understanding what constitutes the criminal environment and its interface with criminal law enforcement is essential in order for agencies to prioritise the allocation of limited resources and that is where strategic intelligence analysis comes in. These are issues for all agencies – enforcement, non-police, and regulatory. The potential strengths of strategic criminal intelligence include the ability to distinguish long-term trends from short-term fluctuations and to provide estimates of the magnitude and character of likely criminal patterns. This point was made in the opening chapter; patterns suggest predictability, and predictability opens the door to proactivity and crime prevention action. A related requirement is the production of accurate assessments of the impact of different crime types on society and suggestions about how to avoid, or at least minimise, them. One of the tasks of this chapter will be to try to explain why strategic analysis might be useful, but we will do so by discussing why it is so hard to implement.

At the outset, it is obvious that the quality of data and the way that it is interpreted determines how the impact of different types of organised crime is understood. Further, over-reliance on law enforcement data places considerable limitations on strategic intelligence analysis. It follows that liaison and information exchange with other agencies holds the promise of improving the quality of strategic assessments by incorporating complimentary (or alternative) views and data. Such was some of the rationale behind the creation of intelligence fusion centres in the United States (see Chapter 13), though a paucity of evaluations as of yet negates any attempt to pass judgement on their effectiveness. Data sharing and evaluations are vital to quality strategic intelligence products, but there are a number of issues to contend with, not least of which are the organisational pathologies of the intelligence system itself. Police intelligence systems tend towards hermetic closure and autopoiesis (Sheptycki, 2002).

There can be an element of self-fulfilling prophecy in police intelligence cycles and it is not difficult to imagine a situation whereby a particular sector of criminal activity remains a high strategic priority because of its already established presence. In this chapter we will pay particular attention to the extent to which intelligence systems do, in fact, create this type of feedback loop and point out the implications that this has for strategic assessments with regard to those types of crime that are not already strategic priorities. Strategic thinking with regards to organised and serious crime also needs to stretch beyond its normal law enforcement confines in order to produce intelligence that suggests preventative measures that have a chance of mitigating the worst aspects of these phenomena in the longer term. We therefore examine how a 'strategic harm'-based approach might realign approaches to strategic intelligence prioritisation. Such an approach opens the door to problem-oriented policing as a preventative solution, informed by a strategic assessment. We begin by examining the relevance of strategic intelligence within the operational and decision-making framework of police organisations.

The relevance of strategic intelligence

Intelligence managers have not been quick to recognise that strategic intelligence must be seen to be relevant, both to other analysts as well as higher echelon policy makers. With regard to the former group, for example, the NSW Police Service undertook a Statewide program to document an Assessment of the Criminal Environment (ACE) for each of the State's 80 local area commands (Gray, 2000). One constant criticism of the program from local intelligence officers was that it was driven from the centre and that it required considerable effort by the local intelligence officers (LIOs). Very often, having completed (often numerous) intelligence reports, LIOs reported being left feeling they received little or nothing in return. Intelligence reports collated centrally were said to disappear into an intelligence 'black-hole' – a space where all information is swallowed-up but from where no light emerges.

Similar observations have been made in the United Kingdom, for example, with regard to organised vehicle theft. There, efforts to centralise data pertaining to vehicle theft required the participation of regional and local intelligence officers in a reporting regime that produced intelligence products by and for centrally located managers of police intelligence. Again, it was not infrequently said by police officers in the field that any intelligence product that did emerge did not adequately reflect the local needs of most police officers working on the problem area (Brown et al, 2003). This is not to suggest that this intelligence reporting regime was entirely without effect. With regard to organised vehicle theft in the United Kingdom, vehicle crime units in local areas did acknowledge operational successes from time-to-time that stemmed from intelligence analysis provided by the (then) National Criminal

Intelligence Service (NCIS). However, such success was not understood in strategic terms, but rather merely pertained to the operational support provided by NCIS to local constabularies.

Likewise, a review of intelligence management in three districts of the New Zealand Police some years ago identified a lack of direction as a problem (Ratcliffe, 2005). Again, strategic support was not well understood, and as a result value was connected to operational outcomes. This realisation (among many) sparked the current reinvigoration of the role of police intelligence in New Zealand within the framework of the New Zealand Crime Reduction Model, based on the three-i model (NZP, 2004).

Strategic intelligence analysts often struggle for positive recognition and legitimacy among a constituency whom they rely on for baseline data. Tactical and operational analysts, detectives and investigators view strategic intelligence work as lacking day-to-day relevance. It is easy to see why. Tactical and operational outcomes can be easily measured, resulting in new operations leading to more arrests – the yardstick of law enforcement. The identification of emerging trends or preventative strategies do not result in 'success' as measured by law enforcement indicators. This causes problems for strategic assessments in two ways. First, there is a resultant lack of rank-and-file support within law enforcement for a process seen as having little relevance. Secondly, difficulties in defining measurable outcomes for strategic intelligence product mean that it is difficult to justify the maintenance of a strategic intelligence staff. The point is made by Harfield, who as an intelligence commander supported one organisational objective (fiscal constraint) by failing to fill a vacant intelligence staff position (MacVean and Harfield, 2008). To the frustration of strategic analysts, the preference for management by objectives – where the cost-benefit analysis of law enforcement performance indicators underwrites management decisions – means that it is extremely difficult to assert the worth of an assessment that aims to predict the scope of criminal behaviour months or years into an uncertain future.

There is a creeping realisation across the field that strategic intelligence has to 'sell' itself to local analysts and front-line personnel. This was appreciated by the Strategic Intelligence Directorate of NCIS who began the practice of sending analysts out to liaise directly with professionals in the field. This not only places analysts closer to the source data so fundamental to the intelligence cycle, it also allows them to explain the utility of the strategic approach to field agents. Temporary secondments and other liaison arrangements are thought to be a good way to generate greater cooperation between agencies situated in different geographical and functional locations in the police sector. It is a way of improving relations in the 'institutional neighbourhood'. Similarly, the Australian Crime Commission employs approximately 80 secondees and about 50 task force members from Australian State police agencies.[1]

---

1   Kevin Kitson, ACC Executive Director, Strategic Outlook and Policy Division, personal communication, 2009.

Selling the intelligence product to senior management and decision-makers closer to the ministerial level is no less difficult for intelligence analysts, and this is the case even when there are specific requests for strategic analysis. Strategic forecasts are cautious in their wording. We would say necessarily so, since they attempt to derive understandings of dynamic processes based on tentative indicators in order to predict an uncertain future. The importance of caveats and cautious language was emphasised in the United Kingdom by the Hutton and Butler inquiries into the circumstances surrounding the death of Dr David Kelly and intelligence on Iraq respectively. As the Butler Inquiry observed, the removal of caveats from the Joint Intelligence Committee's September 2002 dossier that the British government used to justify the Iraq invasion – caveats that could have cast doubt on the fullness and reliability of intelligence contained in the dossier – was a serious failing.

Moreover, strategic crime prevention approaches may require responses outside the police sector. The problem-oriented policing literature is replete with long-term crime prevention solutions that can only be implemented through partnership with non-law enforcement bodies. For example, with regard to organised vehicle theft, better regulation of vehicle licensing and its associated record-keeping (Hill, 1998), and greater scrutiny and regulation of used vehicle retail and repair businesses could be expected to impact significantly on this crime phenomenon (Gant and Grabosky, 2001), but not in ways that are productive for law enforcement performance indicators. For these reasons strategic intelligence approaches lack appeal for many senior managers in law enforcement. Most senior and middle-ranking police officers have detective backgrounds. It is not surprising that more holistic, esoteric and cautious strategic thinking can lack a sense of immediacy and directness to action-oriented managers. It must be remembered that strategic intelligence is relatively new within the policing sector and that many senior officers chalked up successes (by which they gained promotion) under an entirely different regime; one that placed great value on law enforcement skills, that is: nicking villains. Little training is available for senior officers to appreciate the strategic value of quality intelligence products.

Detectives build their role around crime investigation and arrest leading to successful prosecution. To detectives, information equates with evidence and so, all too often, they succumb to the tendency to subvert intelligence into detections by another name. In certain circumstances, the long-entrenched sub-cultural expectations of detective work may reduce the intelligence process to mere evidence gathering and evaluation. This imparts significant risk to both strategic thinking as well as any investigative support role: '[t]here is a perceptual danger that the increasing use of science in seeking evidential certainty in the trial process has created the same public expectation of forensic certainty in intelligence work' (Harfield, 2008a: 1). From the experience of many detectives –and rather analogous to the expression 'When all you have is a hammer, every problem looks like a nail' – an investigation leading to a prosecution is deemed the only response to crime problems. This can even lead to adaptation of legislation from its original purpose in order to achieve a conviction, as with a justification for RICO laws (Racketeer Influenced and Corrupt Organizations legislation originally intended to target US mafia groups) being applied to gang members in the United States (Wheatley, 2008).

In contrast to detectives, strategic analysts are trained to look at information more broadly. They are interested not merely in the evidence in a criminal case, although they can be involved in that too. Rather, intelligence analysis (particularly of the strategic variety) aims at the discovery of trends and patterns, tries to explain why these occur and provide preventative strategies so they do not (Dintino and Martens, 1983). Unfortunately, since the traditional detective role is more long-standing than that of the crime analyst, it is a relatively high-status role within police organisations and key performance indicators often reflect this. That is why there is an observable tendency to co-opt police analysis for the purposes of crime investigation. The detective sub-culture exerts a powerful allure and it is possible to observe that some analysts come to identify with the detective worldview. Celebrating the 'good pinch' is not necessarily antithetical to the analyst's role, but neither is it particu-larly central to strategic intelligence analysis. It is undesirable that crime analysis should become narrowed to a limited set of practices concerned only with law enforcement objectives (Sheptycki, 2003a).

The problems with estimating the impact of crime

Strategic impact assessments that are not offence-specific (such as gang or drug assessments) require that data relating to violence, drugs, and intellectual property theft must be weighed against data relating to stock market and benefit fraud, crimes against the environment, clandestine immigration and paedophilia – to name only a few types of organised and serious crime. The methodological issues that arise are highly com-plex. Decisions about prioritisation are important partly because they set the parameters for gathering the next generation of intelligence data and therefore set the limits of what is known and what is considered to be knowable. That is why methodological issues about measurement and weighting are so important.

What measurement criteria can be brought to bear that make the variety of crime types mentioned above comparable? A growing range of national threat assessments[2] attempt to do just that using both data

2   In Canada from the website of Criminal Intelligence Service Canada <www.cisc.gc.ca>, in the United Kingdom from the Serious Organised Crime Agency <www.soca.gov.uk>, in Australia from the Australian Crime Com-mission <www.crimecommission.gov.au>, and in the United States from a

generated from both inside and outside the police sector and, on that basis, establish a rational basis for future strategic priorities. While questions about data quality can be raised, there is more to the problem than that. Some types of crime (for example, intellectual property theft) are only monetary in nature, while others (for example, sexual victimisation by organised groups of paedophiles) are entirely, or almost entirely, non-monetary. Distortions in the estimation of organised crime inevitably result from reducing everything to the lowest common denominator: money (Sheptycki, 2003a). In much the same reductionist way, Mayhew and Adkins (2003) estimated costs of crime for a wide range of offences in Australia through a complex process of combining police sector and non-police sector data to determine the impact of victim costs, medical costs, lost output, intangible costs (such as pain, suffering, and quality of life impacts), transfer of resource costs, and the costs to the criminal justice system.[3]

Attempts to assess organised crime impact expressed in monetary terms only inadequately express the costs of human life and suffering. Intelligence assessments that rank the negative impact of intellectual property theft higher than an emotive issue such as paedophilia lack credibility not only to senior policy makers, but also to the broader public. The demand for more objective priority setting by governments is likely to produce methodological refinements in this area. This is probably behind the admission in the *UK Threat Assessment* (NCIS, 2001: 115-116) and citing Home Office research study no 217, *The Economic and Social Costs of Crime*, (Brand and Price, 2000), that 'impact analysis needs to be further improved' while also noting the 'inherent danger in only including costs that can be quantified since this can distort the overall picture and provide a misleading guide for policy makers'.

There are few incontestably accurate, objective and reliable indicators to draw on for such an analysis. This point is obscured by the over-reliance of criminal justice system data in intelligence analysis. As noted in the 2000 *UK Threat Assessment*, a considerable number of the available indicators are as much a reflection of law enforcement activity as they are significant measures of the problem (Sheptycki, 2003a). The range of information produced by the police sector itself that is commonly used in crime analysis include: victim reports; witness reports; police reports and data held by other agencies in the police sector (for example, Customs data); crime scene examinations; historical data held by police agencies (for example, Criminal Records Office); prisoner debriefings; technical or

---

(*cont*)

 variety of locations; for example, national drug assessments are produced by the National Drug Intelligence Center <www.usdoj.gov/ndic>, while for money laundering, the Department of Treasury release an occasional assessment <www.treas.gov>.

3 A recent update was provided by Kiah Rollings (2008) including links to relevant US and UK research.

human surveillance products; suspicious transactions reporting; and undercover police operations. This list is graded roughly in terms of the sensitivity of the source. For most intelligence units working in police constabularies in the United Kingdom, the vast majority of analysable intelligence (in the region of 75 per cent) stems from standardised reporting by uniformed patrol officers (Sheptycki 2003a). Similarly, the Australian study of the costs of crime, referred to above, relied heavily on administrative data collected from law enforcement and the criminal justice system. The difficulties with these types of analyses cannot be underestimated. For example, the Australian study noted that, 'Although burglary is a key crime of public concern, Australian data for gauging costs is poor' (Mayhew and Adkins, 2003: 3).

There are clearly some disadvantages when using law enforcement data. The first problem is one of scope. Such data inevitably fail to document the activities of crime groups or problems that have not already come to the attention of law enforcement. In other words, the intelligence may lack validity due to institutional myopia. Specialist units focusing on individual crime phenomena, for example, the problem of football hooligans in the United Kingdom or the Australian 'Swordfish' Task Force that focused on fraud against the federal government, are well placed to produce data showing the extent of their specific problem. However, newly emerging crime issues – for example, identity theft, Internet fraud, and crimes against the environment – may not be on law enforcement's radar due to the lack of specialist units collating and analysing information in these areas.

A further problem relates to an organisational bias towards information collected covertly, with a corollary that open source information is not given the weight and credibility that it perhaps should. Covert information has an inherent attractiveness to decision-makers as it has the allure of information to which others are not privy, with a sometimes mythical suggestion that covert information provides a deeper insight into a criminal problem. The protagonists of organised crime usually wish to conceal information from the police simply to avoid prosecution, rather than to prevent police gaining a strategic advantage, and it is not always clear how some covert information can inform a strategic perspective.

Threat assessments based on police sector data alone are based on historical data that reflect the entrenched and structured collecting mechanisms within national and local agencies. This can cause significant problems when attempts are made to determine new priorities and the reallocation of resources because the reliance on the routine activity of the agency tends to reaffirm the existing status quo. An example of this can be drawn from one of the first tasks of the Australian Crime Commission. Asked by government to examine illegal firearms trafficking[4] a brief scan of the topic showed the paucity of reliable data in an area not previously a major focus for Australian law enforcement (Mouzos, 1999).

---

4   Nick Wolanin, Australian Crime Commission, personal communication, 2003.

Administrative data are of variable quality. This particular problem was identified in Mayhew and Adkin's study (2003) of the economic and social costs of crime in Australia. Police sector data collected in the study tended to reflect police priorities and was more useful for law enforcement applications. Spatio-temporal data (date, time and place) relating to offences are generally more efficiently recorded than the value of goods stolen or the cost of repairs to damaged property because police can use the spatio-temporal data for resource allocation and intelligence-led law enforcement operations. The secondary data analysis that Mayhew and Adkin conducted therefore found police data to be of limited value due to poor recording practices in key areas.[5]

Estimating the impact of organised and serious crime is fraught with difficulties; the data to hand are weak and the way comparisons are drawn across already recognised sectors of organised crime phenomena is poor. These methodological issues must be set beside organisational problems in information sharing.

The problems with sharing information

Knowledge is power and in the intelligence game 'sharing' is not a word that comes easy to many. Much information changes hands in processes that are less information sharing and more 'pay-to-play systems of information trading' (Ratcliffe, 2008: 132). Unfortunately, strategic criminal intelligence processes are further complicated by the requirement for multi-agency information sharing. Associated problems are both technical and cultural. In the United Kingdom, the National Intelligence Model is an attempt to orchestrate the harmonisation of the intelligence process but it has met with slow success, taking years to become embedded within police culture. The police sector in the United Kingdom can be understood to include the police constabularies themselves, plus the British Transport Police, the Civil Nuclear Constabulary (CNC), the Serious Organised Crime Agency (SOCA), the Ministry of Defence Police, the Serious Fraud Office (SFO), Her Majesty's Revenue and Customs (HMRC), the Scottish Crime and Drug Enforcement Agency and the UK Border Agency. It may also be extended to include a host of other governmental agencies such as Jobcentre Plus (the rebranded benefits agency) and the Financial Services Authority (FSA) which also contribute to and draw on information circulating in the intelligence 'system'. Each of these agencies maintains a separate information environment. Although configured differently, similar inter-agency cooperation hurdles faced the team investigating the Nine-Trey subset of the Bloods gang, part of a large investigation spanning the American state of New Jersey (Ratcliffe and Guidetti, 2008). Unlike the UK example above,

---

5   Mayhew, personal communication, 2003. The Mayhew and Adkins study was updated for 2005 by Kiah Rollings (2008).

where various national policing agencies have responsibilities within a single domain, the New Jersey State Police had to work with dozens of agencies that retain hegemonic policing rights to municipalities and counties within the state and often maintain individual information silos.

The intelligence system for the police sector *as a whole* can be characterised as a group of hermetically-sealed information systems based on more or less hierarchical principles of intelligence flow, more or less lubricated by informal communications and the sporadic formal exchange of intelligence in aid of limited law enforcement objectives (Sheptycki, 2003a). The inability to share knowledge is a significant hindrance.

The Australian picture is also instructive in this regard. In Australia, attempts to co-ordinate the police information environment have taken place under the auspices of the Australian Criminal Intelligence Database (ACID), part of the Australian Law Enforcement Intelligence Network (ALEIN). First released in 1989, ACID has become the major primary intelligence database for all Australian police services except the Australian Federal Police and the NSW Police Service. While these two agencies maintain their own databases, there exists an electronic exchange facility with ACID. Two significant features limit ACID. First, the system allows users to 'caveat' intelligence postings and limit access to certain users (a practice known as 'flagging' in the UK context). Often the caveats are legitimate and required by data protection legislation, which limits the sharing of information between agencies. However, informal discussion with a number of intelligence officers suggests that many caveats are unnecessarily placed, with some state police services being worse offenders than others. It is not possible to determine with precision how many caveats are due to institutional friction and intelligence hoarding or because of either a legal requirement or legitimate concerns about operational security.

Some agencies, such as the former National Crime Authority (NCA), formed dedicated Task Forces with representatives from other agencies. Under a task force umbrella, liaison officers became, in effect, NCA members of staff who had access to information generated by the inquiry. To ensure the legal integrity of the dissemination, the information was then caveated with an operational name (such as 'Blade' or 'Swordfish') and stored on ACID. For more general use, the issue of caveating reached a level where the ABCI was forced to introduce a 'bulk caveat removal facility' so that information previously caveated due to sensitivity concerns was made more available when those concerns dissipated over time (APMC, 2002).

The second limiting feature of ACID is funding. While ALEIN was the primary means of intelligence communication across Australia during the 2000 Sydney Olympic games, funding constraints on the ABCI necessitated the introduction of a 'user pays' system for both ALEIN and ACID. The financial constraints within the ABCI continued until its amalgamation with the Office of Strategic Crime Assessments and the National Crime Authority into the Australian Crime Commission

(ACC) in January 2003 (for more thoughts on the challenges and successes of the ACC since its inception, see the chapter by Kevin Rogers at the start of this book).

Cultural barriers to information sharing should also not be underestimated. There is only so much glory to be had from operational successes, yet to achieve those 'wins' often requires a high degree of cooperation between agencies that have previously been in competition and that have had, and often still have, overlapping agendas. As an example of an operation requiring a high degree of cooperation, consider the Agio Task Force. The Agio Task Force was an Australian operation that examined patterns of suspect financial activity. When there was the likelihood of serious criminal activity, the task force passed the information to the relevant law enforcement or compliance agency. Agencies in the partnership included the National Crime Authority (now part of the ACC), the ABCI (again, part of the ACC), Australian Transactions Reports and Analysis Centre (AUSTRAC), the Australian Taxation Office (ATO), the Australian Federal Police (AFP), the Australian Customs Service (ACS), and the Australian Securities and Investments Commission (ASIC). At the time, many of these agencies maintained watching briefs on similar areas, especially the activities of South-East Asian crime groups and the activities of outlaw motorcycle gangs. All of these agencies have analysts trained in financial intelligence analysis.

As Hogan notes, 'the corporate culture of the intelligence community is a culture of secrecy. Much effort is expended to ensure that intelligence is appropriately classified and those who receive it are appropriately cleared' (1994: 15). This can be seen in the earlier example of the extensive use of caveats to limit access to the ACID system. However, it is a reality that many strategic intelligence assessments draw heavily on open source information. Government research agencies, such as the Australian Institute of Criminology and the Research and Statistics Directorate of the UK Home Office, provide public-access assessments that identify long-term trends. These documents often form the starting point for many classified documents. The culture of secrecy that surrounds criminal intelligence assessments can act against the broader interests of the intelligence community when assessments are unnecessarily classified and information is not shared between agencies.

The problem of information sharing is organisational as well as cultural. According to one analysis (Sheptycki 2004) limitations to data sharing were due to a number of 'organisational pathologies'. These pathologies have been described at some length and can only be listed here. They are: the digital divide (resulting from the use of separate and, very often incompatible, computer systems within and between different organisations); linkage blindness (the failure to spot linked interests by partner agencies in the police sector); noise (a glut of often low-grade, intelligence); intelligence overload (the systemic inability to analyse intelligence due to 'noise'); compulsive data demand (the failure to recognise that more data is not necessarily better data); non-reporting and non-recording (the failure of reporting officers to fulfil intelligence reporting requirements); intelligence gaps (a gap in knowledge about a specific crime, series of crimes, or crime type); duplication (the recording of intelligence data by more than one agency in the police sector); institutional friction (poor relations of co-operation between partner agencies in the police sector); intelligence hoarding and information silos (the failure to share intelligence within and between agencies in the police sector); and defensive data concentration (amassing intelligence through compulsive data demand – which paradoxically exacerbates other organisational pathologies such as non-reporting and intelligence overload). These terms are not mutually exclusive, but they do provide a vocabulary for managing some of the difficulties in intelligence sharing across the police sector as a whole.

These organisational pathologies have implications for a range of intelligence products in that the incorporation of data into a given analysis tends to be uneven. The perennial problem of current criminal intelligence priorities is that they are often organised primarily around existing law enforcement collection regimes (and already existing priorities), with other information sources merely 'tacked on' to compliment an assessment that remains predicated on traditional law enforcement outcomes.

The Australian National Crime Authority's (NCA) reference system could be viewed in this light. Between 1984 and 2002, the NCA was issued 'References' by the federal and State governments to investigate specific areas of organised criminality such as; South-East Asian Organised Crime (Task Force Blade); fraud against the Commonwealth (the Swordfish Task Force), established criminal networks (Freshnet Task Force), and the activities of Outlaw Motor Cycle Gangs (Panzer Task Force). In most cases these References endured over many years and were used as the basis for the formation of large-standing task forces (most working part-time on the particular Task Force) focused on that particular activity. These References and their associated Task Forces proved successful in terms of investigation and intelligence insight (because they instituted a compulsive demand for data on these issues) but had the result of focusing the NCA on only those specific areas of organised crime covered by the Reference. The organised crime environment was then periodically defined by the References with the corollary that the NCA was unable to look at the organised crime environment in its entirety and prioritise those areas where its scarce resources could be devoted. In other words, it was not possible to construct a holistic view of the criminal environment and act on identified intelligence gaps.

Counting practices and non-police studies

Even when agencies agree to share information and technical issues of incompatible databases can be overcome, the problems do not end there.

Counting and definition differences hamper the ability of analysts to compare across crime types and across agencies and states. The flagship product of the ABCI (now under the mantle of the ACC), the annual Australian Illicit Drug Report (AIDR) has long lamented this problem in a variety of areas. The AIDR aims to provide a statistical analysis and strategic review of the Australian illicit drug situation from a law enforcement perspective (ABCI 2002). One of the principal findings of a chapter on the proceeds of crime noted that; 'We are not presently in the position to reliably estimate how much illicit drug money is being laundered at any time in Australia. The problem is exacerbated by the differences in the nature of statistical records kept by State, Territory and federal agencies' (ABCI, 2000: 112). Although providing a comprehensive summary of arrest and seizure data, the 2000-2001 report noted that a number of factors, 'limit the ABCI's ability to produce a comprehensive, reliable assessment [of the trends in the supply of and demand for illicit drugs] based on the data supplied' (ABCI, 2002). These problems included:

- lack of uniformity in both recording and storing data on illicit drug arrests and seizures across all States and Territories;
- problems with quality control;
- differences in counting methodologies applied in the jurisdictions;
- differences in definitions of drug consumer and provider offences across jurisdictions;
- differences in the way drugs and offences may be coded; and
- inadequate drug identification.

In Australia, a new initiative is underway to create a model performance measurement framework for drug law enforcement agencies to assess their impact in drug crime reduction (Willis and Homel, 2008); however, across many countries the problems noted above abound and such statistics should be used cautiously in priority setting. More often they are projected as a marker of agency success. For example, annual UK statistics that document drug seizures and arrests, and the confiscation of proceeds of crime, may be read as indicating that law enforcement has made in-roads into drug-related criminal activity. But statistics relating to deaths due to overdose and crime survey data indicate a less sanguine picture. According to the European Monitoring Centre for Drugs and Drug Addiction, the United Kingdom has the highest death-rate due to drug overdose in Europe, and the population of Class A drug users is much younger and getting younger in the United Kingdom than the average in most other European countries (*The Economist*, 10 January 2002). Non-law enforcement data provides a more strategic picture of the drug situation in the United Kingdom, but is a picture that does not paint policing activity in such a positive light. The policy implications of this more strategic view may not be popular in a law enforcement arena where realistic evaluation is secondary to perceived success.

Integration of data sources and views from outside law enforcement can be a problematic area. Even though law enforcement strategic issues are broader than the policing field alone, many organisations still employ police officers as strategic analysts. This can be helpful in a data gathering and liaison function, especially when it is necessary to work with other policing agencies in a collaborative manner towards tactical law enforcement objectives. However, the level of training in strategic intelligence analysis is rarely thorough. Even when training is available, as with the Australian National Strategic Intelligence Course, places are limited. Appreciation of knowledge produced by external studies of a broad social scientific nature is hampered by the lack of training within policing with regard to understanding and applying research methodology. Brown (1996) not only mentions an atmosphere of anti-academia within law enforcement, but also raises some serious concerns regarding the ability of internal police research departments to conduct quality research. With sometimes little enthusiasm to use intelligence resources internally, it is not surprising, as Phillips (2008: 9) notes, that 'commanders have a strong and sometimes sorry record of relying on their preconceptions rather than a current and measured appraisal of the problem in hand. Strong leaders can be personally effective and strategically weak'.

Self-fulfilling prophecies

Strategic analysts know that simply by looking at an area of criminal activity it will become a problem. Often they begin with a scarcity of reliable information and therefore conclude that there is a significant knowledge gap. The next step is to examine the issue further and the awareness of the problem grows. However, strategic analysts seldom set the task in the first instance. Clients, that is, senior policy makers, determine the tasking, and they often do so on the basis of previous intelligence assessments, or what they think they know. There is thus an element of self-fulfilling prophecy resulting from many strategic intelligence assessments, which we describe as a 'positive feedback loop'. The process is roughly as follows. A strategic assessment is commissioned on problem 'A', which draws attention to knowledge gaps that prevent a thorough analysis of it. The client may be persuaded to invest intelligence resources to further examine the issue. A number of analysts are employed to examine 'A' and discover more about the area. The problem continues to grow as an issue because a number of people are now working in the area generating intelligence products that raise the profile of 'A' as a problem. This positive feedback system continually raises 'A' as a significant crime threat.

This scenario can be demonstrated with a Canadian example (Sheptycki 2003b). Throughout the 1990s, the Criminal Intelligence Service of Canada (CISC) annually produced assessments identifying outlaw motorcycle gangs at or near the pinnacle of organised crime in Canada. This consistency is, in part, reflective of the amount of police resources dedicated to monitoring outlaw motorcyclists and only tangentially the result of an accurate measure of their objective threat to Canadian society. This is not to argue that members of such groups do not participate in (sometimes very serious) criminality, or that such crime is not productive of social harm. Persistent newspaper reportage about 'turf wars' between rival criminal gangs in Quebec throughout the 1990s gave such groups an undeniably high public profile. So when the Royal Canadian Mounted Police (RCMP) conducted a survey of local intelligence analysts in order to determine organised crime priorities, outlaw motorcycle gangs featured prominently. However, that survey also contained notable 'blind spots', for example, white collar and economic crime.

The self-fulfilling prophecy may not always be a significant problem. The core activities for organised crime have resilience of their own. Groups that profit from illicit markets, and who use violence to protect their interests, are significant problems. Left to exploit a criminal opportunity unchecked, organised crime groups will grow to fill the niche provided by the opportunity until remedial action is taken. The most reliable indication of future criminal activity is current criminal activity. However, the purpose of strategic intelligence analysis is to rise above the already established intelligence routines so that new types of criminality are identified, and priorities for the allocation of (scarce) resources are set accordingly.

Realigning strategic intelligence priorities

Strategic intelligence priorities originate with decision-makers, but are in turn influenced by existing law enforcement priorities. Thus far in this chapter we have considered how the entrenched law enforcement sub-culture of the police sector shapes the intelligence process in ways that undermine the strategic view. We have looked at methodological problems associated with estimating the impact of organised and serious crime and we have critically examined the nature of the information environment that the strategic intelligence process is embedded in. We have concluded that over-reliance on a limited range of data has real implications for maintaining the intelligence gathering status quo and in doing so, preventing the organisation from identifying new and emerging criminal threats. We characterise this as a positive feedback loop producing self-fulfilling prophecies.

Such problems are not altogether unrecognised in criminal intelligence circles. The value of multi-agency intelligence sharing is frequently cited. For example, networking between professional analysts at a similar level of their respective organisations is one aim of Australia's National Strategic Intelligence Course (Walsh & Ratcliffe, 2005). Face-to-face contact is important. In Australia, the Joint Strategic Intelligence Group

(JSIG) was formed precisely as a result of this recognition. The Joint Strategic Intelligence Group consisted of four senior analysts representing the NCA, AFP, ACS and AUSTRAC. Their aim was to 'improve and refine intelligence sharing arrangements between Justice and Customs agencies and address issues of common concern to the portfolio from a multi-agency perspective' (NCA, 2001: 24). Each analyst was a senior analyst from their agency, able to bring to the table a thorough background in criminal intelligence generally, as well as a solid working knowledge of the data holding of each agency. Similar programs have also been developed in the United Kingdom and elsewhere in the Commonwealth.

Still, the extension of strategic intelligence approaches outside the confines of law enforcement thinking seems unclear. Greater use of non-police sector intelligence sources and greater cooperation with non-police agencies will expand both the scope and range of intelligence. However, much more is required. Strategic thinking should also go beyond law enforcement responses to include a range of other possible solutions. One significant development on this front is the advocacy of the 'strategic harm based approach' (Sheptycki 2003a). The first step in this approach is to establish priorities for strategic criminal intelligence gathering and subsequent analysis based on notions of the social harm caused by different sorts of criminal activity. What is required is a general index of the *social harm* that is not monetary in nature so that organised and serious crime activities can be scaled and compared. The key to this is to reorientate law enforcement logic in the organised crime field in order to focus on crime prevention and harm reduction.

Strategic harm reduction measures call upon a broad range of data sources. With regard to the strategic assessment of organised and serious crime, this approach would look for information relating to:

1. Health-related statistics, such a data from health departments or hospital emergency units relating to violence or deaths due to drug overdose, mortality statistics and other epidemiological data pertaining to physical and mental health;

2. National crime and victimisation survey data;

3. Community crime audits, surveys of local community crime and disorder problems; and

4. A wide variety of data from government ministries, such as departments that deal with the environment, trade, industry and education, as well as census data and other survey research, all of which provide clues as to the 'health of society' that can be used to shed light on particular aspects of crime problems.

Social harm is a reorientation of our ideas of 'crime' away from legalistic definitions to an understanding of harm being more humanistic and localised; as Gilmour (2008) points out, harm is felt subjectively by different communities and is best measured by direct communication.

Because of this subjective nature of social harm, it is difficult to define: what harms you might not harm us. The point is recognised by SOCA in their 2008/9 UK Threat Assessment of Organised Crime (SOCA, 2008: 4):

> The overall aim of the UK Serious Organised Crime Control Strategy is to reduce the harm caused by serious organised crime. Harm remains difficult to define clearly and size accurately, but it is clear that serious organised crime is highly damaging to the UK and UK interests. In addition to the direct and indirect financial losses and costs, there are many other, less quantifiable, consequences; businesses, communities, families, and individuals damaged by the criminal trades, by the fear of crime, and by the sight of criminals carrying on their activities and profiting from them, which, in addition to undermining public confidence, acts as an encouragement to others to become involved in crime.

Hillyard and Tombs (2007) suggest a social harm approach should encompass physical harm, financial/economic harm, emotional/ psychological harm and cultural safety, and it is possible to see how such a wider conceptualisation of social harm is reflective of much of the distress caused by serious and organised crime. Fortunately, there is now evidence of an increasing orientation towards a social harm perspective. As Harfield (2008b: 72) notes, 'perceptions of organized crime have changed and it is now viewed in terms of preventing harm caused, rather than criminality automatically to be prosecuted'.

A growing field concerned with harm reduction can also be found in academic criminology under the rubric of environmental criminology (Brantingham and Brantingham, 1981; Wortley and Mazerolle, 2008). This theoretical and practical node of criminology is concerned with mapping the geography of crime, and particularly to map the 'crime careers' of urban locales (see Weisburd et al, 2004; Chainey and Ratcliffe, 2005). Typically criminologists interested in environmental criminology (not to be confused with 'environmental crime') look at locations associated with high degrees of criminality and compare them with areas where it is lower or absent altogether. The policy concern is that a reputation for criminality may prompt businesses and stable families to relocate from an area, subsequently leading to deterioration in the quality of housing stock and the quality of life. Data used as indicators of social harm to urban communities trapped in this cycle include information about trends in house prices or rental costs over time, as well as insurance data, school truancy rates and other social statistics. These data tap into broader concepts of social harm being associated with the non-fulfilment of the 'pre-requisites for human well-being' (Pemberton, 2007: 37). Use of these data goes beyond mere strategic reckoning or scientific description, and slides into the area of evaluating effectiveness (Maltz, 1990; Maltz and Buslik, 1997). Harm-based modelling is concerned with altering the trajectory of 'community crime careers' by orchestrating a variety of policy interventions that include, but are certainly not limited to, law enforcement interventions.

Problem-oriented policing is a strategy that actively embraces the focus on the spatially-targeted and problem-specific nature of harm-based modelling (Goldstein 1990, 2003). Originally conceived as a response to day-to-day policing problems, it has now grown to represent a methodology to address problems from graffiti to terrorism.[6]

Harm-reduction approaches have achieved the greatest notoriety in the context of drug policy reform. An example of this is the 'Swiss Experiment'. This controlled experiment showed that acquisitive crime by heroin users declined substantially under a prescription regime. Other criteria related to the social well-being of drug takers, such as being able to maintain employment and steady social relationships, and their general physical and psychological health status, also indicated a positive influence attributable to the prescription regime (Killias and Uchtenhagen, 1996).

The results of the Swiss heroin experiment and the efforts of environmental criminologists and proponents of problem-oriented policing all point to strategies that require outcome measures that are different from those that typically shape the criminal intelligence process. Unlike traditional approaches to controlling organised crime, strategic harm-based approaches cannot be assessed on the basis of purely law enforcement outcomes. By its very nature it requires some measure of the social harms due to organised and serious crime, and police sector statistics do not usually provide this type of measure. Some commentators from within policing have pointed to the benefits of greater utilisation of police data, given that for 'most routine policing of local areas, a good deal of information is already "known". This information should be used as the foundations for strategic thinking about how to minimise the harm of violence threatening communities' (Stanko, 2008: 236). And it is likely that the local area context of organised crime will be a significant focus for policing in the immediate future (Gilmour, 2008).

One element of strategic harm-based approaches is the recognition that law enforcement solutions may be iatrogenic. An example of iatrogenesis found currently in the literature pertains to measures of crime group 'disruption'. In the United Kingdom measures of the number of criminal groups 'disrupted' or 'dismantled' were advanced as another law enforcement measurement indicator alongside traditional arrest statistics. These were criticised by the Commons Public Accounts Committee for being too subjective and reports by Her Majesty's Inspectorate of Constabulary (HMIC) noted that disruption was ill-defined (Sheptycki, 2003a). What the reports of the official government agencies did not do was point out that the unintended consequences of 'disruption' could in fact be greater harm. An illustrative example cited by Sheptycki (2003a) concerned that of a mid-level drug dealer who had had monetary assets frozen or confiscated. Dealers in such situations frequently owe money to others. In some instances the pressure to pay

---

6   More information is available through the website of the Center for Problem-Oriented Policing at <www.popcenter.org>.

off debts might lead criminal entrepreneurs to engage in more violent forms of crime (eg, armed robbery) in order to ward off the threats of criminal debtors. What law enforcement officials count as a group 'disrupted', may in fact turn out to be an incentive to more harmful criminal activity.

There is a growing literature on harm reduction and regulatory strategies that is only slowly being integrated with the literature on intelligence-led policing.[7] By concentrating on minimising harm we move beyond the hermetic type of intelligence thinking that currently dominates the field and grasp a more strategic view whereby the knowledge and capacities of a range of organisational entities are strategically mobilised to reduce the impact of organised and serious crime.

Conclusion

Existing routines of intelligence collection are determinative of future crime priorities because they habituate processes for the gathering and analysis of information that will highlight today's crime problems at the possible expense of tomorrow's. Moreover, existing intelligence routines are entrenched in a law enforcement apparatus that can be both inefficient and ineffective, even while it is capable of producing statistics that attest to a modicum of efficiency and effectiveness. In a risk-oriented society, the reliance on law enforcement agencies as the primary source of knowledge about organised crime will continue to be a significant barrier to progress. In the absence of a more holistic social harm orientation, strategic intelligence may lack validity due to institutional myopia and a lack of connectivity to decision-makers in the political spectrum. Specialist units focusing on individual crime phenomena will continue to advertise (often limited) success in a continued battle for scarce resources, but if we are to break out of this cycle and produce a new strategic view, it will be necessary to break old habits. Unfortunately, old habits die hard.

References

ABCI, 2000, *Australian Illicit Drug Report 1998-1999*, Australian Bureau of Criminal Intelligence.

ABCI, 2002, *Australian Illicit Drug Report 2001-2002*, Australian Bureau of Criminal Intelligence.

APMC, 2002, *Annual report on the activities of National Common Police Services 2000-2001*, Australian Police Ministers' Council.

Brand, S and Price, R, 2000, *The Economic and Social Costs of Crime*, Home Office, Research and Development Section Report, no 217.

Brantingham, PJ and Brantingham, PL (eds), 1981, *Environmental Criminology*. Waveland Press.

---

7   Erickson et al, 1997; Grabosky, 1997; and O'Malley, 1999 provide valuable insights into how strategic thinking can be realigned in this way.

Brown, J, 1996, 'Police research: some critical issues', in F Leishman, B Loveday and SP Savage (eds), *Core Issues in Policing*, Longman, pp 178-90.

Brown, R, Clarke, R, Rix, B and Sheptycki, J, 2003, *Intelligence-led Vehicle Crime Reduction; the Role of NCIS*, (unpublished manuscript written for the Home Office Police and Reducing Crime Unit).

Chainey, S and Ratcliffe, JH, 2005, *GIS and Crime Mapping*, Wiley and Sons.

Dintino, JJ and Martens, FT, 1983, *Police Intelligence Systems in Crime Control*, Charles C Thomas.

Erickson, PG, Riley, DM, Cheung, YT and O'Hare, PA, 1997, *Harm Reduction: A New Direction for Drug Policies and Programs*, University of Toronto Press.

Gant, F and Grabosky, PN, 2001, 'The stolen vehicle parts market', *Trends and Issues in Crime and Criminal Justice*, no 215, Australian Institute of Criminology.

Gilmour, S, 2008, 'Understanding organized crime: A local perspective', *Policing: A Journal of Policy and Practice*, vol 2, no 1, 18-27.

Goldstein, H, 1990, *Problem-Oriented Policing*, McGraw-Hill.

Goldstein, H, 2003, 'On further developing problem-oriented policing: The most critical need, the major impediments, and a proposal', in J Knutsson (ed), *Problem-Oriented Policing: From Innovation to Mainstream* (pp 13-47). Criminal Justice Press.

Grabosky, PN, 1997, 'Inside the Pyramid: Towards a Conceptual Framework for the Analysis of Regulatory Systems', *International Journal of the Sociology of Law*, vol 25, no 3, 195-201.

Gray, D, 2000, 'Intelligence driven policing: ACE supports crime reduction', *Australian Criminal Intelligence Digest*, Australian Bureau of Criminal Intelligence, 17, February, pp 26-27.

Harfield, C, 2008a, 'Introduction: Intelligence policing', in Harfield, C, MacVean, A, Grieve, JGD and Phillips, D (eds), *The Handbook of Intelligent Policing: Consilience, Crime Control, and Community Safety* (pp 1-6), Oxford University Press.

Harfield, C, 2008b, 'Paradigms, pathologies, and practicalities – policing organized crime in England and Wales', *Policing: A Journal of Policy and Practice*, vol 2, no 1, 63-73.

Hill, P, 1998, 'Preventing car theft in Australia: "golden opportunity" for partnerships', *Trends and Issues in Crime and Criminal Justice*, no 86, Australian Institute of Criminology.

Hillyard, P and Tombs, S, 2007, 'From 'crime' to social harm?' *Crime, Law & Social Change*, vol 48, no 1-2, 9-25.

Hogan, GP, 1994, '"Open secrets": Rethinking of strategic intelligence', *Journal of the Australian Institute of Professional Intelligence Officers*, vol 3, 13-25.

Killias, M and Uchtenhagen, A, 1996, 'Does medical heroin prescription reduce delinquency among drug addicts? On the evaluation of the Swiss heroin prescription projects and its methodology', *Studies on Crime and Crime Prevention*, vol 5, no 2, pp 245-256.

MacVean, A and Harfield, C, 2008, 'Science or sophistry: Issues in managing analysts and their products', in Harfield, C, MacVean, A, Grieve, JGD and Phillips, D (eds), *The Handbook of Intelligent Policing: Consilience, Crime Control, and Community Safety* (pp 93-104), Oxford University Press.

Maltz, M, 1990, *Measuring the Effectiveness of Organized Crime Control Efforts*, OICJ Press.

Maltz, M and Buslik, M, 1997, 'Power to the People: Crime Mapping and Information Sharing in the Chicago Police Department', in David Weisburd and J, Thomas McEwen (eds), *Crime Mapping and Crime Prevention*, Criminal Justice Press.

Mayhew, P and Adkins, G, 2003, 'Counting the costs of crime in Australia: An update', *Trends and Issues in Crime and Criminal Justice*, no 247, Australian Institute of Criminology.

Mouzos, J, 1999, 'International traffic in small arms: an Australian perspective', *Trends and Issues in Crime and Criminal Justice*, no 104, Australian Institute of Criminology.

NCA, 2001, *National Crime Authority Annual Report 2000-2001*, National Crime Authority.

NCIS, 2001, 'The Threat from Serious and Organised Crime; 2001 UK Threat Assessment' (Confidential Version), National Criminal Intelligence Service.

NZP, 2004, 'New Zealand Police Statement of Intent 2004/2005', New Zealand Police.

O'Malley, Pat, 1999, 'Consuming Risks: Harm Minimization and the Government of 'Drug Users'', in Russell Smandych (ed), *Governable Places: Readings in Governmentality and Crime Control. Advances in Criminology Series*, Dartmouth.

Pemberton, S, 2007, 'Social harm future(s): exploring the potential of the social harm approach', *Crime, Law & Social Change*, vol 48, no 1-2, 27-41.

Phillips, D, 2008, 'Police intelligence systems as a strategic response' in Harfield, C, MacVean, A, Grieve, JGD and Phillips, D (eds), *The Handbook of Intelligent Policing: Consilience, Crime Control, and Community Safety*, Oxford University Press.

Ratcliffe, JH, 2005, 'The effectiveness of police intelligence management: A New Zealand case study', *Police Practice and Research*, vol 6, no 5, 435-451.

Ratcliffe, JH, 2008, *Intelligence-Led Policing*, Willan Publishing.

Ratcliffe, JH & Guidetti, RA, 2008, 'State police investigative structure and the adoption of intelligence-led policing', *Policing: An International Journal of Police Strategies & Management*, vol 31, no 1, 109-128.

Rollings, K, 2008, Counting the costs of crime in Australia: a 2005 update'. *Research and Public Policy Series*, no 91, Australian Institute of Criminology, no. 91.

Sheptycki, JWE, 2002, *In Search of Transnational Policing: Towards a Sociology of Global Policing*, Avebury.

Sheptycki, JWE, 2003a, *Review of the Influence of Strategic Intelligence on Organized Crime Policy and Practice*, Home Office Police and Reducing Crime Unit.

Sheptycki, JWE, 2003b, 'The Governance of Organized Crime in Canada', *The Canadian Journal of Sociology*, vol 28, no 4, 489-516.

Sheptycki, JWE, 2004, 'Organizational pathologies in police intelligence systems; some contributions to the lexicon of intelligence-led policing', *European Journal of Criminology*, vol 1, no 3, 307-332.

SOCA, 2008, *UK Threat Assessment of Serious Organised Crime 2008/9*, Serious Organised Crime Agency.

Stanko, B, 2008, 'Strategic intelligence: Methodologies for understanding what police services already 'know' to reduce harm', in Harfield, C, MacVean, A, Grieve, JGD and Phillips, D (eds), *The Handbook of Intelligent Policing: Consilience, Crime Control, and Community Safety*, Oxford University Press.

Walsh, P and Ratcliffe, JH, 2005, 'Strategic criminal intelligence education: A collaborative approach', *International Association of Law Enforcement Intelligence Analysts*, vol 16, no 2, 152-166.

Weisburd, D, Bushway, S, Lum, C and Yang, S-M, 2004, 'Trajectories of crime at places: A longitudinal study of street segments in the City of Seattle', *Criminology*, vol 42, no 2, 283-321.

Wheatley, J, 2008, 'The flexibility of RICO and its use on street gangs engaging in organized crime in the United States', *Policing: A Journal of Policy and Practice*, vol 2, no 1, 82-91.

Willis, K and Homel, P, 2008, 'Measuring the performance of drug law enforcement', *Policing: A Journal of Policy and Practice*, vol 2, no 3, 311-321.

Wortley, R, and Mazerolle, L (eds), 2008, *Environmental Criminology and Crime Analysis*, Willan Publishing.

Index

9/11 terrorist attacks, 14, 26, 205, 223
analysis
  competing hypothesis, 142, 178
  content, 116
  criminal market, 149
  Delphi, 133, 180
  exploratory tools, 124
  Ishikawa diagrams, 136, 174
  mind mapping, 216
  morphological, 140
  paralysis-by, 112, 114
  PESTEL, 139, 149
  process mapping, 130-1
  resiliency theory, 152
  secondary data, 120
  SWOT, 135
  structured vs intuitive, 125
  trend, 132
  see also futures work
Association of Chief Police Officers
  (ACPO) 54
  influential reports, 33
  see also Baumber report, Pearce
  report
Audit Commission, 35, 45, 51, 237
Australian Bureau of Criminal
  Intelligence, 13, 16-21
Australian Crime Commission, 13,
  68, 82, 254
  performance, 25
  structure and function, 24
Australian Criminal Intelligence
  Database (ACID), 256
Australian Customs Service, 17, 23
Australian Federal Police, 16, 128,
  212
Australian Illicit Drug Data Report,
  120, 259
Australian Institute of Criminology,
  14, 18, 82, 122
Australian Law Enforcement
  Intelligence Network (ALIEN),
  256

Australian Securities and
  Investments Commission
  (ASIC), 19
Australian Security and Intelligence
  Organisation (ASIO), 15-6, 24
Australian Transaction Reports and
  Analysis Centre (AUSTRAC), 19
Bali terrorist attacks, 26
Baumber report, 33, 48, 50
Black Bob Craufurd, 30, 42
Black September faction, 14
black swans, 1
Bogdanos, Matthew, 223
British Crime Survey, 104
Butler Inquiry, 1, 109
Canter, David, 34
Carter, David, 188
CCTV, 34, 44
Center for Problem-Oriented
  Policing, 122
Christopher, Steve, 51
client
  identifying, 66
  implicit/explicit engagement
  with, 70
  managing, 68-75
  multiple, 69, 198
collators, 92
collection
  classical model, 87
  covert collectors, 100-1, 239
  phenomena research, 87
  push model, 94, 100
  social science model, 87, 112
  theoretical approaches, 86
Commissions, 17
  Australian Commission of
  Inquiry into Drugs (Williams
  Commission), 16
  Royal Commission into the
  Federated Ships Painters and
  Dockers Union (Costigan
  Commission), 16

Commonwealth Law Enforcement
  Arrangements Review (CLER),
  19, 22
Commonwealth Law Enforcement
  Board (CLEB), 22
Community/crime reduction
  partnerships, 6, 10, 34, 198
Compstat, 212
Condon, Sir Paul, 36
crime
  cocaine and heroin, 104, 143
  costs of, 157, 253
  cross border/regional, 57, 62
  drivers, 172
  drug importation (as example),
    139
  franchising (as example), 181
  hate, 117
  high-tech, 105
  mobile phone theft, 96-7
  money laundering (as example),
    119
  Outlaw Motor Cycle Gangs
    (OMCGs), 258
  patterns, 2
  property (as example), 137
  terrorism (as example), 141
  volume, 58
Criminal Intelligence Service
  Canada (CISC), 152, 154, 260
criminal
  leaders, 59
  specialists, 58
De Bono, Edward, 198
decision-making, 4, 8, 10, 75
  framework, 249
  influencing, 187, 195
  relationship with analysts, 189,
    196
  sophistication of structure, 200-1
deductive reasoning, 127, 168
defence, 9, 68, 87
demand gap, 49
detectives (investigators), 47, 101,
  196, 252
  in disguise, 30
  view of intelligence, 4, 251
Disruption Attribute Tool, 162

Dutch Parliamentary Commission
  on Organised Crime, 156
environmental criminology, 263
European Convention on Human
  Rights, 55
European Court of Human Rights,
  35
Federal Bureau of Investigation
  (FBI), 33
Flood, Brian, 37
future scenarios, 8, 180
futures work
  analogies, 180
  Devil's advocate, 183
  drivers, 270
  events, 269
  force field, 176-7
  futures wheel, 173
  indications and warnings system,
    see indictors, early warning
  key assumptions, 165
  patterns, 270
  scenario methods, 181
  time frames, 168
  time-impact, see trend
  trend, 174
  wildcards, 183
  written estimates, 171
Gantt charts, 209
Gardner, Howard, 197
Gaspar, Roger, 37, 241
Gill, Peter, 243
Glasses Guide, 31
Goldwater-Nichols Reorganization
  Act, 232
Grieve, John, 86
Gross, Hans, 29
Harfield, Clive, 115, 251, 263
harm, 148, 154, 157, 178
  social, 263, 265
  strategic harm approach, 249, 262
Hatherill, George, 31
Heads of Commonwealth
  Operational Law Enforcement
  Agencies (HOCOLEA), 22
Heuer, Richards, 143
Hilton Hotel bombing, Sydney, 15
Hogan, GP, 257
Home Office, 26, 30, 32, 122, 157

Hutton Inquiry, 1
hypotheses, 95, 114
indicators
  early warning, 142, 145, 184
  protective factors, 150
  risk factors, 150
inductive reasoning, 126, 168
informants, 30, 32, 33, 50, 239
intelligence model
  Canadian Criminal Intelligence
    Model, 163
  European Intelligence Model, 64,
    189
  three-i model, 9-10
  security intelligence
    model/policy, as, 24, 26
  Victoria Police Intelligence
    Model, 215
  see also National Intelligence
    Model
Intelligence Product Framework,
  190
intelligence
  analyst educational level, 121
  assets, 61
  black hole, 4, 249
  case support, 189, 191
  common standards, 48
  community, 31
  cycle, 7, 9 (limitations), 83, 90,
    112-3
  definitions, 6, 19, 28
  doctrine, 50
  estimative, 159, 166-7
  gaps, 160
  indicators, 97
  information designed for action,
    as 28-9
  instantiation criteria, 28
  legislative basis, 24
  management of units, 49, 71
  operational, 6
  opportunity, 94
  product proposal example,
    78-80, 231
  relevance, 249
  resourcing, 20
  strategic, see strategic intelligence

self-fulfilling prophecy, 85, 89, 94,
  238, 249, 260
tactical, 6 , 189, 218
theory of control, 3
training, 20, 219, 228
triangulation, 99
intelligence-led policing, 29, 35, 38,
  45, 160, 162, 198
  definition, 4
interagency collaboration, 222, 255
  governance process, 226
  Memorandum of
    Understanding, 225
  stakeholders, 226
  unity of purpose, 224
investigations, 21, 93, 102
Ishikawa, Kaoru, 136
John, Tim, 240
Joint Intelligence Committee
  (JIC), 87
KGB, 205
knowledge sharing, 229
knowledge workers, 235, 241
leadership, 37
liaison officers, 250
logical fallacies, 127
MacVean, Allyson, 115
Maguire, Mike, 240
Mathams, RH, 76
McDowell, Don, 87, 134
megatrends, 132, 174
Metropolitan Police, 29, 37
  C11, 32
  Criminal Investigation
    Department (CID), 30, 32
  intelligence section, 31
  Flying Squad, 31
  Special Duty Squad, 30
  Stolen Car Squad, 31
Mintzberg, Henry, 196
mission creep, 76, 121
Mission Essential Task List
  (METL), 225
National Crime Authority, 13, 16-7,
  64, 258
National Criminal Intelligence
  Service (NCIS), 53
National Criminal Justice Reference
  Service, 122

National Intelligence Model, 5, 37,
51-2, 86, 163
analytical toolkit, 188
control strategy, 60-1, 239
origin of name, 53
origins, 51
tactical menu, 57, 60-1
tasking and coordinating process,
60, 62, 195, 231, 239
National Intelligence Requirement
(NIR), 87
national security, 68, 166, 198, 223
National Strategic Intelligence
Course (NSIC), 21, 233, 260-1
New Jersey State Police, 118, 148,
188, 256
New South Wales Crime
Commission, 18
New Zealand Police, 189, 250
Newman, Sir Kenneth, 34, 44
Nicholl, Jonathan, 92
Non-government organisations
(NGOs), 75-80 (as example),105
Office of National Assessments
(ONA), 14
Office of Strategic Crime
Assessments (OSCA), 22-4
open source information, 106, 254
Operation Anchorage, 128-9
organisational culture, 94, 102, 193
partnerships (*see also* Community
partnerships), 37
Pearce report, 33, 49-50
Pease, Ken, 194
Peterson, Marilyn, 72
Phillips, Sir David, 2, 8, 108, 260
Pickpockets Handbook, 31
Police Service of Northern Ireland
(PSNI), 189
police
Operation Nine Connect, 118
operations, 35
over-reliance on data, 248
Policing with Intelligence, 242
policing
community, 34, 48
problem-oriented, 3, 48, 251, 264
see also intelligence-led policing

Powis, David, 32-3
privacy, 35
proactivity, 2, 47
definition, 35
producer-client model, 69
profiling
behavioural, 34
geographic, 34
project management
audit, 213
champion, 214
culture of collaboration, 227
defined, 206
phases, 207-213
project plan, 207
theory, 204
Project Nimbus, 210
Protective Security Review, 15
Queensland Criminal Justice
Commission, 18
Racketeer Influenced and Corrupt
Organizations (RICO)
legislation, 252
Ratcliffe, Jerry, 255
recommendations, 11, 82, 97, 138,
160, 193, 200
PIER, 194
Regulation of Investigative Power
Act 2000, 35, 55
Reiner, Robert, 28
research
academic, 110
action, 118
applied, 119
internal, 93
literature review, 108-9
qualitative, 116, 147
quantitative, 116, 147
time pressures, 109, 111
resource allocation, 53
risk assessment, 155
risk
management, 55
law enforcement, to, 59
Rossmo, D Kim, 34
Rowan, Sir Charles, 30, 42
Royal Canadian Mounted Police
(RCMP), 153, 162, 261

Rumsfeld, Donald, 85
Scotland Yard (*see* Metropolitan
    Police)
security clearance/classification,
    74, 193
Senge, Peter, 128
Serious Organised Crime Agency
    (SOCA), 37, 82, 160
Shulsky, Abram, 125
Sleipnir, 153-4
Standing Advisory Committee on
    Organised Crime and Criminal
    Intelligence (SCOCCI), 24
Standing Committee on
    Commonwealth/State
    cooperation for Protection
    Against Violence
    (SAC-PAV), 15, 17
Stanko, Betsy, 117, 264
strategic intelligence
    requirements, 86
strategic intelligence, 242
    analyst's role, 11, 71, 81, 83
    capabilities, 26

defining, 5, 53, 186, 243
institutional context, 13, 236
manager's role, 71, 232
place within law enforcement, 13
Sun Tzu, 28, 38
surveillance, 30, 32, 239
Swiss heroin experiment, 264
Systems for Investigation and
    Detection, 35
Szent-Györgyi, Albert, 85
Tackling Crime Effectively, 237, 242
task definition, 66-84, 231
threat assessments
    national, 157
    risk, and, 8, 147, 178
    traditional role, 47-8
    UK, 52, 61, 87, 243, 253
    vulnerability, 155
triage process, 3
victims, 57, 105
Victoria Police, 212
Whitechapel Murders (1888), 30